THE
HIAWATHA LEGENDS.

D0027269

Cover: Oil Painting by John Heath
Illustrations: by John Evans

THE MYTH OF HIAWATHA
AND
OTHER ORAL LEGENDS, MYTHOLOGIC AND
ALLEGORIC, OF THE NORTH AMERICAN INDIANS

by
HENRY R. SCHOOLCRAFT, LL.D.

Published by
Avery Color Studios, Inc.
Gwinn, Michigan 49841

ISBN 0-932212-35-2
Library of Congress Card No. 84-70272

First Edition–February 1984
Reprinted–August 1985
Reprinted–November 1987
Reprinted–May 1990
Reprinted–July 1991
Reprinted–July 1992
Reprinted–April 1994
Reprinted–January 1997
Reprinted–May 2001

Entered according to the Act of Congress, in the year 1856, by

HENRY R. SCHOOLCRAFT

in the Clerk's Office of the District Court of the United States
in and for the Eastern District of Pennsylvania

The Myth
of
H I A W A T H A,
and

OTHER ORAL LEGENDS,
Mythologic and Allegoric,
of the

NORTH AMERICAN INDIANS.

BY
HENRY R. SCHOOLCRAFT, LL. D.

1984

This edition typeset and reproduced from the original format printed by J.B. Lippincott & Co., Philadelphia, and Trubner & Co., London, in 1856.

Henry W. Longfellow.

398.208997
S372h

Alpine #15

704

TO
PROF. HENRY WADSWORTH LONGFELLOW.

SIR:—

Permit me to dedicate to you, this volume of Indian myths and legends, derived from the story-telling circle of the native wigwams. That they indicate the possession, by the Vesperic tribes, of mental resources of a very characteristic kind— furnishing, in fact, a new point from which to judge the race, and to excite intellectual sympathies, you have most felicitously shown in your poem of Hiawatha. Not only so, but you have demonstrated, by this pleasing series of pictures of Indian life, sentiment, and invention, that the theme of the native lore reveals one of the true sources of our literary independence. Greece and Rome, England and Italy, have so long furnished, if they have not exhausted, the field of poetic culture, that it is, at least, refreshing to find both in theme and metre, something new.

Very truly yours,
HENRY R. SCHOOLCRAFT.

GERMANTOWN COMMUNITY LIBRARY
GERMANTOWN, WI 53022
MAR 1 1 2004

PREFACE.

THERE is but one consideration of much moment necessary to be premised respecting these legends and myths. It is this: they are versions of oral relations from the lips of the Indians, and are transcripts of the thought and invention of the aboriginal mind. As such, they furnish illustrations of Indian character and opinions on subjects which the ever-cautious and suspicious minds of this people have, heretofore, concealed. They place the man altogether in a new phasis. They reflect him as he is. They show us what he believes, hopes, fears, wishes, expects, worships, lives for, dies for. They are always true to the Indian manners and customs, opinions and theories. They never rise above them; they never sink below them. Placing him in almost every possible position, as a hunter, a warrior, a magician, a pow-wow, a medicine man, a meda, a husband, a father, a friend, a foe, a stranger, a wild singer of songs to monedos or fetishes, a trembler in terror of demons and wood genii, and of ghosts, witches, and sorcerers—now in the enjoyment of plenty in feasts—now pale and weak with abstinence in fasts; now transforming beasts and birds, or plants and trees into men, or men into beasts by necromancy; it is impossible not to perceive what he perpetually thinks, believes, and feels. The very language of man is employed, and his vocabulary is not enlarged by words and phrases foreign to it. Other sources of information depict his exterior habits and outer garb and deportment; but in these legends and myths, we perceive the interior man, and are made cognizant of the secret workings of his mind, and heart, and soul.

To make these collections, of which the portions now submitted are but a part, the leisure hours of many seasons, passed in an official capacity in the solitude of the wilderness far away from society, have been employed, with the study of the languages, and with the very best interpreters. They have been carefully translated, written, and rewritten, to obtain their true spirit and meaning, expunging passages, where it was necessary to avoid tediousness of narration, triviality of

GERMANTOWN COMMUNITY LIBRARY
GERMANTOWN, WI 53022

circumstance, tautologies, gross incongruities, and vulgarities; but adding no incident and drawing no conclusion, which the verbal narration did not imperatively require or sanction. It was impossible to mistake the import of terms and phrases where the means of their analysis were ample. If the style is sometimes found to be bald, and of jejune simplicity, the original is characteristically so. Few adjectives are employed, because there are few in the original.* The Indian effects his purposes, almost entirely, by changes of the verb and demonstrative pronoun, or by adjective inflections of the substantive. Good and bad, high and low, black and white, are in all cases employed in a transitive sense, and with strict relation to the objects characterized. The Indian compound terms are so descriptive, so graphic, so local, so characterizing, yet so flexible and transpositive, that the legends derive no little of their characteristic features as well as melody of utterance from these traits. Sometimes these terms cannot be literally translated, and they cannot, in these cases, be left out without damaging the stories.

With regard to the thought-work of the legends, those who have deemed the Indians exclusively a cruel and blood-thirsty race, always seeking revenge, always invoking evil powers, will not be disappointed that giants, enchanters, demons, and dark supernatural agencies, should form so large a part of the dramatis personae. Surprise has been expressed,* that the kindlier affections come in for notice at all, and particularly at the occurrence of such refined and terse allegories as the origin of Indian Corn, Winter and Spring, and the poetic conception of the Celestial Sisters, & c. I can only add, that my own surprise was as great when these traits were first revealed. And the trait may be quoted to show how deeply the tribes have wandered away from the type of the human race in which love and affection absorb the heart; and how little, indeed, we know of their mental character.

When the volumes of Algic Researches, in 1839, were published, the book-trade had hardly awakened to that wide and

* If Edwards the younger, to whom the Mohican was familiar from his childhood, could say, that he doubted whether there were any true adjectives in that language, it can easily be imagined that the subtlety of the transitive principle had not been sufficiently analyzed; but the remark is here quoted in relation to the paucity of adjectives.
* *Vide* Criterion, No. XXIII. P. 361.

diffusive impulse which it has since received. No attention had been given to topics so obscure as inquiries into the character of the Indian mind—if, indeed, it was thought the Indian had any mind at all. It was still supposed that the Indian was, at all times and in all places, "a stoic of the woods," always statuesque, always formal, always passionless, always on stilts, always speaking in metaphors, a cold embodiment of bravery, endurance, and savage heroism. Writers depicted him as a man who uttered nothing but high principles of natural right, who always harangued eloquently, and was ready, with unmoved philosophy on all occasions, to sing his death-song at the stake to show the world how a warrior should die.

These legends have been out of print several years. They are now reproduced, with additional legendary lore of this description from the portfolios of the author, in a revised, and, it is believed, a more terse, condensed, and acceptable form, both in a literary and business garb. The songs and chants which form so striking a part of the original legends, and also the poetic use of aboriginal ideas, are transferred to the end of the volume, and will thus, it is apprehended, relieve and simplify the text.

HENRY R. SCHOOLCRAFT.

WASHINGTON, D.C., *April* 28, 1856.

TABLE OF CONTENTS

SUPPLEMENTARY INTRODUCTION
By Larry B. Massie, Allegan, Michigan

To *The Myth of Hiawatha* by Henry Rowe Schoolcraft

Even in today's less culturally conscious society, school-children soon become familiar with *The Song of Hiawatha.* Longfellow's epic poem has become part of America's folklore.

Yet few Americans, including residents of Schoolcraft County in Michigan's Upper Peninsula or of the village of Schoolcraft in Kalamazoo County, realize that Longfellow based his poem upon genuine Chippewa legends first collected and published by Henry Rowe Schoolcraft. In the 19th century Schoolcraft was nationally known as a pioneer ethnologist, Indian agent, and author of hundreds of articles and over twenty books. Today he stands in danger of becoming one of the "lost men of American history."

Henry Rowe Schoolcraft was born in a small village west of Albany, New York in 1793. Villagers remembered him as a youth early bent on scholarship. As a teenager he supplied original poetry and essays to local newspapers and edited his own manuscript magazine devoted to philosophy and literature. He initially followed his father into the profession of glass manufacturing. But the Treaty of Ghent in 1815 allowed an influx of cheap British glass into America, ruining the industry and forcing Schoolcraft out of business. He turned to the west to make his fortune. In 1818 he traveled to the western frontier to spend a winter observing the lead mining region of Missouri. He published his first book in 1819, *A View of the Lead Mines of Missouri.* This scientific account earned Schoolcraft a national reputation as a mineralogist and attracted the attention of Secretary of War John C. Calhoun who was interested in developing America's natural resources.

Calhoun invited Schoolcraft to Washington where he impressed President James Monroe and other cabinet members with his expertise. These important contacts brought Schoolcraft the opportunity to serve as mineralogist on an expedition then being fitted up to explore the wilderness of the upper

Great Lakes. The expedition left Detroit on May 24, 1820 under the direction of Territory of Michigan Governor Lewis Cass. The arduous canoe voyage which first brought School- craft to the north country proved a milestone in the develop- ment of his career. He found a life-long friend in Lewis Cass and furthered his reputation as a scientific explorer through his account of the expedition, *Narrative Journal of Travels through the Northwestern Regions*... (Albany, 1821).

In 1822 Schoolcraft accepted the newly created position of Indian agent for the Upper Great Lakes with headquarters at Sault Ste. Marie. Despite his new title, Schoolcraft remained quite ignorant of Indian culture. However, Lewis Cass, a pioneer student of Indian life, showed him a questionnaire concerning Indian social characteristics which he was cir- culating throughout the northern frontier. This sparked a similiar interest in Schoolcraft. Upon his arrival at the Sault he began to study the native Chippewa.

Throughout the following decade Schoolcraft periodically journeyed to uncharted areas of the Lake Superior region, most notably in 1832 when he discovered the source of the Mississippi River at Itasca Lake. While so engaged he dili- gently collected information about Indian life. His position as Indian Agent at Sault Ste. Marie from 1822-1833 and at Mackinac Island from 1833-1836 and as Superintendent of Indian Affairs for Michigan at Detroit with summers on Mackinac Island from 1836-1841 allowed him to interview hundreds of Indians and traders.

Schoolcraft helped found the State Historical Society of Michigan in 1828 and the Algic Research Society in 1832 and served in the Territorial Legislature from 1828-1832. These activities brought further contacts with others interested in preserving information about the Indians. But Schoolcraft's greatest successes in collecting ethnology came through his relationship with the Johnston family of Sault Ste. Marie. He recorded in his private journal on July 28, 1822: "I have in fact stumbled, as it were, on the only family in Northwest America who could in Indian lore have acted as my guide, philosopher, and friend."

John Johnston, "patriarch of the Sault," was born in Ireland in 1762. He emigrated to Montreal in 1790 to seek his fortune and to Sault Ste. Marie in 1793, where he developed a lucrative fur trading business. He married a remarkable woman, renamed Susan, the daughter of a famous Chippewa Chief,

Waub Ojeeg of La Pointe, a renowned story teller. At his substantial clapboard dwelling at the Sault (which is still standing) Johnston created an oasis of culture on the frontier. The Johnston children received a hybrid education. He trained them in the classics at home and sent them to private schools in Canada for finishing, and Susan enculturated them in the language and customs of her people.

Schoolcraft stayed with the Johnstons when he first arrived at his new post in 1822. He became a fast friend of John and Susan Johnston and the following year married their beautiful daughter Jane, "the northern Pocahontas." For decades the Johnstons assisted Schoolcraft in collecting, translating and interpreting Chippewa legends. As the daughter of a celebrated chief, Susan provided many unusual contacts, while Jane and especially her brother George proved invaluable as translators. Schoolcraft remained interested in all aspects of Indian life, but perhaps as a result of the unique opportunities presented through his relationship with the Johnstons, he became increasingly concerned with preserving and promoting the oral myths of the Chippewa, known as lodge stories.

Schoolcraft began publishing his collections in 1826 in the form of a manuscript magazine, *The Literary Voyager,* which he circulated among the winterbound residents of the Sault. In 1837 he began refining his impressive collection of Chippewa myths which he published in two volumes as Algic Researches... (New York, 1839). While not a popular success, this work brought Schoolcraft scholarly acclaim. He included other Chippewa legends in his *Oneota, or The Red Race of America...* first issued in eight parts in 1844-45 and later reissued under various titles. In 1847 Schoolcraft relocated to Washington, D.C. to serve as special agent in the Office of Indian Affairs and authorized by Congress to gather, collect and edit information on all American Indians. He spent the next decade working on his massive magnum opus, *Historical and Statistical Information Respecting the History, Condition and Prospects of the Indian Tribes of the United States* (Philadelphia, 1851-57). This monumental six volume series also contains many Chippewa lodge stories.

One reader in particular found Schoolcraft's Indian legends of intriguing interest - Henry Wadsworth Longfellow. He recorded: "I pored over Mr. Schoolcraft's writings nearly three years, before I resolved to appropriate something of them to my own use." In 1854 Longfellow began work on an

15

epic poem based largely on Schoolcraft's collections. He first titled the work **Manabozho,** after the legendary Algonquin messenger of the Great Spirit but he later shifted to **Hiawatha,** the Iroquois version of the same legend. *The Song of Hiawatha* appeared November 10, 1855 and met with phenomenal success for a poem, selling 50,000 copies within fifteen months. In his notes to the first edition Longfellow cited as his chief authority,"...the various and valuable writings of Mr. Schoolcraft, to whom the literary world is greatly indebted for his indefatigable zeal in rescuing from oblivion so much of the legendary lore of the Indians." He acknowledged that "the scene of the poem is among the Ojibways on the southern shore of Lake Superior, in the region between the Pictured Rocks and the Grand Sable" - a major collecting area for Schoolcraft.

However, *Hiawatha's* tremendous popularity did not go unchallenged by the critics. Some reviewers, including Edgar Allen Poe, then suffering a particularly vitriolic jealous streak, leveled charges of plagarism against Longfellow. They accused him of stealing Hiawatha's plot and poetic measure from the ancient Finnish epic, *The Kalevala.* For generations scholars had been gathering examples of nearly forgotten Finnish rune songs. Elias Lonrrot, Finnish poet, published an arrangement of these legends in 1835 and an expanded version in 1849. *The Kalevala* and *The Song of Hiawatha* contain some similarities of theme and arrangement as do most of the other national epics including the Illiad, the Song of Roland, and the Nibelungenlied. Longfellow, read *The Kalevala* and was undoubtedly influenced to the extent, that he choose for *Hiawatha* the same unusual trochaic meter in which the Finnish epic was recorded. Longfellow, in fact, became the first to popularize, in English, the use of that lilting poetic measure. In view of the later settlement of the north country by Finnish immigrants, it perhaps would be appropriate for *Hiawatha* and *The Kalevala* to have originated from the same source. However the similarities in plot appear to be purely coincidental.

It was partially to quell this criticism and undoubtedly to take advantage of *Hiawatha's* market that Schoolcraft issued an enlarged and popularized edition of *Algic Researches* in 1856 as *The Myth of Hiawatha.* While *The Song of Hiawatha* was published in Boston by Ticknor and Fields and *The Myth of Hiawatha* in Philadelphia by J.B. Lippincott the volumes resemble a set. As issued in their original cloth-covered boards their size, spine labeling, and blind-stamped cover decoration are virtually identical.

While Longfellow with Schoolcraft's assistance effectively exhonorated himself of the plagiarism charges, vestiges of the attack periodically reappeared. Nathan Haskell Dole wrote a scholarly introduction comparing *The Kalevala* and *Hiawatha* in an 1898 edition of *Hiawatha* which should have forever vindicated Longfellow. But as late as 1939, Malcolm Bingay resurrected the controversy in his column in the Detroit *Free Press*. Chase Osborne, former Michigan governor and long time champion of the north country and its heroes, soon set him straight. Chase and Stellanova Osborn's *Schoolcraft-Longfellow-Hiawatha* (Lancaster, Penn., 1942) should be consulted for additional information on the plagiarism controversy, a detailed biography and bibliography of Schoolcraft, and an annotated version of *Hiawatha*.

The 1856 collection of Chippewa myths which is reprinted in this volume proved greater popular success than the earlier *Algic Researches*. That same year an abridgment of some of the legends appeared as *The Indian Fairy Book*. Other editions appeared under various imprints, titles, and degrees of bowdlerization in 1857, 1869, 1877, and 1916. Mentor L. Williams edited a scholarly version in 1956.

Schoolcraft died on December 10, 1864 in Washington and was buried in the Congressional Cemetery, thus ending a colorful life of adventure and scholarship. He left a legacy of literature which comprises the single most important 19th century source for the study of the American Indians. All of Schoolcraft's books have become scarce and sought-after collector's items in their original form, commanding high prices in the antiquarian book market. Avery Color Studios by reprinting one of Schoolcraft's most interesting works in an inexpensive format has rendered a distinct service to modern readers. This volume should be required reading for anyone interested in the American Indian, Great Lakes history, or who has fallen under the lure of the north - "the Hiawatha country."

INTRODUCTION.

HITHERTO, Indian opinion, on abstract subjects, has been a sealed book. It has been impossible to extract the truth from his evasive replies. If asked his opinion of religion in the abstract, he knows not the true meaning of the term. His ideas of the existence of a Deity are vague, at best; and the lines of separation between it and necromancy, medical magic, and demonology are too faintly separated to allow him to speak with discrimination. The best reply, as to his religious views, his mythology, his cosmogony, and his general views as to the mode and manifestations of the government and providences of God, are to be found in his myths and legends. When he assembles his lodge-circle, to hear stories, in seasons of leisure and retirement in the depths of the forest, he recites precisely what he believes on these subjects. That restlessness, suspicion, and mistrust of motive, which has closed his mind to inquiry, is at rest here. If he mingles fiction with history, there is little of the latter, and it is very easy to see where history ends and fiction begins. While he amuses his hearers with tales of the adventures of giants and dwarfs, and the conflicts of Manito with Manito, fairies and enchanters, monsters and demons, he also throws in some few grains of instruction, in the form of allegory and fable, which enable us to perceive glimpses of the heart and its affections.

It is also by his myths that we are able to trace connections with the human family in other parts of the world. Yet, where the analogies are so general, there is a constant liability to mistakes. Of these foreign analogies of myth lore, the least tangible, it is believed, is that which has been suggested with the Scandinavian mythology. That mythology is of so marked and peculiar a character, that it has not been distinctly traced out of the great circle of tribes of the Indo-Germanic family. Odin, and his terrific pantheon of war-gods and social deities, could only exist in the dreary latitudes of storms and fire, which produce a Hecla and a Maelstrom. These latitudes have invariably produced nations, whose influence has been felt in an elevating power over the world; and whose tracks have everywhere been marked by the highest evidences of inductive intellect, centralizing energy, and practical wisdom and forecast. From such a source the Indian could have derived none of his vague symbolisms and mental idiosyncrasies, which have left him, as he is found to-day, without a government and without a God. Far more probable is it, in seeking for analogies to his mythology and cosmogony, to resort to the era of that primal reconstruction of the theory of a Deity, when the human philosophy in the oriental world ascribed the godship of the universe to the subtile, ineffable, and indestructible essences of fire and light, as revealed in the sun. Such were the errors of the search for divine truth, power, and a controllable Deity, which early developed themselves in the dogmas of the Assyrians, Egyptians, Persians, and wandering hordes of Northern Asia.

Authors inform us that the worship of the sun lies at the foundation of all the ancient mythologies, deeply enveloped as they are, when followed over Asia Minor and Europe, in symbolic and linguistical subtleties and refinements. The symbolical fires erected on temples and altars to Baal, Chemosh, and Moloch, burned brightly in the valley of the Euphrates,* long before the pyramids of Egypt were erected, or its priestly-hoarded hieroglyphic wisdom resulted in a phonetic alphabet. In Persia, these altars were guarded and religiously fed by a consecrated body of magical priesthood, who recognized a Deity in the essence of an eternal fire and a world-pervading light.

The same dogma, derived eastwardly and not westwardly through Europe, was fully installed at Atacama and Cuzco, in Peru, at Cholulu, on the magnificent and volcano-lighted peaks of Mexico; and along the fertile deltas of the Mississippi valley. Altar-beds for a sacred fire, lit to the Great Spirit, under the name and symbolic form of Ceezis, or the sun, where the frankincense of the nicotiana was offered, with hymns and genuflections, have been discovered, in many instances, under the earth-heaps and artificial mounds and places of sepulture of the ancient inhabitants. Intelligent Indians yet living, among the North American tribes, point out the symbol of the sun, in their ancient muzzinabikons, or rock-inscriptions, and also amid the idiographic tracery and bark-scrolls of the

* Gross.

19

hieratic and magical medicine songs.

With a cosmogony which ascribes the creation of the Geezha Monedo, who is symbolized by the sun, the myth of Hiawatha is almost a necessary consequence in carrying out his mundane intentions to the tribes, who believed themselves to be peculiar objects of his love and benevolence. This myth is noticed by the earliest explorers of this continent, who have bestowed attention on the subject, under the various names of Inigorio, Yoskika, Taren-Yawagon, Atahentsic, Manabozho, and Micabo. A mythology appears indispensable to a rude and ignorant race like the Indians. Their vocabulary is nearly limited to objects which can be seen and handled. Abstractions are only reached by the introduction of some term which restores the idea. The Deity is a mystery, of whose power they must chiefly judge by the phenomena before them. Everything is mysterious which is not understood; and, unluckily, they understand little or nothing. If any phenomenon, or existence not before them, is to be described, the language must be symbolic. The result is, that the Indian languages are peculiarly the languages of symbols, metaphors, and figures. Without this feature, everything not in the departments of eating, drinking, and living, and the ordinary transactions of the chase and forest, would not be capable of description.

When the Great Sacred White Hare of Heaven, the Manabozho of the Algrics, and Hiawatha of the Iroquois, kills the Great Misshikinabik, or prince of serpents, it is understood that he destroys the great power of evil. It is a deity whom he destroys, a sort of Typhon or Ahriman in the system. It is immediately found, on going to his lodge, that it is a man, a hero, a chief, who is sick, and he must be cured by simples and magic songs like the rest of the Indians. He is surrounded with Indian doctors, who sing magic songs. He has all the powers of a deity, and, when he dies, the land is subjected to a flood; from which Hiawatha alone escapes. This play between the zoonic and mortal shapes of heroes must constantly be observed, in high as well as in ordinary characters. To have the name of an animal, or bird, or reptile, is to have his powers. When Pena runs, on a wager of life, with the Great Sorcerer, he changes himself sometimes into a partridge, and sometimes into a wolf, to outrun him.

The Indian's necessities of language at all times require personifications and linguistic creations. He cannot talk on abstract topics without them. Myths and spiritual agencies are constantly required. The ordinary domestic life of the Indian is described in plain words and phrases, but whatever is mysterious or abstract must be brought under mythological figures and influences. Birds and quadrupeds must be made to talk. Weeng is the spirit of somnolency in the lodge stories. He is provided with a class of little invisible emissaries, who ascend the forehead, armed with tiny war-clubs, with which they strike the temples, producing sleep. Pauguk is the personification of death. He is armed with a bow and arrows, to execute his mortal functions. Hosts of a small fairy-like creation, called Ininees, little men, or Pukwudj Ininees, vanishing little men, inhabit cliffs, and picturesque and romantic scenes. Another class of marine or water spirits, called Nebunabaigs, occupy the rivers and lakes. There is an articulate voice in all the varied sounds of the forest—the groaning of its branches, and the whispering of its leaves. Local Manitos, or fetishes, inhabit every grove; and hence he is never alone.

To facilitate allusion to the braggadocio, or the extravagant in observation, the mythos of Iagoo is added to his vocabulary. The North and the South, the East and the West, are prefigured as the brothers of Hiawatha, or the laughter-provoking Manabozho. It is impossible to peruse the Indian myths and legends without perceiving the governing motives of his reasons, hopes, wishes, and fears, the principles of his actions, and his general belief in life, death, and immortality. He is no longer an enigma. They completely unmask the man. They lay open his most secret theories of the phenomena of spirit life; of necromancy, witchcraft, and demonology; and, in a special manner, of the deep and wide-spread prevalence throughout the world of Indian opinion, of the theory and power of local Manitos. It is here that the Indian prophet, powwow, or jossakeed, throws off his mask, and the Indian religionist discloses to us the secrets of his fasts and dreams. His mind completely unbends itself, and the man lives over, in imagination, both the sweet and the bitter scenes of a hunter's life. To him the clouds, which chase each other, in brilliant hues and constantly changing forms, in the heavens, constitute a species of wild pictography, which he can interpret. The phenomena of storms and meteorological changes connect themselves, in the superstitious mind, with some engrossing mythos or symbol. The eagle, the kite, and the hawk, who fly to great heights, are deemed to be con-

GERMANTOWN COMMUNITY LIBRARY
GERMANTOWN, WI 53022
21

versant with the aerial powers, who are believed to have an influence over men, and hence the great regard which is paid to the flight of these birds in their war and hieratic songs.

Fictitious tales of imaginary Indian life, and poems on the aboriginal model, have been in vogue almost from the days of the discovery. But what has been fancied as life in the forest, has had no little resemblance to those Utopian schemes of government and happiness which rather denote 'the human mind run mad, than supply models to guide judgment or please philosophy. In general, these attempts have held up high principles of thought and action in a people, against truth, observation, and common sense. High heroic action, in the Indian, is the result of personal education in endurance, supported by pride of character; and if he can ever be said to rejoice in suffering, it is in the spirit of a taunt to his enemy. This error had been so long prevalent, that when, in 1839, the author submitted a veritable collection of legends and myths from the Indian wigwams, which reflected the Indian life as it is, it was difficult, and almost impossible, to excite interest in the theme, in the trade. He went to England and the continent, in hopes of better success. But, although philanthropists and men of letters and science appreciated the subject, as historical elements in the history of the human mind, the booksellers of London, Paris, Leipsic, and Frankfort-on-the-Main, to whose notice the subject was brought, exhibited very nearly the same nonchalant tone; and had it not been for the attractive poetic form in which one of our most popular and successful bards has clothed some of these wild myths, the period of their reproduction is likely to have been still further postponed.

In now submitting so large a body of matter, respecting the mental garniture of a poeple whose fate and fortunes have excited so much interest, the surprise is not that we know so little of their mental traits, but that, with so little research and inquiry, we should know anything at all. They have only been regarded as the geologist regards boulders, being not only out of place, but with not half the sure guides and principles of determining where they came from, and where the undisturbed original strata remain. The wonder is not that, as boulder-tribes, they have not adopted our industry and Christianity, and stoutly resisted civilization, in all its phases, but that, in spite of such vital truths, held up by all the Colonies and States, and by every family of them, they have not long since died out and become extinguished. No English colony could live three or four centuries, in any isolated part of the world, without the plough, the school-book, and the Bible; it would die out, of idleness and ignorance. If one century has kicked the Indian in America harder than another, it is because the kicks of labor, art, and knowledge are always the hardest, and in the precise proportion to the contiguity of the object.

By obtaining—what these legends give—a sight of the inner man, we are better able to set a just estimate on his character, and to tell what means of treatment are best suited for his reclamation. That forbearance, kindness, and teaching are best adapted to the object, there is no doubt. We are counselled to forgive an erring brother seventy and seven times. If, as some maintain, wrongfully, we believe, the Indian is not, in a genealogical sense, of the same stock, yet is he not, in a moral sense, a brother? If the knowledge of his story-telling faculty has had any tendency to correct the evils of false popular opinion respecting him, it has been to show that the man talks and laughs like the rest of the human family; that it is fear that makes him suspicious, and ignorance super-stitious; that he is himself the dupe of an artful forest priest-hood; and that his cruelty and sanguinary fury are the effects of false notions of fame, honor, and glory. He is always, and at all times and places, under the strong influence of hopes and fears, true or false, by which he is carried forward in the changing scenes of war and peace. Kindness never fails to soften and meliorate his feelings, and harshness, injury, and contempt to harden and blunt them. Above all, it is shown that, in the recesses of the forest, he devotes a portion of his time to domestic and social enjoyment, in which the leading feature is the relation of traditionary legends and tales. Heroes and heroines, giants and dwarfs, spirits, Monetos or local gods, demons, and deities pass in review. It is chiefly by their misadventures and violations of the Indian theories, that the laugh is sought to be raised. The *dramatis persona* are true transcripts of Indian life; they never rise above it, or express a sentiment or opinion which is not true to Indian society; nor do they employ words which are not known to their vocabulary. It is in these legends that we obtain their true views of life and death, their religion, their theory of the state of the dead, their mythology, their cosmogony, their notions of astrology, and often of their biography and history—for the boundaries between history and fiction are vaguely defined. These stories are often told, in seasons of great severity in the depth of the winter, to an eagerly listening group, to while away the hour, and divert attention from the pressing claims of hunger. Under such circumstances to dole away time which has no value to him, and to cheat hunger and want, is esteemed a trait of philosophy. If there is a morsel to eat in the lodge, it is given to the children. The women imitate this stoicism and devotion of the men. Not a tone in the narration tells of dismay in their domestic circumstances, not an eye acknowledges the influence of grief. Tell me whether the dignity of this position is not worthy of remembrance. The man, it may be, shall pass away from the earth, but these tributes to the best feelings of the heart will remain, while these simple tales and legendary creations consitute a new point of character by which he should be judged. They are, at least, calculated to modify our views of the man, who is not always a savage, not always a fiend.

HIAWATHA;

OR,

MANABOZHO.

THE myth of the Indians of a remarkable personage, who is called Manabozho by the Algonquins, and Hiawatha by the Iroquois, who was the instructor of the tribes in arts and knowledge, was first related to me in 1822, by the Chippewas of Lake Superior. He is regarded as the messenger of the Great Spirit, sent down to them in the character of a wise man, and a prophet. But he comes clothed with all the attributes of humanity, as well as the power of performing miraculous deeds. He adapts himself perfectly to their manners, and customs, and ideas. He is brought up from a child among them. He is made to learn their mode of life. He takes a wife, builds a lodge, hunts and fishes like the rest of them, sings his war songs and medicine songs, goes to war, has his triumphs, has his friends and foes, suffers, wants, hungers, is in dread or joy—and, in fine, undergoes all the vicissitudes of his fellows. His miraculous gifts and powers are always adapted to his situation. When he is swallowed by a great fish, with his canoe, he escapes by the exertion of these powers, but always, as much as possible, in accordance with Indian maxims and means. He is provided with a magic canoe, which goes where it is bid; yet, in his fight with the great wampum prince, he is counselled by a woodpecker to know where the vulnerable point of his antagonist lies. He rids the earth of monsters and giants, and clears away windfalls, and obstructions to the navigation of streams. But he does not do these feats by miracles; he employs strong men to help him. When he means to destroy the serpents, he changes himself into an old tree, and stands on the beach till they come out of the water to bask in the sun. Whatever man could do, in strength or wisdom, he could do. But he never does things above the comprehension or belief of his people; and whatever else he is, he is always true to the character of an Indian.

This myth is one of the most general in the Indian country. It is the prime legend of their mythology. He is talked of in every winter lodge—for the winter season is the only time devoted to such narrations. The moment the leaves come out, stories cease in the lodge. The revival of spring in the botanical world opens, as it were, so many eyes and ears to listen to the tales of men; and the Indian is far too shrewd a man, and too firm a believer in the system of invisible spirits by which he is surrounded, to commit himself by saying a word which they, with their acute senses on the opening of the spring, can be offended at.

He leaps over extensive regions of country like an ignis fatuus. He appears suddenly like an avater, or saunters over weary wastes a poor and starving hunter. His voice is at one moment deep and sonorous as a thunder-clap, and at another clothed with the softness of feminine supplication. Scarcely any two persons agree in all the minor circumstances of the story, and scarcely any omit the leading traits. The several tribes who speak dialects of the mother language from which the narration is taken, differ, in like manner, from each other in the particulars of his exploits. His birth and parentage are mysterious. Story says his grandmother was the daughter of the moon. Having been married but a short time, her rival attracted her to a grape-vine swing on the banks of a lake, and by one bold exertion pitched her into its centre, from which she fell through to the earth. Having a daughter, the fruit of her lunar marriage, she was very careful in instructting her, from early infancy, to beware of the west wind, and never, in stooping, to expose herself to its influence. In some unguarded moment this precaution was neglected. In an instant, the gale accomplished its Tarquinic purpose.

Very little is told of his early boyhood. We take him up in the following legend at a period of advanced youth, when we find him living with his grandmother. And at this time he possessed, although he had not yet *exercised*, all the anomalous and contradictory powers of body and mind, of manship and divinity, which he afterward evinced. The timidity and rawness of the boy quickly gave way in the courageous developments of the man. He soon evinced the sagacity, cunning, perseverance, and heroic courage which constitute the admiration of the Indians. And he relied largely upon these in the gratification of an ambitious, vain-glorious, and mischief-loving disposition. In wisdom and energy he was superior to any one who had ever lived before. Yet he was simple when circumstances required it, and was ever the object of tricks and ridicule in others. He could transform himself into any animal he pleased, being man or manito, as circumstances rendered necessary. He often conversed with animals, fowls, reptiles, and fishes. He deemed himself related to them, and invariably addressed them by the term "my brother;" and one of his greatest resources, when hard pressed, was to change himself into their shapes.

Manitoes constitute the great power and absorbing topic of Indian lore. Their agency is at once the groundwork of their mythology and demonology. They supply the machinery of their poetic inventions, and the belief in their multitudinous existence exerts a powerful influence upon the lives and character of individuals. As their manitoes are of all imaginary kinds, grades, and powers, benign and malicious, it seems a grand conception among the Indians to create a personage strong enough in his necromantic and spiritual powers to baffle the most malicious, beat the stoutest, and overreach the most cunning. In carrying out this conception in the following myth, they have, however, rather exhibited an incarnation of the power of Evil than of the genius of Be-

27

nevolence.

Manabozho was living with his grandmother near the edge of a wide prairie. On this prairie he first saw animals and birds of every kind. He there also saw exhibitions of divine power in the sweeping tempests, in the thunder and lightning, and the various shades of light and darkness, which form a never-ending scene of observation. Every new sight he beheld in the heavens was a subject of remark; every new animal or bird an object of deep interest; and every sound uttered by the animal creation a new lesson, which he was expected to learn. He often trembled at what he heard and saw. To this scene his grandmother sent him at an early age to watch. The first sound he heard was that of the owl, at which he was greatly terrified, and, quickly descending the tree he had climbed, he ran with alarm to the lodge. "Noko! Noko!"* he cried, "I have heard a monedo." She laughed at his fears, and asked him what kind of a noise it made. He answered, "It makes a noise like this: Ko-ko-ko-ho." She told him that he was young and foolish; that what he had heard was only a bird, deriving its name from the noise it made.

He went back and continued his watch. While there, he thought to himself, "It is singular that I am so simple, and my grandmother so wise, and that I have neither father nor mother. I have never heard a word about them. I must ask and find out." He went home and sat down silent and dejected. At length his grandmother asked him, "Manabozho, what is the matter with you?" He answered, "I wish you would tell me whether I have any parents living, and who my relatives are." Knowing that he was of a wicked and revengeful disposition, she dreaded telling him the story of his parentage, but he insisted on her compliance. "Yes," she said, "you have a father and three brothers living. Your mother is dead. She was taken without the consent of her parents by your father the West. Your brothers are the North, East, and South, and, being older than yourself, your father has given them great power with the winds, according to their names. You are the youngest of his children. I have nourished you from your infancy, for your mother died in giving you birth, owing to the ill treatment of your father. I have no relations besides you this side of the planet in which I was born, and from which I was precipitated by female jealousy. Your mother was my

---

* An abbreviated term for "my grandmother," derived from *no-ke-miss.*

only child, and you are my only hope."

He appeared to be rejoiced to hear that his father was living, for he had already thought in his heart to try and kill him. He told his grandmother he should set out in the morning to visit him. She said it was a long distance to the place where Ningabiun* lived. But that had no effect to stop him, for he had now attained manhood, possessed a giant's height, and was endowed by nature with a giant's strength and power. He set out and soon reached the place, for every step he took covered a large surface of ground. The meeting took place on a high mountain in the West. His father was very happy to see him. He also appeared pleased. They spent some days in talking with each other. One evening Manabozho asked his father what he was most afraid of on earth. He replied, "Nothing." "But is there not something you dread here? tell me." At last his father said, yielding, "Yes, there is a black stone found in such a place. It is the only thing earthly I am afraid of; for if it should hit me or any part of my body, it would injure me very much." He said this as a secret, and in return asked his son the same question. Knowing each other's power, although the son's was limited, the father feared him on account of his great strength. Manabozho answered, "Nothing!" intending to avoid the question, or to refer to some harmless object as the one of which he was afraid. He was asked again and again, and answered, "Nothing!" But the West said, "There must be something you are afraid of." "Well! I will tell you," says Manabozho, "what it is." But, before he would pronounce the word, he affected great dread. "Ie-ee— Ie-ee—it is—it is," said he, "yeo! yeo!* I cannot name it: I am seized with a dread." The West told him to banish his fears. He commenced again, in a strain of mock sensitiveness repeating the same words; at last he cried out, "It is the root of the apukwa."* He appeared to be exhausted by the effort of pronouncing the word, in all this skillfully acting a studied part.

Some time after he observed, "I will get some of the black rock." The West said, "Far be it from you; do not do so, my son." He still persisted. "Well," said the father, "I will also

* This is a term for the west wind. It is a derivative from *Kabian-oong*, the proper appellation for the occident.
* An interjection indicating pain.
* The scirpus, or bulrush.

get the apukwa root." Manabozho immediately cried out, "*Kago! Kago!*"* affecting, as before, to be in great dread of it, but really wishing, by this course, to urge on the West to procure it, that he might draw him into combat. He went out and got a large piece of the black rock, and brought it home. The West also took care to bring the dreaded root.

In the course of conversation he asked his father whether he had been the cause of his mother's death. The answer was "Yes!" He then took up the rock and struck him. Blow led to blow, and here commenced an obstinate and furious combat, which continued several days. Fragments of the rock, broken off under Manabozho's blows, can be seen in various places to this day."* The root did not prove as mortal a weapon as his well-acted fears had led his father to expect, although he suffered severely from the blows. This battle commenced on the mountains. The West was forced to give ground. Manabozho drove him across rivers, and over mountains and lakes, and at last he came to the brink of this world.

"Hold!" cried he, "my son; you know my power, and that it is impossible to kill me. Desist, and I will also portion you out with as much power as your brothers. The four quarters of the globe are already occupied; but you can go and do a great deal of good to the people of this earth, which is infested with large serpents, beasts, and monsters,* who make great havoc among the inhabitants. Go and do good. You have the power now to do so, and your fame with the beings of this earth will last forever. When you have finished your work, I will have a place provided for you. You will then go and sit with your brother Kabibboonocca in the north."

*The Northern Indians, when traveling in company with each other, or with white persons who possess their confidence, so as to put them at ease, are in the habit of making frequent allusions to Manabozho and his exploits. "There," said a young Chippewa, pointing to some huge boulders of greenstone, "are pieces of the rock broken off in Manabozho's combat with his father." "This is the duck," said an Indian interpreter on the sources of the Mississippi, "that Manabozho kicked." "Under that island," said a friend conversant with their language, "under that island Manabozho lost a beaver."

* The term weendigo, translated here monster is commonly applied, at this time, by the Indians, to cannibals. Its ancient use appears, however, to have embraced giants and anomalous voracious beasts of the land, to the former existence of which, on this Continent, their traditions refer.

The word genabik, rendered serpent, appears likewise to have been used in a generic sense for amphibious animals of large and venomous character. When applied to existing species of serpents, it requires an adjective prefix or qualifying term.

Manabozho was pacified. He returned to his lodge, where he was confined by the wounds he had received. But from his grandmother's skill in medicines he was soon recovered. She told him that his grandfather, who had come to the earth in search of her, had been killed by MEGISSOGWON,* who lived on the opposite side of the great lake. "When he was alive," she continued, "I was never without oil to put on my head, but now my hair is fast falling off for the want of it." "Well!" said he, "Noko, get cedar bark and make me a line, whilst I make a canoe." When all was ready, he went out to the middle of the lake to fish. He put his line down, saying, "Me-she-nah-ma-gwai (the name of the kingfish), take hold of my bait." He kept repeating this for some time. At last the king of the fishes said, "Manabozho troubles me. Here, Trout, take hold of his line." The trout did so. He then commenced drawing up his line, which was very heavy, so that his canoe stood nearly perpendicular; but he kept crying out, "Wha-ee-he! wha-ee-he!" till he could see the trout. As soon as he saw him, he spoke to him. "Why did you take hold of my hook? Esa! esa!* you ugly fish." The trout, being thus rebuked, let go.

Manabozho put his line again in the water, saying, "King of fishes, take hold of my line." But the king of the fishes told a monstrous sunfish to take hold of it; for Manabozho was tiring him with his incessant calls. He again drew up his line with difficulty, saying as before, "Wha-ee-he! wha-ee-he!" while his canoe was turning in swift circles. When he saw the sunfish, he cried, "Esa! esa! you odious fish! why did you dirty my hook by taking it in your mouth? Let go, I say, let go." The sunfish did so, and told the king of fishes what Manabozho said. Just at that moment the bait came near the king, and hearing Manabozho continually crying out, "Me-she nah-ma-gwai, take hold of my hook," at last he did so, and allowed himself to be drawn up to the surface, which he had no sooner reached than, at one mouthful, he took Manabozho and his canoe down. When he came to himself, he found that he was in the fish's belly, and also his canoe. He now turned his thoughts to the way of making his escape. Looking in his canoe, he saw his war-club, with which he immediately struck the heart of the fish. He then a felt sudden motion, as if he were moving with great velocity. The fish observed to the others,

* The wampum or pearl feather.
* An interjection equivalent to shame! shame!

31

"I am sick at stomach for having swallowed this dirty fellow Manabozho." Just at this moment he received another severe blow on the heart. Manabozho thought, "If I am thrown up in the middle of the lake, I shall be drowned; so I must prevent it." He drew his canoe and placed it across the fish's throat, and just as he had finished the fish commenced vomiting, but to no effect. In this he was aided by a squirrel, who had accompanied him unperceived until that moment. This animal had taken an active part in helping him to place his canoe across the fish's throat. For this act he named him, saying, "For the future, boys shall always call you Ajidaumo."*

He then renewed his attack upon the fish's heart, and succeeded, by repeated blows, in killing him, which he first knew by the loss of motion,and by the sound of the beating of the body against the shore. He waited a day longer to see what would happen. He heard birds scratching on the body, and all at once the rays of light broke in. He could see the heads of gulls, who were looking in by the opening they had made. "Oh!" cried Manabozho, "my younger brothers, make the opening larger, so that I can get out." They told each other that their brother Manabozho was inside of the fish. They immediately set about enlarging the orifice, and in a short time liberated him. After he got out he said to the gulls, "For the future you shall be called Kayoshk* for your kindness to me."

The spot where the fish happened to be driven ashore was near his lodge. He went up and told his grandmother to go and prepare as much oil as she wanted. All besides, he informed her, he should keep for himself.

Some time after this, he commenced making preparations for a war excursion against the Pearl Feather, the Manito who lived on the opposite side of the great lake, who had killed his grandfather. The abode of this spirit was defended, first, by fiery serpents, who hissed fire so that no one could pass them; and, in the second place, by a large mass of gummy matter lying on the water, so soft and adhesive, that whoever attempted to pass, or whatever came in contact with it, was sure to stick there.

He continued making bows and arrows without number,

* Animal tail, or bottom upward.
* A free translation of this expression might be rendered, noble scratchers, or grabbers.

but he had no heads for his arrows. At last Noko told him that an old man who lived at some distance could make them. He sent her to get some. She soon returned with her conaus or wrapper full.* Still he told her he had not enough, and sent her again. She returned with as much more. He thought to himself, "I must find out the way of making these heads." Cunning and curiosity prompted him to make the discovery. But he deemed it necessary to deceive his grandmother in so doing. "Noko," said he, "while I take my drum and rattle, and sing my war songs, go and try to get me some *larger* heads for my arrows, for those you brought me are all of the same size. Go and see whether the old man cannot make some a little larger." He followed her as she went, keeping at a distance, and saw the old artificer at work, and so discovered his process. He also beheld the old man's daughter, and perceived that she was very beautiful. He felt his breast beat with a new emotion, but said nothing. He took care to get home before his grandmother, and commenced singing as if he had never left his lodge. When the old woman came near, she heard his drum and rattle, without any suspicion that he had followed her. She delivered him the arrow-heads.

One evening the old woman said, "My son, you ought to *fast* before you go to war, as your brothers frequently do, to find out whether you will be successful or not."* He said he had

* The conaus is the most ancient garment known to these tribes, being a simple extended single piece, without folds. The word is the apparent root of godaus, a female garment. Waub-e-wion, a blanket, is a comparatively modern phrase for a wrapper, signifying, literally, a white skin with the wool on.

* Fasts. The rite of fasting is one of the most deep-seated and universal in the Indian ritual. It is practiced among all the American tribes, and is deemed by them essential to their success in life in every situation. No young man is fitted and prepared to begin the career of life until he has accomplished his great fast. Seven days appear to have been the ancient maximum limit of endurance, and the success of the devotee is inferred from the length of continued abstinence to which he is known to have attained. These fasts are anticipated by youth as one of the most important events of life. They are awaited with interest, prepared for with solemnity, and endured with a self-devotion bordering on the heroic. Character is thought to be fixed from this period, and the primary fast, thus prepared for and successfully established, seems to hold that relative importance to subsequent years that is attached to a public profession of religious faith in civilized communities. It is at this period that the young men and the young women "see visions and dream dreams," and fortune or misfortune is predicted from the guardian spirit chosen during this, to them, religious ordeal. The hallucinations of the mind are taken for

divine inspiration. The effect is deeply felt and strongly impressed on the mind; too deeply, indeed, to be ever obliterated in after life. The father in the circle of his lodge, the hunter in the pursuit of the chase, and the warrior in the field of battle, think of the guardian genius which they fancy to accompany them, and trust to his power and benign influence under every circumstance. This genius is the absorbing theme of their silent meditations, and stands to them in all respects in place of the Christian's hope, with the single difference that, however deeplymused upon, the *name* is never uttered, and every circumstance connected with its selection, and the devotion paid to it, is most studiously and professedly concealed even from their nearest friends.

Fasts in subsequent life appear to have for their object a renewal of the powers and virtues which they attribute to the rite. And they are observed more frequently by those who strive to preserve unaltered the ancient state of society among them, or by men who assume austere habits for the purpose of acquiring influence in the tribe, or as preparatives for war or some extraordinary feat. It is not known that there is any fixed day observed as a general fast. So far as a rule is followed, a general fast seems to have been observed in the spring, and to have *preceded* the general customary feasts at that season.

It will be inferred from these facts, that the Indians believe fasts to be very meritorious. They are deemed most acceptable to the Manitoes or spirits whose influence and protection they wish to engage or preserve. And it is thus clearly deducible, that a very large proportion of the time devoted by the Indians to secret worship, so to say, is devoted to these guardian or intermediate spirits, and not to the Great Spirit or Creator.

no objection, and immediately commenced a fast for several days. He would retire every day from the lodge so far as to be out of reach of his grandmother's voice. It seems she had indicated this spot, and was very anxious he should fast there, and not at another place. She had a secret motive, which she carefully hid from him. Deception always begets suspicion. After a while he thought to himself, "I must find out why my grandmother is so anxious for me to fast at this spot." Next evening he went but a short distance. She cried out, "A little farther off;" but he came nearer to the lodge, and cried out in a low, counterfeited voice, to make it appear that he was distant. She then replied, "That is far enough." He had got so near that he could see all that passed in the lodge. He had not been long in his place of concealment, when a paramour in the shape of a bear entered the lodge. He had very long hair. They commenced talking about him, and appeared to be improperly familiar. At that time people lived to a very great age, and he perceived, from the marked attentions of this visitor, that he did not think a grandmother too old to be pleased with such attentions. He listened to their conversation some time. At last he determined to play the visitor a trick. He took some fire, and when the bear had turned his back, touched his long hair. When the animal felt the flame, he jumped out, but the open air only made it burn the fiercer, and he was seen running off in a full blaze.

Manabozho ran to his customary place of fasting, and assuming a tone of simplicity, began to cry out, "Noko! Noko! is it time for me to come home?" "Yes," she cried. When he came in she told him what had taken place, at which he appeared to be very much surprised.

After having finished his term of fasting and sung his warsong—from which the Indians of the present day derive the custom—he embarked in his canoe, fully prepared for war. In addition to the usual implements, he had a plentiful supply of oil. He travelled rapidly night and day, for he had only to will or speak, and the canoe went. At length he arrived in sight of the fiery serpents. He stopped to view them. He saw they were some distance apart, and that the flame only which issued from them reached across the pass. He commenced talking as a friend to them; but they answered, "We know you, Manabozho, you cannot pass." He then thought of some expedient to deceive them, and hit upon this. He pushed his canoe as near as possible. All at once he cried out, with a loud and terrified voice, "What is that behind you?" The serpents instantly turned their heads, when, at a single word, he passed them. "Well!" said he, placidly, after he had got by, "how do you like my exploit?" He then took up his bow and arrows, and with deliberate aim shot them, which was easily done, for the serpents were stationary, and could not move beyond a certain spot. They were of enormous length and of a bright color.

Having overcome the sentinel serpents, he went on in his magic canoe till he came to a soft gummy portion of the lake, called PIGIU-WAGUMEE or Pitchwater. He took the oil and rubbed it on his canoe, and then pushed into it. The oil softened the surface and enabled him to slip through it with ease, although it required frequent rubbing, and a constant reapplication of the oil. Just as his oil failed, he extricated himself from this impediment, and was the first person who ever succeeded in overcoming it.

He now came in view of land, on which he debarked in safety, and could see the lodge of the Shining Manito, situated on a hill. He commenced preparing for the fight, putting his arrows and clubs in order, and just at the dawn of day began his attack, yelling and shouting, and crying with triple voices, "Surround him! surround him! run up! run up!" making it appear that he had many followers. He advanced crying out, "It was you that killed my grandfather," and with this shot his arrows. The combat continued all day. Manabozho's arrows had no effect, for his antagonist was clothed with pure wampum. He was now reduced to three arrows, and it was only by extraordinary agility that he could escape the blows which the Manito kept making at him. At that moment a large woodpecker (the ma-ma) flew past, and lit on a tree. "Manabozho," he cried, "your adversary has a vulnerable point; shoot at the lock of hair on the crown of his head." He shot his first arrow so as only to draw blood from that part. The Manito made one or two unsteady steps, but recovered himself. He began to parley, but, in the act, received a second arrow, which brought him to his knees. But he again recovered. In so doing, however, he exposed his head, and gave his adversary a chance to fire his third arrow, which penetrated deep, and brought him a lifeless corpse to the ground. Manabozho uttered his saw-saw-quan, and taking his scalp as a trophy, he called the woodpecker to come and receive a reward for his information. He took the blood of the Manito and rubbed it on the woodpecker's* head, the feathers of which are red to this day.

After this victory he returned home, singing songs of triumph and beating his drum. When his grandmother heard him, she came to the shore and welcomed him with songs and dancing. Glory fired his mind. He displayed the trophies he had brought in the most conspicuous manner, and felt an unconquerable desire for other adventures. He felt himself urged by the consciousness of his power to new trials of bravery, skill, and necromantic prowess. He had destroyed the Manito of Wealth, and killed his guardian serpents, and eluded all his charms. He did not long remain inactive. His next adventure was upon the water, and proved him the prince of fishermen. He captured a fish of such monstrous size, that the fat and oil he obtained from it formed a small lake. He therefore invited all the animals and fowls to a banquet, and he made the order in which they partook of this repast the measure of their fatness. As fast as they arrived, he told them to plunge in. The bear came first, and was followed by the deer, opossum, and such other animals as are noted for

* The tuft feathers of the red-headed woodpecker are used to ornament the stems of the Indian pipe, and are symbolical of valor.

36

their peculiar fatness at certain seasons. The moose and bison came tardily. The partridge looked on till the reservoir was nearly exhausted. The hare and marten came last, and these animals have, consequently, no fat. When this ceremony was over, he told the assembled animals and birds to dance, taking up his drum and crying, "New songs from the south, come, brothers, dance." He directed them to pass in a circle around him, and to shut their eyes. They did so. When he saw a fat fowl pass by him, he adroitly wrung off its head, at the same time beating his drum and singing with greater vehemence, to drown the noise of the fluttering, and crying out, in a tone of admiration, "That's the way, my brothers, *that's* the way." At last a small duck (the diver), thinking there was something wrong, opened one eye and saw what he was doing. Giving a spring, and crying "Ha-ha-a! Manabozho is killing us," he made for the water. Manabozho followed him, and, just as the duck was getting into the water, gave him a kick, which is the cause of his back being flattened and his legs being straightened out backward, so that when he gets on land he cannot walk, and his tail feathers are few. Meantime the other birds flew off, and the animals ran into the woods.

After this Manabozho set out to travel. He wished to outdo all others, and to see new countries. But after walking over America and encountering many adventures, he became satisfied as well as fatigued. He had heard of great feats in hunting, and felt a desire to try his power in that way. One evening, as he was walking along the shores of a great lake, weary and hungry, he encountered a great magician in the form of an old wolf, with six young ones, coming towards him. The wolf, as soon as he saw him, told his whelps to keep out of the way of Manabozho, "for I know," continued he, "that it is him that we see yonder." The young wolves were in the act of running off, when Manabozho cried out, "My grandchildren, where are you going? Stop, and I will go with you." He appeared rejoiced to see the old wolf, and asked him whither he was journeying. Being told that they were looking out for a place, where they could find most game, to pass the winter, he said he should like to go with them, and addressed the old wolf in the following words: "Brother, I have a passion for the chase; are you willing to change me into a wolf?" He was answered favorably, and his transformation immediately effected.

Manabozho was fond of novelty. He found himself a wolf corresponding in size with the others, but he was not quite satisfied with the change, crying out, "Oh, make me a little larger." They did so. "A little larger still," he exclaimed. They said, "Let us humor him," and granted his request. "Well," said he, "*that* will do." He looked at his tail. "Oh!" cried he, "do make my tail a little longer and more bushy." They did so. They then all started off in company, dashing up a ravine. After getting into the woods some distance, they fell in with the tracks of moose. The young ones went after them, Manabozho and the old wolf following at their leisure. "Well," said the wolf, "who do you think is the fastest of the boys? can you tell by the jumps they take?" "Why," he replied, "that one that takes such long jumps, he is the fastest, to be sure." "Ha! ha! you are mistaken," said the old wolf. "He makes a good start, but he will be the first to tire out; this one, who appears to be behind, will be the one to kill the game." They then came to the place where the boys had started in chase. One had dropped his small bundle. "Take that, Manabozho," said the old wolf. "Esa," he replied, "what will I do with a dirty dogskin?" The wolf took it up; it was a beautiful robe. "Oh, I will carry it now," said Manabozho. "Oh no," replied the wolf, who at the moment exerted his magic power; "it is a robe of pearls!" And from this moment he omitted no occasion to display his superiority, both in the hunter's and magician's art, above his conceited companion. Coming to a place where the moose had lain down, they saw that the young wolves had made a fresh start after their prey. "Why," said the wolf, "this moose is poor. I know by the tracks, for I can always tell whether they are fat or not." They next came to a place where one of the wolves had bit at the moose, and had broken one of his teeth on a tree. "Manabozho," said the wolf, "one of your grandchildren has shot at the game. Take his arrow; there it is." "No," he replied; "what will I do with a dirty dog's tooth!" The old man took it up, and behold! it was a beautiful silver arrow. When they overtook the youngsters, they had killed a very fat moose. Manabozho was very hungry; but, alas! such is the power of enchantment, he saw nothing but the bones picked quite clean. He thought to himself, "Just as I expected, dirty, greedy fellows!" However, he sat down without saying a word. At length the old wolf spoke to one of the young ones, saying, "Give some meat to your grandfather." One of them obeyed, and, coming near to Manabozho, opened his mouth as if he was about to vomit. He jumped up, saying, "You filthy dog, you have eaten so much that your stomach refuses to hold it. Get you gone into some other place." The old wolf, hearing the abuse, went a little to one side to see, and behold, a heap of fresh ruddy meat, with the fat, lying all ready prepared. He was followed by Manabozho, who, having the enchantment instantly removed, put on a smiling face. "Amazement!" said he; "how fine the meat is." "Yes," replied the wolf; "it is always so with us; we know our work, and always get the best. It is not a long tail that makes a hunter." Manabozho bit his lip.

They then commenced fixing their winter quarters, while the youngsters went out in search of game, and soon brought in a large supply. One day, during the absence of the young wolves, the old one amused himself in cracking the large bones of a moose. "Manabozho," said he, "cover your head with the robe, and do not look at me while I am at these bones, for a piece may fly in your eye." He did as he was told; but, looking through a rent that was in the robe, he saw what the other was about. Just at that moment a piece flew off and hit him on the eye. He cried out, "Tyau, why do you strike me, you old dog?" The wolf said, "You must have been looking at me." But deception commonly leads to falsehood. "No, no," he said, "why should I want to look at you?" "Manabozho," said the wolf, "you *must* have been looking, or you would not have got hurt." "No, no," he replied again, "I was not. I will repay the saucy wolf this," thought he to himself. So, next day, taking up a bone to obtain the marrow, he said to the wolf, "Cover your head and don't look at me, for I fear a piece may fly in your eye." The wolf did so. He then took the leg-bone of the moose, and looking first to see if the wolf was well covered, he hit him a blow with all his might. The wolf jumped up, cried out, and fell prostrate from the effects of the blow." "Why," said he, "do you strike me so?" "Strike you!" he replied; "no, you must have been looking at me." "No," answered the wolf, "I say I have not." But he persisted in the assertion,and the poor magician had to give up.

Manabozho was an expert hunter when he earnestly undertook it. He went out one day and killed a fat moose. He was very hungry, and sat down to eat. But immediately he fell into great doubts as to the proper point to begin. "Well," said he, "I do not know where to commence. At the head? No! People will laugh, and say 'he ate him backward.' " He went to the side. "No!" said he, "they will say I ate sideways." He then went to the hind-quarter. "No!" said he, "they will say I ate him forward. I will commence *here*, say what they will." He took a delicate piece from the rump, and was just ready to put it in his mouth, when a tree close by made a creaking noise, caused by the rubbing of one large branch against another. This annoyed him. "Why!" he exclaimed, "I cannot eat when I hear such a noise. Stop! stop!" said he to the tree. He was putting the morsel again to his mouth, when the noise was repeated. He put it down, exclaiming, "I *cannot eat* with such a noise;" and immediately left the meat, although very hungry, to go and put a stop to the noise. He climbed the tree and was pulling at the limb, when his arm was caught between the two branches so that he could not extricate himself. While thus held fast, he saw a pack of wolves coming in the direction towards his meat. "Go that way! go that way!" he cried out; "what would you come to get here?" The wolves talked among themselves and said, "Manabozho must have something there, or he would not tell us to go another way." "I begin to know him," said an old wolf, "and all his tricks. Let us go forward and see." They came on, and finding the moose, soon made way with the whole carcass. Manabozho looked on wishfully to see them eat till they were fully satisfied, and they left him nothing but the bare bones. The next heavy blast of wind opened the branches and liberated him. He went home, thinking to himself, "See the effect of meddling with frivolous things when I had certain good in my possession."

Next day the old wolf addressed him thus: "My brother, I am going to separate from you, but I will leave behind me one of the young wolves to be your hunter." He then departed. In the act Manabozho was disenchanted, and again resumed his mortal shape. He was sorrowful and dejected, but soon resumed his wonted air of cheerfulness. The young wolf who was left with him was a good hunter, and never failed to keep the lodge well supplied with meat. One day he addressed him as follows: "My grandson, I had a dream last night, and it does not pretend good. It is of the large lake which lies in *that* direction (pointing). You must be careful never to cross it, even if the ice should appear good. If you should come to it at night weary or hungry, you must make the circuit of it." Spring commenced, and the snow was melting fast before the rays of the sun, when one evening the wolf came to this lake, weary with the day's chase. He disliked to go so far to make the circuit of it. "Hwooh!" he exclaimed, "there can be no great harm in trying the ice, as it appears to be sound. Nesho* is over cautious on this point." But he had not got half way across when the ice gave way and he fell in, and was immediately seized by the serpents, who knew it was Manabozho's grandson, and were thirsting for revenge upon him. Manabozho sat pensively in his lodge.

Night came on, but no son returned. The second and third night passed, but he did not appear. He became very desolate and sorrowful. "Ah!" said he, "he must have disobeyed me, and has lost his life in that lake I told him of. Well!" said he at last, "I must mourn for him." So he took coal and blackened his face. But he was much perplexed as to the right mode. "I wonder," said he, "how I must do it? I will cry 'Oh! my grandson! Oh! my grandson!'" He burst out a laughing. "No! no! that won't do. I will try so—'Oh! my heart! Oh! my heart! ha! ha! ha!' That won't do either. I will cry, 'Oh my grandson *obiquadj!*'"* This satisfied him, and he remained in his lodge and fasted, till his days of mourning were over. "Now," said he, "I will go in search of him." He set out and travelled some time. At last he came to a great lake. He then raised the same cries of lamentation for his grandson which had pleased him. He sat down near a small brook that emptied itself into the lake, and repeated his cries. Soon a bird called *Ke-ske-mun-i-see** came near to him. The bird inquired, "What are you doing here?" "Nothing," he replied; "but can you tell me whether any one lives in this lake, and what brings you here yourself?" "Yes!" responded the bird; "the Prince of Serpents lives here, and I am watching to see whether the obiquadj of Manabozho's grandson will not drift ashore, for he was killed by the serpents last spring. But are you not Manabozho himself?" "No," he answered, with his usual deceit; "how do you think *he* could get to this place? But tell me, do the serpents ever appear? when? and where? Tell me all about their habits." "Do you see that beautiful white sandy beach?" said the bird. "Yes!" he answered. "It is there," continued the Kingfisher, "that they bask in the sun. Before they come out, the lake will appear perfectly calm; not even a ripple will appear. After midday (na-wi-qua) you will see them."

* That part of the intestines of a fish, which by its expansion from air in the first stage of decomposition, causes the body to rise and float. The expression here means float.
* The Alcedo or Kingfisher.

41

"Thank you," he replied; "I am Manabozho himself. I have come in search of the body of my son, and to seek my revenge. Come near me that I may put a medal round your neck as a reward for your information." The bird unsuspectingly came near, and received a white medal, which can be seen to this day.* While bestowing the medal, he attempted slyly to wring the bird's head off, but it escaped him, with only a disturbance of the crown feathers of its head, which are rumpled backward. He had found out all he wanted to know, and then desired to conceal the knowledge of his purposes by killing his informant.

He went to the sandy beach indicated, and transformed himself into an oak stump. He had not been there long before he saw the lake perfectly calm. Soon hundreds of monstrous serpents came crawling on the beach. One of the number was beautifully white. He was the prince. The others were red and yellow. The prince spoke to those about him as follows: "I never saw that black stump standing there before. It may be Manabozho. There is no knowing but he may be somewhere about here. He has the power of an evil genius, and we should be on our guard against his wiles." One of the large serpents immediately went and twisted himself around it to the top, and pressed it very hard. The greatest pressure happened to be on his throat; he was just ready to cry out when the serpent let go. Eight of them went in succession and did the like, but always let go at the moment he was ready to cry out. "It cannot be him," they said. "He is too great a weak-heart* for that." They then coiled themselves in a circle about their prince. It was a long time before they fell asleep. When they did so, Manabozho took his bow and arrows, and cautiously stepping over the serpents till he came to the prince, drew up his arrow with the full strength of his arm, and shot him in the left side. He then gave a saw-saw-quan,* and ran off at full speed. The sound uttered by the snakes on seeing their prince mortally wounded, was horrible. They cried, "Manabozho has killed our prince; go in chase of him." Meantime he ran over hill and valley, to gain the interior of the country, with all his strength and speed, treading a mile at a step. But his pursuers were also spirits, and he could hear that something was approaching him fast. He made for the highest mountain,

---

* This bird nas a white spot on the breast, and a tufted head.
* Shau-go-dai-a, i.e., a Coward.
* The war-cry.

42

and climbed the highest tree on its summit, when, dreadful to behold, the whole lower country was seen to be overflowed, and the water was gaining rapidly on the high lands. He saw it reach to the foot of the mountain, and at length it came up to the foot of the tree, but there was no abatement. The flood rose steadily and perceptibly. He soon felt the lower part of his body to be immersed in it. He addressed the tree: "Grandfather, stretch yourself." The tree did so. But the waters still rose. He repeated his request, and was again obeyed. He asked a third time, and was again obeyed; but the tree replied, "It is the last time; I cannot get any higher." The waters continued to rise till they reached up to his chin, at which point they stood, and soon began to abate. Hope revived in his heart. He then cast his eyes around the illimitable expanse, and spied a loon. "Dive down, my brother," he said to him, "and fetch up some earth, so that I can make a new earth." The bird obeyed, but rose up to the surface a lifeless form. He then saw a muskrat. "Dive!" said he, "and if you succeed, you may hereafter live either on land or water, as you please; or I will give you a chain of beautiful little lakes, surrounded with rushes, to inhabit." He dove down, but he floated up senseless. He took the body and breathed in his nostrils, which restored him to life. "Try again," said he. The muskrat did so. He came up senseless the second time, but clutched a little earth in one of his paws, from which, together with the carcass of the dead loon, he created a new earth as large as the former had been, with all living animals, fowls and plants.

As he was walking to survey the new earth, he heard some one singing. He went to the place, and found a female spirit, in the disguise of an old woman, singing these words, and crying at every pause:—

"Ma nau bo sho, O do zheem un,
Ogeem au wun, Onis sa waun,
Hee-Ub bub ub bub (crying).
Dread Manabozho in revenge,
For his grandson lost—
Has killed the chief—the king."

"Noko," said he, "what is the matter?" "Matter!" said she, "where have you been, not to have heard how Manabozho shot my son, the prince of serpents, in revenge for the loss of his nephew, and how the earth was overflowed, and created anew?

43

So I brought my son, here, that he might kill and destroy the inhabitants, as he did on the former earth. But," she continued, casting a scrutinizing glance, "N'yau! indego Manabozho! hub! ub! ub! ub! Oh, I am afraid you are Manabozho!" He burst out into a laugh to quiet her fears. "Ha! ha! ha! how can that be? Has not the old earth perished, and all that was in it?" "Impossible! impossible!" "But, Noko," he continued, "what do you intend doing with all that cedar cord on your back?" "Why," said she, "I am fixing a snare for Manabozho, if he should be on this earth; and, in the mean time, I am looking for herbs to heal my son. I am the only person that can do him any good. He always gets better when I sing—

" 'Manabozho a ne we guawk,
Koan dan mau wah, ne we guawk,
Koan dan mau wah, ne we guawk.'
It is Manabozho's dart,
I try my magic power to withdraw."

Having found out, by conversation with her, all he wished, he put her to death. He then took off her skin, and assuming this disguise, took the cedar cord on his back, and limped away singing her songs. He completely aped the gait and voice of the old woman. He was met by one who told him to make haste; that the prince was worse. At the lodge, limping and muttering, he took notice that they had his grandson's hide to hang over the door. "Oh dogs!" said he; "the evil dogs!" He sat down near the door, and commenced sobbing like an aged woman. One observed, "Why don't you attend the sick, and not set there making such a noise?" He took up the poker and laid it on them, mimicking the voice of the old woman. "Dogs that you are! why do you laugh at me? You know very well that I am so sorry that I am nearly out of my head." With that he approached the prince, singing the songs of the old woman, without exciting any suspicion. He saw that his arrow had gone in about one half its length. He pretended to make preparations for extracting it, but only made ready to finish his victim; and giving the dart a sudden thrust, he put a period to the prince's life. He performed this act with the power of a giant, bursting the old woman's skin, and at the same moment rushing through the door, the serpents following him, hissing and crying out, "Perfidy! murder! vengeance! it is Manabozho." He immediately transformed himself into a wolf, and ran over the plain

44

with all his speed, aided by his father the West Wind. When he got to the mountains he saw a badger. "Brother," said he, "make a hole quick, for the serpents are after me." The badger obeyed. They both went in, and the badger threw all the earth backward, so that it filled up the way behind.

The serpents came to the badger's wauzh,* and decided to watch. "We will starve him out," said they; so they continued watching. Manabozho told the badger to make an opening on the other side of the mountain, from which he could go out and hunt, and bring meat in. Thus they lived some time. One day the badger came in his way and displeased him. He immediately put him to death, and threw out his carcass, saying, "I don't like you to be getting in my way so often."

After living in this confinement for some time alone, he decided to go out. He immediately did so; and after making the circuit of the mountain, came to the corpse of the prince, who had been deserted by the serpents to pursue his destroyer. He went to work and skinned him. He then drew on his skin, in which there were great virtues, took up his war-club, and set out for the place where he first went in the ground. He found the serpents still watching. When they saw the form of their dead prince advancing towards them, fear and dread took hold of them. Some fled. Those who remained Manabozho killed. Those who fled went towards the South.

Having accomplished the victory over the reptiles, Manabozho returned to his former place of dwelling, and married the arrow-maker's daughter.

After Manabozho had killed the Prince of Serpents, he was living in a state of great want, completely deserted by his powers, as a deity, and not able to procure the ordinary means of subsistence. He was at this time living with his wife and children, in a remote part of the country, where he could get no game. He was miserably poor. It was winter, and he had not the common Indian comforts.

He said to his wife, one day, "I will go out a walking, and see if I cannot find some lodges." After walking some time he saw a lodge at a distance. The children were playing at the door. When they saw him approaching they ran into the lodge, and told their parents that Manabozho was coming. It was the residence of the large redheaded Woodpecker. He came to the lodge door and asked him to enter. He did so. After some time,

* A burrow.

45

the Woodpecker, who was a magician, said to his wife. "Have you nothing to give Manabozho? he must be hungry." She answered, "No." In the centre of the lodge stood a large white tamarack-tree. The Woodpecker flew on to it, and commenced going up, turning his head on each side of the tree, and every now and then driving in his bill. At last he drew something out of the tree, and threw it down, when, behold! a fine, fat raccoon on the ground. He drew out six or seven more. He then descended, and told his wife to prepare them. "Manabozho," he said, "this is the only thing we eat. What else can we give you?" "It is very good," replied Manabozho. They smoked their pipes and conversed with each other. After eating, the great spirit-chief got ready to go home. The Woodpecker said to his wife, "Give him what remains of the raccoons to take home for his children." In the act of leaving the lodge he dropped intentionally one of his mittens, which was soon after observed. "Run," said the Woodpecker to his eldest son, "and give it to him. But don't give it into his hand; throw it at him, for there is no knowing him, he acts so curiously." The boy did as he was bid. "Nemesho" (my grandfather), said he, as he came up to him, "you have left one of your mittens—here it is." "Yes," said he, affecting to be ignorant of the circumstance, "it is so. But don't throw it, you will soil it on the snow." The lad, however, threw it, and was about to return. "List," said Manabozho, "is that all you eat—do you eat nothing else with the raccoon?" "No," replied the young Woodpecker. "Tell your father," he answered, "to come and visit me, and let him bring a sack. I will give him what he shall eat with his raccoon meat." When the young one reported this to his father, the old man turned up his nose at the invitation. "What does the old fellow think he has got!" exclaimed he.

Some time after the Woodpecker went to pay a visit to Manabozho. He was received with the usual attention. It had been the boast of Manabozho, in former days, that he could do what any other being in the creation could, whether man or animals. He affected to have the sagacity of all animals, to understand their language, and to be capable of exactly imitating it. And in his visits to men, it was his custom to return, exactly, the treatment he had received. He was very ceremonious in following the very voice and manner of his entertainers. The Woodpecker had no sooner entered his lodge, therefore, than he commenced playing the mimic. He had previously directed his wife to change his lodge, so as to inclose a large dry tam-

46

arack-tree. "What can I give you?" said he to the Woodpecker; "but as we eat, so shall you eat." He then put a long piece of bone in his nose, in imitation of the bill of this bird, and jumping on the tamarack-tree, attempted to climb it, doing as he had seen the Woodpecker do. He turned his head first on one side, then on the other. He made awkward efforts to ascend, but continually slipped down. He struck the tree with the bone in his nose, until at last he drove it so far up his nostrils that the blood began to flow, and he fell down senseless at the foot of the tree. The Woodpecker started after his drum and rattle to restore him, and having got them, succeeded in bringing him to. As soon as he came to his senses, he began to lay the blame of his failure to his wife, saying to his guest, "Nemesho, it is this woman relation of yours—*she* is the cause of my not succeeding. She has rendered me a worthless fellow. Before I took her I could also get raccoons." The Woodpecker said nothing, but flying on the tree, drew out several fine raccoons. "Here," said he, "this is the way *we* do," and left him with apparent contempt.

Severe weather continued, and Manabozho still suffered for the want of food. One day he walked out, and came to a lodge, which was occupied by the Moose (Moz). The young Mozonsug* saw him and told their father Manabozho was at the door. He told them to invite him in. Being seated, they entered into conversation. At last the Moose, who was a Meeta, said, "What shall we give Manabozho to eat? We have nothing." His wife was seated with her back toward him, making garters. He walked up to her, and untying the covering of the armlet from her back, cut off a large piece of flesh from the square of her shoulder.* He then put some medicine on it, which immediately healed the wound. The skin did not even appear to have been broken, and his wife was so little affected by it, that she did not so much as leave off her work, till he told her to prepare the flesh for eating. "Manabozho," said he, "this is all we eat,

*Diminutive form, plural number, of the noun Moz.

* The dress of the females in the Odjibwa nation, consists of sleeves, open on the inner side of the arm from the elbow up, and terminating in large square folds, falling from the shoulders, which are tied at the back of the neck with ribbon or binding. The sleeves are separately made, and not attached to the breast garment, which consists of square folds of cloth, ornamented and sustained by shoulder straps. To untie the sleeves or armlets, as is here described, is therefore to expose the shoulders, but not the back—a simple device, quickly accomplished, by which the magician could readily exercise his art almost imperceptibly to the object.

and it is all we can give you."

After they had finished eating, Manabozho set out for home, but intentionally, as before, dropped one of his *minjekawun*, or mittens. One of the young Moose took it to him, telling him that his father had sent him with it. He had been cautioned not to hand it to him, but to throw it at him. Having done so, contrary to the remonstrance of Manabozho, he was going back, when the latter cried out, "BAKAH! BAKAH!* Is *that** the only kind of meat you eat? Tell me." "Yes," answered the young man, "that is all; we have nothing else." "Tell your father," he replied, "to come and visit me, and I will give him what you shall eat with your meat." The old Moose listened to this message with indignity. "I wonder what he thinks he has got, poor fellow!"

He was bound, however, to obey the invitation, and went accordingly, taking along a cedar sack, for he had been told to bring one. Manabozho received him in the same manner he had himself been received—repeating the same remarks, and attempted to supply the lack of food in the same manner. To this end he had requested his wife to busy herself in making garters. He arose and untied the covering of her back as he had seen the Moose do. He then cut her back shockingly, paying no attention to her cries or resistance, until he saw her fall down, from the loss of blood. "Manabozho," said the Moose, "you are killing your wife." He immediately ran for his drum and rattle, and restored her to life by his skill. He had no sooner done this than Manabozho began to lay the blame of his ill success on his wife. "Why, Nemesho," said he, "this woman, this relation of yours—she is making me a most worthless fellow. Formerly, I procured my meat in this way. But now I can accomplish nothing."

The Moose then cut large pieces of flesh off his own thighs, without the least injury to himself, and gave them to Manabozho, saying, with a contemptuous air, "This is the way *we* do." He then left the lodge.

* Stop! stop!
* It is difficult to throw into the English pronoun the whole of the meaning of the Indian. Pronouns in this language being, like other parts of speech, transitive; they are at once indicative both of the actor, personal, and relative, and the nature of the object, or subject of the action, or relation. This, and that, are not used in the elementary form these pronouns invariably possess in the English. Inflections are put to them indicating the class of natural objects to which they refer. A noun masculine or feminine, requiring an animate pronoun, a noun inanimate, a pronoun inanimate.

After these visits Manabozho was sitting pensively in his lodge one day, with his head down. He heard the wind whistling around it, and thought, by attentively listening, he could hear the voice of some one speaking to him. It seemed to say to him: "Great chief, why are you sorrowful? Am not I your friend—your guardian Spirit?" He immediately took up his rattle, and without leaving his sitting posture, began to sing the chant which at the close of every stanza has the chorus of "WHAW LAY LE AW." When he had devoted a long time to this chant, he laid his rattle aside, and determined to fast. For this purpose he went to a cave, and built a very small fire, near which he laid down, first telling his wife that neither she nor the children must come near him till he had finished his fast. At the end of seven days he came back to the lodge, pale and emaciated. His wife in the meantime had dug through the snow, and got a small quantity of the root called truffles. These she boiled and set before him. When he had finished his repast, he took his large bow and bent it. Then placing a strong arrow to the string, he drew it back, and sent the arrow, with the strength of a giant, through the side of his bark lodge. "There," said he to his wife, "go to the outside, and you will find a large bear, shot through the heart." She did so, and found one as he had predicted.

He then sent the children out to get red willow sticks. Of these he cut off as many pieces, of equal length, as would serve to invite his friends to a feast. A red stick was sent to each one, not forgetting the Moose and the Woodpecker.

When they arrived, they were astonished to see such a profusion of meat cooked for them, at such a time of scarcity. Manabozho understood their glances, and felt a conscious pride in making such a display. "Akewazi," said he, to one of the oldest of the party, "the weather is very cold, and the snow lasts a long time. We can kill nothing now but small squirrels. And I have sent for you to help me eat some of them." The Woodpecker was the first to put a mouthful of the bear's meat to his mouth, but he had no sooner begun to taste it, than it changed into a dry powder, and set him coughing. It appeared as bitter as ashes. The Moose felt the same effect, and began to cough. Each one, in turn, was added to the number of coughers. But they had too much sense of decorum, and respect for their entertainer, to say anything. The meat looked very fine. They thought they would try more of it. But the more they ate the faster they coughed and the louder became

49

the uproar, until Manabozho, exerting his former power, which he now felt to be renewed, transformed them all into the ADJIDAMO, or squirrel, an animal which is still found to have the habit of barking, or coughing, whenever it sees any one approach its nest.

The story of this chief of northern myths is dropped in my notes at this point of his triumph over the strongest of the reptile race. But his feats and adventures by land and sea do not terminate here. There is scarcely a prominent lake, mountain, precipice, or stream in the northern part of America, which is not hallowed in Indian story by his fabled deeds. Further accounts will be found in several of the subsequent tales, which are narrated by the Indians in an independent form, and may be now appropriately left as they were found, as episodes, detached from the original story. To collect all these and arrange them in order would be an arduous labor; and, after all, such an arrangement would lack consistency and keeping, unless much of the thread necessary to present them in an English dress were supplied by alteration, and transposition. The portions above narrated present a beginning and an end, which could hardly be said of the loose and disjointed fragmentary tales referred to. How long Manabozho lived on earth is not related. We hear nothing more of his grandmother; every mouth is filled with his queer adventures, tricks, and sufferings. He was everywhere present where danger presented itself, power was required, or mischief was going forward. Nothing was too low or trivial for him to engage in, nor too high or difficult for him to attempt. He affected to be influenced by the spirit of a god, and was really actuated by the malignity of a devil. The period of his labors and adventures having expired, he withdrew to dwell with his brother in the North, where he is understood to direct those storms which proceed from the points west of the pole. He is regarded as the spirit of the northwest tempests, but receives no worship from the present race of Indians. It is believed by them that he is again to appear, and to exercise an important power in the final disposition of the human race.

In this singular tissue of incongruities may be perceived some ideas probably derived from Asiatic sources. It will be found in the legends of the visitors to the Sun and Moon, and of the white stone canoe, that Manabozho was met on the way, and he is represented as expressing a deep repentance for the bad acts he had committed while on earth. He is, however, found exercising the vocation of a necromancer; has a jossakecd's lodge, from which he utters oracles; and finally transforms on the spot two of the party,who had consulted him, and asked the gift of immortality, the one into a cedartree, and the other into a block of granite.

Manabozho is regarded by the Indians as a divine benefactor, and is admired and extolled as the personification of strength and wisdom. Yet he constantly presents the paradox of being a mere mortal; is driven to low and common expedients; and never utters a sentiment wiser or better than the people among whom he appears. The conception of a divinity, pure, changeless, and just, as well as benevolent, in the distribution of its providences, has not been reached by any traits exhibited in the character of this personage. And if such notions had ever been conceived by the ancestors of the present race of Indians in the East, they have been obliterated, in the course of their long, dark, and hopeless pilgrimage in the forests of America. The prevalence of this legend, among the Indian tribes, is extensive.

The character, the place, which he holds in the Indian mythology are further denoted in the 5th vol. of my *Hist.*, p. 417, where he is represented as giving passage to souls on their way through the regions of space, to the Indian paradise; and also in the legend of the White Stone Canoe. The general myth, is recognized in the legend of the Iroquois, under the name of Hiawatha, and Tarenyawazon. See *Notes on the Iroquois*, page 270 (1846), and also in the 3d vol. *Hist.*, p. 314. Mr. Longfellow has given prominence to it, and to its chief episodes, by selecting and generalizing such traits as appeared best susceptible of poetic uses.

PAUP-PUK-KEEWISS.

THE vernal equinox in the north, generally takes place while the ground is covered with snow, and winter still wears a polar aspect. Storms of wind and light drifting snow, expressively called *poudre* by the French, and peewun by the Indians, fill the atmosphere, and render it impossible to distinguish objects at a short distance. The fine powdery flakes of snow are driven into the smallest crannies of buildings and fixtures, and seem to be endowed with a subtle power of insinuation, which renders northern joinerwork but a poor defence. It is not uncommon for the sleeper, on waking up in the morning, to find heaps of snow, where he had supposed himself quite secure on lying down.

Such seasons are, almost invariably, times of scarcity and hunger with the Indians, for the light snows have buried up the traps of the hunters, and the fishermen are deterred from exercising their customary skill in decoying fish through orifices cut in the ice. They are often reduced to the greatest straits, and compelled to exercise their utmost ingenuity to keep their children from starving. Abstinence, on the part of the elder members of the family, is regarded both as a duty and a merit. Every effort is made to satisfy the importunity of the little ones for food, and if there be a storyteller in the lodge, he is sure to draw upon his cabin lore, to amuse their minds, and beguile the time.

In these storms, when each inmate of the lodge has his *conaus*, or wrapper, tightly drawn around him, and all are cowering around the cabin fire, should some sudden puff of wind drive a volume of light snow into the lodge, it would scarcely happen, but that some one of the group would cry out, "Ah, Pauppukkeewiss is now gathering his harvest," an expression which has the effect to put them all into good humor.

Pauppukkeewiss was a crazy brain, who played many queer tricks, but took care, nevertheless, to supply his family and children with food. But, in this, he was not always successful. Many winters have passed since he was overtaken; at this very season of the year, with great want, and he, with his whole family, was on the point of starvation. Every resource seemed to have failed. The snow was so deep, and the storm continued so long, that he could not even find a partridge or a hare. And his usual resource of fish had entirely failed. His lodge stood in a point of woods, not far back from the shores of the Gitchiguma, or great water, where the autumnal storms had piled up the ice into high pinnacles, resembling castles.

"I will go," said he to his family one morning, "to these castles, and solicit the pity of the spirits who inhabit them, for I know that they are the residence of some of the spirits of Kabiboonoka." He did so, and found that his petition was not disregarded. They told him to fill his mushkemoot, or sack, with the ice and snow, and pass on toward his lodge, without looking back, until he came to a certain hill. He must then drop it and leave it till morning, when he would find it filled with fish.

They cautioned him, that he must by no means look back, although he would hear a great many voices crying out to him, in abusive terms, for these voices were nothing but the wind playing through the branches of the trees. He faithfully obeyed the injunction, although he found it hard to avoid turning round, to see who was calling out to him. And when he visited his sack in the morning, he found it filled with fish.

It chanced that Manabozho visited him on the morning that he brought home the sack of fish. He was invited to partake of a feast, which Pauppukkeewiss ordered to be prepared for him. While they were eating, Manabozho could not help asking him, by what means he had procured such an abundance of food, at a time when they were all in a state of starvation.

Pauppukkeewiss frankly told him the secret, and repeated the precautions which were necessary to insure success. Manabozho determined to profit by his information, and as soon as he could, he set out to visit the icy castles. All things happened as he had been told. The spirits seemed propitious, and told him to fill and carry. He accordingly filled his sacks with ice and snow, and proceeded rapidly toward the hill of transmutation. But as he ran he heard voices calling out behind him. "Thief! thief! He he stolen fish from Kabiboonoka," cried one. "Mukumik! mukumik! Take it away! Take it away!" cried another.

In fine, his ears were so assailed by all manner of opprobrious terms, that he could not avoid turning his head, to see who it was that thus abused him. But his curiosity dissolved the charm. When he came to visit his bags next morning, he found them filled with ice and snow. A high drifting snow storm never fails to bring up this story. The origin of this queer character is a queer as his acts are phantastic. The myth asserts, that a man of large stature, and great activity of mind and body, found himself standing alone on a prairie. He thought to himself, "How came I here? Are there no beings on this earth but myself? I must travel and see. I must walk till I find the abodes of men." So soon as his mind was made up, he set out, he knew not where, in search of habitations. No obstacles could divert him from his purpose. Neither prairies, rivers, woods, nor storms had the effect to daunt his courage or turn him back. After travelling a long time he came to a wood, in which he saw decayed stumps of trees, as if they had been cut in ancient times, but no other traces of men. Pursuing his journey, he found more recent marks of the same kind; and after this, he came to fresh traces of human beings; first their footsteps, and then the wood they had cut, lying in heaps. Continuing on, he emerged towards dusk from the forest, and beheld at a distance a large village of high lodges, standing on rising ground. He said to himself, "I will arrive there on a run." Off he started with all his speed; on coming to the first large lodge, he jumped over it. Those within saw something pass over the opening, and then heard a thump on the ground.

"What is that?" they all said.

One came out to see, and invited him in. He found himself in company with an old chief and several men, who were seated in the lodge. Meat was set before him, after which the chief asked him where he was going and what his name was. He answered, that he was in search of adventures, and his name was Paup-Puk-Keewiss. A stare followed.

"Paup-Puk-Keewiss!"* said one to another, and a general titter went round.

He was not easy in his new position; the village was too small to give him full scope for his powers, and after a short stay he made up his mind to go farther, taking with him a young man who had formed a strong attachment for him, and might serve him as his mesh-in-au-wa.* They set out together, and when his companion was fatigued with walking, he would show him a few tricks, such as leaping over trees, and turning round on one leg till he made the dust fly, by which he was mightily pleased, although it sometimes happened that the character of these tricks frightened him.

One day they came to a very large village, where they were well received. After staying in it sometime, they were informed of a number of manitoes who lived at a distance, and who made it a practice to kill all who came to their lodge. Attempts had been made to extirpate them, but the war-parties who went out for this purpose were always unsuccessful. Paup-Puk-Keewiss determined to visit them, although he was advised not to do so. The chief warned him of the danger of the visit; but, finding him resolved,

"Well," said he, "if you will go, being my guest, I will send twenty warriors to serve you."

He thanked him for the offer. Twenty young men were ready at the instant, and they went forward, and in due time

---

* This word appears to be derived from the same root as *Paup-puk-ke-nay*, a grasshopper, the inflection *iss* making it personal. The Indian idea is that of harum scarum. He is regarded as a foil to Manabozho, with whom he is frequently brought into contact in aboriginal story craft.

* This is an official who bears the pipe for the ruling chief, and is an inferior dignity in councils.

described the lodge of the manitoes. He placed his friend and the warriors near enough to see all that passed, while he went alone to the lodge. As he entered he saw five horrid-looking manitoes in the act of eating. It was the father and his four sons. They looked hideous; their eyes were swimming low in their heads, as if half starved. They offered him something to eat, which he refused.

"What have you come for?" said the old one.

"Nothing," Paup-Puk-Keewiss answered.

They all stared at him.

"Do you not wish to wrestle?" they all asked.

"Yes," he replied.

A hideous smile came over their faces.

"*You* go," they said to the eldest brother.

They got ready, and were soon clinched in each other's arms for a deadly throw. He knew their object—his death—his *flesh* was all they wanted, but he was prepared for them.

"Haw! haw!"* they cried, and soon the dust and dry leaves flew about as if driven by a strong wind.

The manito was strong, but Paup-Puk-Keewiss soon found that he could master him: and, giving him a trip, he threw him with a giant's force head foremost on a stone, and he fell like a puffed thing.

The brothers stepped up in quick succession, but he put a number of tricks in force, and soon the whole four lay bleeding on the ground. The old manito got frightened and ran for his life. Paup-Puk-Keewiss pursued him for sport; sometimes he was before him, sometimes flying over his head. He would now give him a kick, then a push or a trip, till he was almost exhausted. Meantime his friend and the warriors cried out, "Ha! ha! a! ha! ha! a! Paup-Puk-Keewiss is driving him before him." The manito only turned his head now and then to look back; at last, Paup-Puk Keewiss gave him a kick on his back, and broke his back bone; down he fell, and the blood gushing out of his mouth prevented him from saying a word. The warriors piled all the bodies together in the lodge, and then took fire and burned them. They all looked with deep interest at the quantity of human bones scattered around.

Paup-Puk-Keewiss then took three arrows, and after having performed a ceremony to the Great Spirit, he shot one into the

* This is a studied perversion of the interjection *Ho.* In another instance (vide Wassamo) it is rendered *Hoke.*

56

air, crying, with a loud voice,

"*You* who are lying down, rise up, or you will be hit!" The bones all moved to one place. He shot the second arrow, repeating the same words, when each bone drew towards its fellow-bone; the third arrow brought forth to life the whole multitude of people who had been killed by the manitoes. Paup-Puk Keewiss then led them to the chief of the village who had proved his friend, and gave them up to him. Soon after the chief came with his counsellors.

"Who is more worthy," said he, "to rule than you? *You* alone can defend them."

Paup-Puk-Keewiss thanked him, and told him he was in search of more adventures. The chief insisted. Paup-Puk Keewiss told him to confer the chieftainship on his friend, who, he said, would remain while he went on his travels. He told them that he would, some time or other, come back and see them.

"Ho! ho! ho!" they all cried, "come back again and see us," insisting on it. He promised them he would, and then set out alone.

After travelling some time he came to a large lake; on looking about, he discovered a very large otter on an island. He thought to himself, "His skin will make me a fine pouch," and immediately drew up, at long shots, and drove an arrow into his side. He waded into the lake, and with some difficulty dragged him ashore. He took out the entrails, and even then the carcass was so heavy that it was as much as he could do to drag it up a hill overlooking the lake. As soon as he got him up into the sunshine, where it was warm, he skinned him, and threw the carcass some distance thinking the war-eagle would come, and he should have a chance to get his skin and feathers as head ornaments. He soon heard a rushing noise in the air, but could see nothing; by and by, a large eagle dropped, as if from the air, on the otter's carcass. He drew his bow, and the arrow passed through under both his wings. The bird made a convulsive flight upwards with such force, that the heavy carcass (which was nearly as big as a moose) was borne up several feet. Fortunately, both claws were fastened deeply into the meat, the weight of which soon brought the bird down. He skinned him, crowned his head with the trophy, and next day was on his way, on the lookout for something new.

After walking a while he came to a lake, which flooded the trees on its banks; he found it was only a lake made by beavers.

He took his station on the elevated dam, where the stream escaped, to see whether any of the beavers would show themselves. He soon saw the head of one peeping out of the water to see who disturbed them.

"My friend," said Paup-Puk-Keewiss, "could you not turn me into a beaver like yourself?" for he thought , if he could become a beaver, he would see and know how these animals lived.

"I do not know," replied the beaver; "I will go and ask the others."

Soon all the beavers showed their heads above the water, and looked to see if he was armed; but he had left his bow and arrows in a hollow tree at a short distance. When they were satisfied, they all came near.

"Can you not, with all your united power," said he, "turn me into a beaver? I wish to live among you."

"Yes," answered their chief; "lay down;" and he soon found himself changed into one of them.

"You must make me *large*," said he; "*larger* than any of you."

"Yes, yes!" said they. "By and by, when we get into the lodge, it shall be done."

In they all dove into the lake; and, in passing large heaps of limbs and logs at the bottom, he asked the use of them; they answered, "It is for our winter's provisions."* When they all got into the lodge, their number was about one hundred. The lodge was large and warm.

"Now we will make you large," said they. "Will *that* do?" exerting their power.

"Yes," he answered, for he found he was ten times the size of the largest.

"You need not go out," said they. "We will bring your food into the lodge, and you will be our chief."

"Very well," Paup-Puk-Keewiss answered. He thought, "I will stay here and grow fat at their expense. But, soon after, one ran into the lodge out of breath, saying, "We are visited by Indians." All huddled together in great fear. The water began to *lower*, for the hunters had broken down the dam, and they soon heard them on the roof of the lodge breakig it up. Out jumped all the beavers into the water, and so escaped. Paup-Puk-Keewiss tried to follow them; but, alas! they had made

* We may mention, for the youth who may read these tales, that beavers live by gnawing the bark of trees.

58

him so large that he could not creep out of the hole. He tried to call them back, but to no effect; he worried himself so much in trying to escape, that he looked like a bladder. He could not turn himself back into a man, although he heard and understood all the hunters said. One of them put his head in at the top of the lodge.

"*Ty-au!*" cried he; "*Tut Ty-au!* Me-shau-mik— king of the beavers is in." They all got at him, and knocked his skull till it was as soft as his brains. He thought, as well as ever he did, although he was a beaver. Seven or eight of them then placed his body on poles and carried him home. As they went, he reflected in this manner: "What will become of me? my ghost or shadow will not die after they get me to their lodges." Invitations were immediately sent out for a grand feast. The women took him out into the snow to skin him; but, as soon as his flesh got cold, his *Jee-bi* went off.

Paup-Puk-Kewiss found himself standing near a prairie, having reassumed his mortal shape. After walking a distance, he saw a herd of elk feeding. He admired the apparent ease and enjoyment of their life, and thought there could be nothing pleasanter than the liberty of running about and feeding on the prairies. He asked them if they could not turn him into their shape.

"Yes," they answered, after a pause. "Get down on your hands and feet." And he soon found himself an elk.

"I want big horns, big feet," said he; "I wish to be very large."

"Yes! yes!" they said.

"There!" exerting their power; "are you big enough?"

"Yes!" he answered, for he saw that he was very large. They spent a good time in grazing and running. Being rather cold one day, he went into a thick wood for shelter, and was followed by most of the herd. They had not been long there before some elks from behind passed the others like a strong wind. All took the alarm, and off they ran, he with the rest.

"Keep out on the plains," they said.

But he found it was too late, as they had already got entangled in the thick woods. Paup-Puk-Keewiss soon smelt the hunters, who were closely following his trail, for they had left all the others and followed him. He jumped furiously, and broke down saplings in his flight, but it only served to retard his progress. He soon felt an arrow in his side; he jumped over trees in his agony, but the arrows clattered thicker and thicker upon his sides, and at last one entered his heart. He fell to the ground, and heard the whoop of triumph sounded by the hunters. On coming up, they looked on the carcass with astonishment, and with their hands up to their mouths exclaimed Ty-au! Ty-au! There were about sixty in the party, who had come out on a special hunt, as one of their number had, the day before, observed his *large tracks* on the plains. After skinning him and his flesh getting cold, his *Jee-bi* took its flight from the carcass, and he again found himself in human shape, with a bow and arrows.

But his passion for adventure was not yet cooled; for, on coming to a large lake with a sandy beach, he saw a large flock of brant, and, speaking to them, asked them to turn him into a brant.

"Yes," they replied.

"But I want to be very large," he said.

"Very well," they answered; and he soon found himself a large brant, all the others standing gazing in astonishment at his large size.

"You must fly as leader," they said.

"No," answered Paup-Puk-Kewiss, "I will fly behind."

"Very well," they said. "One thing more we have to say to you. You must be careful, in flying, not to look *down*, for something may happen to you."

"Well! it is so," said he; and soon the flock rose up into the air, for they were bound north. They flew very fast, he behind. One day, while going with a strong wind, and as swift as their wings could flap, while passing over a large village, the Indians raised a great shout on seeing them, particularly on Paup-Puk-Keewiss's account for his wings were broader than two large aupukwa.* They made such a noise, that he forgot what had been told him, about looking down. They were now going as swift as arrows; and, as soon as he brought his neck in and stretched it down to look at the shouters, his tail was caught by the wind, and over and over he was blown. He tried to right himself, but without success. Down, down he went, making more turns than he wished for, from a height of several miles. The first thing he knew was, that he was jammed into a large hollow tree. To get back or forward was out of the question, and there he remained till his brant life was ended by starvation. His *Jee-bi* again left the carcass, and he once more found himself in the shape of a human being.

*Mats.

Travelling was still his passion; and, while travelling, he came to a lodge in which were two old men with heads white from age. They treated him well, and he told them that he was going back to his village to see his friends and people. They said they would aid him, and pointed out the direction he should go; but they were deceivers. After walking all day, he came to a lodge looking very much like the first, with two old men in it with white heads. It was, in fact the very same lodge, and he had been walking in a circle; but they did not undeceive him, pretending to be strangers, and saying, in a kind voice, "We will show you the way." After walking the third day and coming back to the same place, he found them out in their tricks, for he had cut a notch on the doorpost.

"Who are you," said he to them, "to treat me so?" and he gave one a kick and the other a slap, which killed them. Their blood flew against the rocks near the lodge, and this is the reason there are red streaks in them to this day. He then burned their lodge down, and freed the earth of two pretended good men, who were manitoes.

He then continued his journey, not knowing exactly which way to go. At last he came to a big lake. He got on the highest hill to try and see the opposite side, but he could not. He then made a canoe, and took a sail into the lake. On looking into the water, which was very clear, before he got to the abrupt depth, he saw the bottom covered with dark fishes, numbers of which he caught. This inspired him with a wish to return to his village and to bring his people to live near this lake. He went on, and towards evening came to a large island, where he encamped and ate the fish he had speared.

Next day he returned to the main land, and, in wandering along the shore, he encountered a more powerful manito than himself, called Manabozho. He thought best, after playing him a trick, to keep out of his way. He again thought of returning to his village; and, transforming himself into a partridge, took his flight towards it. In a short time he reached it, and his return was welcomed with feastings and songs. He told them of the lake and the fish, and persuaded them all to remove to it, as it would be easier for them to live there. He immediately began to remove them by short encampments, and all things turned out as he had said. They caught abundance of fish. After this, a messenger came for him in the shape of a bear, who said that their king wished to see him immediately at his village. Paup-Puk-Keewiss was ready in an instant; and, getting on to the messenger's back, off he ran. Towards evening they went up a high mountain, and came to a cave where the bear-king lived. He was a very large person, and made him welcome by inviting him into his lodge. As soon as propriety allowed, he spoke, and said that he had sent for him on hearing that he was the chief who was moving a large party towards his hunting-grounds.

"You must know," said he, "that you have no right there. And I wish you would leave the country with your party, or else the strongest force will take possession."

"Very well," replied Paup-Puk-Keewiss. "So be it." He did not wish to do anything without consulting his people; and besides, he saw that the bear-king was raising a war party. He then told him he would go back that night. The bear-king left him to do as he wished, but told him that one of his young men was ready at his command; and, immediately jumping on his back, Paup-Puk-Keewiss rode home. He assembled the village, and told the young men to kill the bear, make a feast of it, and hang the head outside the village, for he knew the bear spies would soon see it, and carry the news to their chief.

Next morning Paup-Puk-Keewiss got all his young warriors ready for a fight. After waiting one day, the bear war-party came in sight, making a tremendous noise. The bear-chief advanced, and said that he did not wish to shed the blood of the young warriors; but that if he, Paup-Puk-Keewiss, consented they two would have a race, and the winner should kill the losing chief, and all his young men should be slaves to the other. Paup-Puk-Keewiss agreed, and they ran before all the warriors. He was victor, and came in first; but, not to terminate the race too soon, he gave the bear-chief some specimens of his skill and swiftness by forming eddies and whirlwinds with the sand, as he leaped and turned about him. As the bear-chief came up, he drove an arrow through him, and a great chief fell. Having done this, he told his young men to take all those blackfish (meaning the bears), and tie them at the door of each lodge, that they might remain in future to serve as servants.

After seeing that all was quiet and prosperous in the village, Paup-Puk-Keewiss felt his desire for adventure returning. He took a kind leave of his friends and people, and started off again. After wandering a long time, he came to the lodge of Manabozho, who was absent. He thought he would play him a trick, and so turned everything in the lodge upside down, and killed his chickens. Now Manabozho calls all the fowls of the air his chickens; and among the number was a raven, the meanest of birds, which Paup-Puk-Keewiss killed and hung up by the neck to insult him. He then went on till he came to a very high point of rocks running out into the lake, from the top of which he could see the country back as far as the eye could reach. While sitting there, Manabozho's mountain chickens flew round and past him in great numbers. So, out of spite, he shot them in great numbers, for his arrows were sure and the birds very plenty, and he amused himself by throwing the birds down the rocky precipice. At length a wary bird cried out, "Paup-Puk-Keewiss is killing us. Go and tell our father." Away flew a delegation of them, and Manabozho soon made his appearance on the plain below. Paup-Puk-Keewiss made his escape on the opposite side. Manabozho cried out from the mountain—

"The earth is not so large but I can get up to you." Off Paup-Puk-Keewis ran, and Manabozho after him. He ran over hills and prairies with all his speed, but still saw his pursuer hard after him. He thought of this expedient. He stoppped and climbed a large pine-tree, stripped it of all its green foilage, and threw it to the winds, and then went on. When Manabozho reached the spot,the tree addressed him.

"Great chief," said the tree, "will you give me my life again? Paup-Puk-Keewiss has killed me."

"Yes," replied Manabozho; and it took him some time to gather the scattered foliage, and then renewed the pursuit. Paup-Puk-Keewiss repeated the same thing with the hemlock, and with various other trees, for Manabozho would always stop to restore what he had destroyed. By this means he got in advance; but Manabozho persevered, and was fast over-taking him, when Paup-Puk-Keewiss happened to see an elk. He asked him to take him on his back, which the elk did, and for some time he made great progress, but still Manabozho was in sight. Paup-Puk-Keewiss dismounted, and, coming to a large sandstone rock, he broke it in pieces and scattered the grains. Manabozho was so close upon him at this place that he had almsot caught him; but the foundation of the rock cried out,

"Haye! Ne-me-sho, Paup-Puk-Keewiss has spoiled me. Will. you not restore me to life?"

"Yes," replied Manabozho; and he restored the rock to its previous shape. He then pushed on in the pursuit of Paup-Puk-

Keewiss, and had got so near as to put out his arm to seize him; but Paup-Puk-Keewiss dodged him, and immediately raised such a dust and commotion by whirlwinds as made the trees break, and the sand and leaves dance in the air. Again and Manabozho's hand was put out to catch him; but he dodged him at every turn, and kept up such a tumult of dust, that in the thickest of it, he dashed into a hollow tree which had been blown down, and changed himself into a snake, and crept out at the roots. Well that he did; for at the moment he had got out, Manabozho, who is Ogee-bau-ge-mon,* struck it with his power, and it was in fragments. Paup-Puk-Kewiss was again in human shape; again Manabozho pressed him hard. At a distance he saw a very high bluff of rock jutting out into the lake, and ran for the foot of the precipice, which was abrupt and elevated. As he came near, the local manito of the rock opened his door and told him to come in. The door was no sooner closed than Manabozho knocked.

"Open it!" he cried, with a loud voice.

The manito was afraid of him, but he said to his guest—

"Since I have sheltered you, I would sooner die with you than open the door.

"Open it!" Manabozho again cried.

The manito kept silent. Manabozho, however, made no attempt to open it by force. He waited a few moments. "Very well," he said; "I give you only till night to live." The manito trembled, for he knew he would be shut up under the earth.

Night came. The clouds hung low and black, and every moment the forked lightning would flash from them. The black clouds advanced slowly, and threw their dark shadows afar, and behind there was heard the rumbling noise of the coming thunder. As they came near to the precipice, the thunders broke, the lightning flashed, the ground shook, and the solid rocks split, tottered, and fell. And under their ruins where crushed the mortal bodies of Paup-Puk-Keewiss and the manito.

It was only then that Paup-Puk-Keewiss found he was really dead. He had been killed in different animal shapes; but now his body, in human shape, was crushed. Manabozho came and took their Jee-bi-ug, or spirits.

"You," said he to Paup-Puk-Keewiss, "shall not be again permitted to live on the earth. I will give you the shape of the

* A species of lightning.

64

war-eagle, and you will be the chief of all fowls, and your duty shall be to watch over their destinies."

OSSEO,

OR

THE SON OF THE EVENING STAR.

ALGONQUIN LEGEND.

THERE once lived an Indian in the north, who had ten daughters, all of whom grew up to womanhood. They were noted for their beauty, but especially Oweenee, the youngest, who was very independent in her way of thinking. She was a great admirer of romantic places and paid very little attention to the numerous young men who came to her father's lodge for the purpose of seeing her. Her elder sisters were all solicited in marriage from their parents, and one after another, went off to dwell in the lodges of their husbands, or mothers-in-law, but she would listen to no proposals of the kind. At last she married an old man called OSSEO, who was scarcely able to walk, and was too poor to have things like others. They jeered and laughed at her, on all sides, but she seemed to be quite happy, and said to them. "It is my choice and you will see in the end, who has acted the wisest." Soon after, the sisters and their husbands and their parents were all invited to a feast, and as they walked along the path, they could not help pitying their young and handsome sister, who had such an unsuitable mate. Osseo often stopped and gazed upwards, but they could perceive nothing in the direction he looked, unless it was the faint glimmering of the evening star They heard him muttering to himself as they went along, and one of the elder sisters caught the words, "Sho-wain-ne-me-shin nosa."* "Poor old man," said she, "he is talking to his father, what a pity it is, that he would not fall and break his neck, that our sister might have a handsome young husband." Presently they passed a large hollow log, lying with one end toward the path. The moment Osseo, who was of the turtle totem, came to it, he stopped short,

* Pity me, my father.

66

uttered a loud and peculiar yell, and then dashing into one end of the log, he came out at the other, a most beautiful young man, and springing back to the road, he led off the party with steps as light as the reindeer.* But on turning round to look for his wife, behold, she had been changed into an old, decrepit woman, who was bent almost double, and walked with a cane. The husband, however, treated her very kindly, as she had done him during the time of his enchantment, and constantly addressed her by the term of ne-ne-moosh-a, or my sweetheart.

When they came to the hunter's lodge with whom they were to feast, they found the feast ready prepared, and as soon as their entertainer had finished his harangue (in which he told them his feasting was in honor of the Evening or Woman's Star), they began to partake of the portion dealt out, according to age and character, to each one. The food was very delicious, and they were all happy but Osseo, who looked at his wife and then gazed upward, as if he was looking into the substance of the sky. Sounds were soon heard, as if from far-off voices in the air, and they became plainer and plainer, till he could clearly distinguish some of the words.

"My son—my son," said the voice, "I have seen your afflictions and pity your wants. I come to call you away from a scene that is stained with blood and tears. The earth is full of sorrows. Giants and sorcerers, the enemies of mankind, walk abroad in it, and are scattered throughout its length. Every night they are lifting their voices to the Power of Evil, and every day they make themselves busy in casting evil in the hunter's path. You have long been their victim, but shall be their victim no more. The spell you were under is broken. Your evil genius is overcome. I have cast him down by my superior strength, and it is this strength I now exert for your happiness. Ascend, my son—ascend into the skies, and partake of the feast I have prepared for you in the stars, and bring with you those you love.

"The food set before you is enchanted and blessed. Fear not to partake of it. It is endowed with magic power to give immortality to mortals, and to change men to spirits. Your bowls and kettles shall be no longer wood and earth. The one shall become silver, and the other wampum. They shall shine like fire, and glisten like the most beautiful scarlet. Every female shall also change her state and looks, and no longer be

---

* The C. Sylvestris inhabits North America, north of latitude 46°.

67

doomed to laborious tasks. She shall put on the beauty of the starlight, and become a shining bird of the air, clothed with shining feathers. She shall dance and not work—she shall sing and not cry."

"My beams," continued the voice, "shine faintly on your lodge, but they have a power to transform it into the lightness of the skies, and decorate it with the colors of the clouds. Come, Osseo, my son, and dwell no longer on earth. Think strongly on my words, and look steadfastly at my beams. My power is now at its height. Doubt not—delay not. It is the voice of the Spirit of the stars that calls you away to happiness and celestial rest."

The words were intelligible to Osseo, but his companions thought them some far-off sounds of music, or birds singing in the woods. Very soon the lodge began to shake and tremble, and they felt it rising into the air. It was too late to run out, for they were already as high as the tops of the trees. Osseo looked around him as the lodge passed through the topmost boughs, and behold! their wooden dishes were changed into shells of a scarlet color, the poles of the lodge to glittering wires of silver, and the bark that covered them into the gorgeous wings of insects. A moment more, and his brothers and sisters, and their parents and friends, were transformed into birds of various plumage. Some were jays, some partridges and pigeons, and others gay singing birds, who hopped about displaying their glittering feathers, and singing their song. But OWEENEE still kept her earthy garb, and exhibited all the indications of extreme age. He again cast his eyes in the direction of the clouds, and uttered that peculiar yell, which had given him the victory at the hollow log. In a moment the youth and beauty of his wife returned; her dingy garments assumed the shining appearance of green silk, and her cane was changed into a silver feather. The lodge again shook and trembled, for they were now passing through the uppermost clouds, and they immediately after found themselves in the Evening Star, the residence of Osseo's father.

"My son," said the old man, "hang that cage of birds, which you have brought along in your hand, at the door, and I will inform you why you and your wife have been sent for." Osseo obeyed the directions, and then took his seat in the lodge. "Pity was shown to you," resumed the king of the star, "on account of the contempt of your wife's sister, who laughed at her ill fortune, and ridiculed you while you were under the power of that wicked spirit, whom you overcame at the log. That spirit

68

lives in the next lodge, being a small star you see on the left of mine, and he has always felt envious of my family, because we had greater power than he had, and especially on account of our having had the care committed to us of the female world. He failed in several attempts to destroy your brothers-in-law and sisters-in-law, but succeeded at last in transforming yourself and your wife into decrepit old persons. You must be careful and not let the light of his beams fall on you, while you are here, for therein is the power of his enchantment; a ray of light is the bow and arrows he uses."

Osseo lived happy and contented in the parental lodge, and in due time his wife presented him with a son, who grew up rapidly, and was the image of his father. He was very quick and ready in learning everything that was done in his grandfather's dominions, but he wished also to learn the art of hunting, for he had heard that this was a favorite pursuit below. To gratify him, his father made him a bow and arrows, and he then let the birds out fo the cage that he might practise in shooting. He soon became expert, and the very first day brought down a bird, but when he went to pick it up, to his amazement, it was a beautiful young woman with the arrow sticking in her breast. It was one of his younger *aunts*. The moment her blood fell upon the surface of that pure and spotless planet, the charm was dissolved. The boy immediately found himself sinking, but was partly upheld, by something like wings, till he passed through the lower clouds, and he then suddenly dropped upon a high, romantic island in a large lake. He was pleased on looking up, to see all his aunts and uncles following him in the form of birds, and he soon discovered the silver lodge, with his father and mother, descending with its waving barks looking like so many insects' gilded wings. It rested on the highest cliffs of the island, and here they fixed their residence. They all resumed their natural *shapes*, but were diminished to the *size* of faires: as a mark of homage to the King of the Evening Star, they never failed, on every pleasant evening, during the summer season, to join hands, and dance upon the top of the rocks. These rocks were quickly observed by the Indians to be covered, in moonlight evenings, with a larger sort of PUK WUDJ ININEES, or little men, and were called Mish-in-e-mok-in-ok-ong, or turtle spirits, and the island is named from them to this day.* Their

* Michilimackinac, the term alluded to, is the original French orthography of MISH EN I MOK IN ONG, the *local* form (sing. and plu.), of Turtle Spirits.

69

KWASIND,

OR
THE FEARFULLY STRONG MAN.

PAUWATING* was a village where the young men amused themselves very much in ancient times, in sports and ball-playing.

One day, as they were engaged in their sports, one of the strongest and most active, at the moment he was about to succeed in a trial of lifting, slipped and fell upon his back. "Ha! ha! ha!" cried the lookers-on, "you will never rival Kwasind." He was deeply mortified, and when the sport was over, these words came to his mind. He could not recollect any man of this name. He thought he would ask the old man, the story-teller of the village, the next time he came to the lodge. The opportunity soon occurred.

"My grandfather," said he, "who was Kwasind? I am very anxious to know what he could do."

"Kwasind," the old man replied, "was a listless idle boy. He would not play when the other boys played, and his parents could never get him to do any kind of labor. He was always making excuses. His parents took notice, however, that he fasted for days together, but they could not learn what spirit he supplicated, or had chosen as the guardian spirit to attend him through life. He was so inattentive to his parents' requests, that he, at last, became a subject of reproach.

" 'Ah,' said his mother to him one day, 'is there any young man of your age, in all the village, who does so little for his parents? You neither hunt nor fish. You take no interest in anything, whether labor or amusement, which engages the attention of your equals in years. I have often set my nets* in the coldest days of winter, without any assistance from you.

---

* i.e. Place of shallow cataract, named *Sault de Ste. Marie* on the arrival of the French. This is the *local* form of the word, the substantive proper terminates in EEG.

71

* Nets are set in winter, in high northern latitudes, through orifices cut in the ice.

And I have taken them up again, while you remained inactive at the the lodge fire. Are you not ashamed of such idleness? Go, I bid you, and wring out that net, which I have just taken from the water.'

"Kwasind saw that there was a determination to make him obey. He did not, therefore, make any excuses, but went out and took up the net. He carefully folded it, doubled and redoubled it, forming it into a roll, and then with an easy twist of his hands wrung it short off, with as much ease as if every twine had been a thin brittle fibre. Here they at once saw the secret of his reluctance. He possessed supernatural strength.

"After this, the young men were playing one day on the plain, where there was lying one of those large, heavy, black pieces of rock, which Manabozho is said to have cast at his father. Kwasind took it up with much ease, and threw it into the river. After this, he accompanied his father on a hunting excursion into a remote forest. They came to a place where the wind had thrown a great many trees into a narrow pass. 'We must go the other way,' said the old man, 'it is impossible to get the burdens through this place.' He sat down to rest himself, took out his smoking apparatus, and gave a short time to reflection. When he had finished, Kwasind had lifted away the largest pine trees, and pulled them out of the path.

"Sailing one day in his canoe, Kwasind saw a large furred animal, which he immediately recognized to be the king of beavers. He plunged into the water in pursuit of it. His companions were in the greatest astonishment and alarm, supposing he would perish. He often dove down and remained a long time under water, pursuing the animal from island to island; and at last returned with the kingly prize. After this, his fame spread far and wide, and no hunter would presume to compete with him.

"He helped Manabozho to clear away the obstructions in the streams, and to remove the great wind-falls of trees from the valleys, the better to fit them for the residence of man.

"He performed so many feats of strength and skill, that he excited the envy of the Puck-wudj In-in-ee-sug, or fairies, who conspired against his life. 'For,' said they, 'if this man is suffered to go on, in his career of strength and exploits, we shall presently have no work to perform. Our agency in the affairs of men must cease. He will undermine our power, and drive us, at last, into the water, where we must all perish, or be devoured by the wicked Neebanawbaig.'*

"The strength of Kwasind was all concentrated in the crown of his head. This was, at the same time, the only vulnerable part of his body; and there was but one species of weapon which could be successfully employed in making any impression upon it. The fairies carefully hunted through the woods to find this weapon. It was the burr or seed vessel of the white pine. They gathered a quantity of this article, and waylaid Kwasind at a point on the river, where the red rocks jut into the water, forming rude castles—a point which he was accustomed to pass in his canoe. They waited a long time, making merry upon these rocks, for it was a highly romantic spot. At last the wished-for object appeared; Kwasind came floating calmly down the stream, on the afternoon of a summer's day, languid with the heat of the weather, and almost asleep. When his canoe came directly beneath the cliff, the tallest and stoutest fairy began the attack. Others followed his example. It was a long time before they could hit the vulnerable part, but success at length crowned their efforts, and Kwasind sunk, never to rise more.

"Ever since this victory, the Puck Wudj Ininee have made that point of rock a favorite resort. The hunters often hear them laugh, and see their little plumes shake as they pass this scene on light summer evenings.

"My son," continued the old man, "take care that you do not imitate the faults of Kwasind. If he had not so often exerted his strength merely for the sake of *boasting*, he would not, perhaps, have made the fairies feel jealous of him. It is better to use the strength you have, in a quiet useful way, than to sigh after the possession of a giant's power. For if you run, or wrestle, or jump, or fire at a mark, only as well as your equals in years, nobody will envy you. But if you would needs be a Kwasind, you must expect a Kwasind's fate."

* A kind of water spirits.

THE JEEBI,

OR

TWO GHOSTS.

FROM THE ODJIBWA.

THERE lived a hunter in the north who had a wife and one child. His lodge stood far off in the forest, several days' journey from any other. He spent his days in hunting, and his evenings in relating to his wife the incidents that had befallen him. As game was very abundant, he found no difficulty in killing as much as they wanted. Just in all his acts, he lived a peaceful and happy life.

One evening during the winter season, it chanced that he remained out later than usual, and his wife began to feel uneasy, for fear some accident had befallen him. It was already dark. She listened attentively, and at last heard the sound of approaching footsteps. Not doubting it was her husband, she went to the door and beheld two strange females. She bade them enter, and invited them to remain.

She observed that they were total strangers in the country. There was something so peculiar in their looks, air, and manner, that she was uneasy in their company. They would not come near the fire; they sat in a remote part of the lodge, were shy and taciturn, and drew their garments about them in such a manner as nearly to hide their faces. So far as she could judge, they were pale, hollow-eyed, and long-visaged, very thin and emaciated. There was but little light in the lodge, as the fire was low, and served by its fitful flashes, rather to increase than dispel their fears. "Merciful spirit!" cried a voice from the opposite part of the lodge, "there are two corpses clothed with garments." The hunter's wife turned around, but seeing nobody, she concluded the sounds were but gusts of wind. She trembled, and was ready to sink to the earth.

Her husband at this moment entered and dispelled her

fears. He threw down the carcass of a large fat deer. "Behold what a fine and fat animal," cried the mysterious females, and they immediately ran and pulled off pieces of the whitest fat,* which they ate with greediness. The hunter and his wife looked on with astonishment, but remained silent. They supposed their guests might have been famished. Next day, however, the same unusual conduct was repeated. The strange females tore off the fat and devoured it with eagerness. The third day the hunter thought he would anticipate their wants by tying up a portion of the fattest pieces for them, which he placed on the top of his load. They accepted it, but still appeared dissatisfied, and went to the wife's portion and tore off more. The man and his wife felt surprised at such rude and unaccountable conduct, but they remained silent, for they respected their guests, and had observed that they had been attended with marked good luck during the residence of these mysterious visitors.

In other respects, the deportment of the females was strictly unexceptionable. They were modest, distant, and silent. They never uttered a word during the day. At night they would occupy themselves in procuring wood, which they carried to the lodge, and then returning the implements exactly to the places in which they had found them, resume their places without speaking. They were never known to stay out until daylight. They never laughed or jested.

The winter had nearly passed away, without anything uncommon happening, when, one evening, the hunter stayed out very late. The moment he entered and laid down his day's hunt as usual before his wife, the two females began to tear off the fat, in so unceremonious a way, that her anger was excited. She constrained herself, however, in a measure, but did not conceal her feelings, although she said but little. The guests observed the excited state of her mind, and became unusually reserved and uneasy. The good hunter saw the change, and carefully inquired into the cause, but his wife denied having used any hard words. They retired to their couches, and he tried to compose himself to sleep, but could not, for the sobs and sighs of the two females were incessant. He arose on his couch and addressed them as follows:—

"Tell me," said he, "what is it that gives you pain of mind,

---

* The fat of animals is esteemed by the N.A. Indians among the choicest parts.

and causes you to utter those sighs. Has my wife given you offence, or trespassed on the rights of hospitality?"

They replied in the negative. "We have been treated by you with kindness and affection. It is not for any slight we have received that we weep. Our mission is not to you only. We come from the land of the dead to test mankind, and to try the sincerity of the living. Often we have heard the bereaved by death say that if the dead could be restored, they would devote their lives to make them happy. We have been moved by the bitter lamentations which have reached the place of the dead, and have come to make proof of the sincerity of those who have lost friends. Three moons were allotted us by the Master of life to make the trial. More than half the time had been successfully past, when the angry feelings of your wife indicated the irksomeness you felt at our presence, and has made us resolve on our departure."

They continued to talk to the hunter and his wife, gave them instructions as to a future life, and pronounced a blessing upon them.

"There is one point," they added, "of which we wish to speak. You have thought our conduct very strange in rudely possessing ourselves of the choicest parts of your hunt. *That* was the point of trial selected to put you to. It is the wife's peculiar privilege. For another to usurp it, we knew to be the severest trial of her, and consequently of your temper and feelings. We know your manners and customs, but we came to prove you, not by a compliance with them, but a violation of them. Pardon us. We are the agents of him who sent us. Peace to your dwelling, adieu!"

When they ceased, total darkness filled the lodge. No object could be seen. The inmates heard the door open and shut, but they never say more of the two JEEBI-UG.

The hunter found the success which they had promised. He became celebrated in the chase, and never wanted for anything. He had many children, all of whom grew up to manhood, and health; peace, and long life were the rewards of his hospitality.

76

IAGOO.

CHIPPEWA.

IAGOO is the name of a personage noted in Indian lore for having given extravagant narrations of whatever he had seen, heard, or accomplished. It seems that he always saw extraordinary things, made extraordinary journeys, and performed extraordinary feats. He could not look out of his lodge and see things as other men did. If he described a bird, it had a most singular variety of brilliant plumage. The animals he met with were all of the monstrous kind; they had eyes like orbs of fire, and claws like hooks of steel, and could step over the top of an Indian lodge. He told of a serpent he had seen, which had hair on its neck like a mane, and feet resembling a quadruped; and if one were to take his own account of his exploits and observations, it would be difficult to decide whether his strength, his activity, or his wisdom should be most admired.

Iagoo did not appear to have been endowed with the ordinary faculties of other men. His eyes appeared to be magnifiers, and the tympanum of his ears so constructed that what appeared to common observers to be but the sound of a zephyr, to him had a far closer resemblance to the noise of thunder. His imagination appeared to be of so exuberant a character, that he scarcely required more than a drop of water to construct an ocean, or a grain of sand to form the earth. And he had so happy an exemption from both the restraints of judgment and moral accountability, that he never found the slightest difficulty in accommodating his facts to the most enlarged credulity. Nor was his ample thirst for the marvellous ever quenched by attempts to reconcile statements the most strange, unaccountable, and preposterous.

Such was Iagoo, the Indian story-teller, whose name is associated with all that is extravagant and marvelous, and has long been established in the hunter's vocabulary as a perfect synonym for liar, and is bandied about as a familiar proverb. If a hunter or warrior, in telling his exploits, undertakes to embellish them; to overrate his merits, or in any other way to excite the incredulity of his hearers, he is liable to be rebuked with the remark, "So here we have Iagoo come again." And he seems to hold the relative rank in oral narration which our written literature awards to Baron Munchausen, Jack Falstaff, and Captain Lemuel Gulliver.

Notwithstanding all this, there are but a few scraps of his actual stories to be found. He first attracted notice by giving an account of a water lily, a single leaf of which, he averred, was sufficient to make a petticoat and upper garments for his wife and daughter. One evening he was sitting in his lodge, on the banks of a river, and hearing the quacking of ducks on the stream, he fired through the lodge door at a venture. He killed a swan that happened to be flying by, and twenty brace of ducks in the stream. But this did not check the force of his shot; they passed on, and struck the heads of two loons, at the moment they were coming up from beneath the water, and even went beyond and killed a most extraordinary large fish called Moshkeenozha.* On another occasion he had killed a deer, and after skinning it, was carrying the carcass on his shoulders, when he spied some stately elks on the plain before him. He immediately gave them chase, and had run, over hill and dale, a distance of half a day's travel, before he recollected that he had the deer's carcass on his shoulders.

One day, as he was passing over a tract of *mushkeeg* or bogland, he saw mosquitoes of such enormous size, that he staked his reputation on the fact that a single wing of one of the insects was sufficient for a sail to his canoe, and the proboscis as big as his wife's shovel. But he was favored with a still more extraordinary sight, in a gigantic ant, which passed him, as he was watching a beaver's lodge, dragging the entire carcass of a hare.

At another time, for he was ever seeing or doing something wonderful, he got out of smoking weed, and in going into the woods in search of some, he discovered a bunch of the red willow, or maple bush, of such a luxuriant growth, that he was industriously occupied half a day walking round it.

* The muscalunge.

SHAWONDASEE.

FROM THE MYTHOLOGY OF THE ODJIBWAS.

MUDJEKEWIS and nine brothers conquered the Mamoth Bear, and obtained the Sacred Belt of Wampum, the great object of previous warlike enterprise, and the great means of happiness to men. The chief honor of this achievement was awarded to Mudjekewis, the youngest of the ten, who received the government of the West Winds. He is therefore called KABEYUN, the father of the winds. To his son, WABUN, he gave the East; to SHAWONDASEE, the south, and to KABIBO-NOKKA, the north. Manabozho being an illegitimate son, was left unprovided. When he grew up, and obtained the secret of his birth, he went to war against his father, KABEYUN, and having brought the latter to terms, he received the government of the Northwest Winds, ruling jointly with his brother KABIBONOKKA the tempests from that quarter of the heavens.

Shawondasee is represented as an affluent, plethoric old man, who has grown unwieldy from repletion, and seldom moves. He keeps his eyes steadfastly fixed on the north. When he sighs, in autumn, we have those balmy southern airs, which communicate warmth and delight over the northern hemisphere, and make the *Indian Summer*.

One day, while gazing toward the north, he beheld a beautiful young woman of slender and majestic form, standing on the plains. She appeared in the same place for several days, but what most attracted his admiration, was her bright and flowing locks of yellow hair. Ever dilatory, however, he contented himself with gazing. At length he saw, or fancied he saw, her head enveloped in a pure white mass like snow. This excited his jealousy toward his brother Kabibonokka, and he threw out a succession of short and rapid sighs—when lo! the air was filled with light filaments of a silvery hue, but the object of his affections had forever vanished. In reality, the southern airs had blown off the fine-winged seed-vessels of the prairie dandelion.

"My son," said the narrator, "it is not wise to differ in our tastes from other people; nor ought we to put off, through slothfulness, what is best done at once. Had Shawondasee conformed to the tastes of his countrymen, he would not have been an admirer of *yellow* hair; and if he had evinced a proper activity in his youth, his mind would not have run flower-gathering in his age."

PUCK WUDJ ININEES,

OR

THE VANISHING LITTLE MEN.

AN ÓDJIBWA MYTH OF FAIRIES.

THERE was a time when all the inhabitants of the earth had died, excepting two helpless children, a baby boy and a little girl. When their parents died, these children were asleep. The little girl, who was the elder, was the first to wake. She looked around her, but seeing nobody besides her little brother, who lay asleep, she quietly resumed her bed. At the end of ten days her brother moved without opening his eyes. At the end of ten days more he changed his position, lying on the other side.

The girl soon grew up to woman's estate, but the boy increased in stature very slowly. It was a long time before he could even creep. When he was able to walk, his sister made him a little bow and arrows, and suspended around his neck a small shell, saying you shall be called WA-DAIS-AIS-IMID, or He of the Little Shell. Every day he would go out with his little bow, shooting at the small birds. The first bird he killed was a tomtit. His sister was highly pleased when he took it to her. She carefully skinned and stuffed it, and put it away for him. The next day he killed a red squirrel. His sister preserved this too. The third day he killed a partridge (Peena), which she stuffed and set up. After this, he acquired more courage, and would venture some distance from home. His skill and success as a hunter daily increased and he killed the deer, bear, moose, and other large animals inhabiting the forest. In fine he became a great hunter.

He had now arrived to maturity of years, but remained a perfect infant in stature. One day, walking about, he came to a small lake. It was in the winter season. He saw a man on the ice killing beavers. He appeared to be a giant. Comparing himself to this great man he appeared no bigger than an insect. He seated himself on the shore, and watched his movements. When the large man had killed many beavers, he put them on a hand sled which he had, and pursued his way home. When he saw him retire, he followed him, and wielding his magic shell, cut off the tail of one of the beavers, and ran home with his trophy. When the tall stranger reached his lodge, with his sled load of beavers, he was surprised to find the tail of one of them gone, for he had not observed the movements of the little hero of the shell.

The next day WA-DIS-AIS-IMID, went to the same lake. The man had already fixed his load of beavers on his *odaw bon*, or sled, and commenced his return. But he nimbly ran forward, and overtaking him, succeeded, by the same means, in securing another of the beaver's tails. When the man saw that he had lost another of this most esteemed part of the animal, he was very angry. I wonder, said he, what dog it is, that has thus cheated me. Could I meet him, I would make his flesh quiver at the point of my lance. Next day he pursued his hunting at the beaver dam near the lake, and was followed again by the little man of the shell. On this occasion the hunter had used so much expedition, that he had accomplished his object, and nearly reached his home, before our tiny hero could overtake him. He nimbly drew his shell and cut off another beaver's tail. In all these pranks, he availed himself of his power of invisibility, and thus escaped observation. When the man saw that the trick had been so often repeated, his anger was greater than ever. He gave vent to his feelings in words. He looked carefully around to see whether he could discover any tracks. But he could find none. His unknown visitor had stepped so lightly as to leave no track.

Next day he resolved to disappoint him by going to his beaver pond very early. When WA-DAIS-AIS-IMID reached the place, he found the fresh traces of his work, but he had already returned. He followed his tracks, but failed to overtake him. When he came in sight of the lodge the stranger was in front of it. employed in skinning his beavers. As he stood looking at him, he thought, I will let him see me. Presently the man, who proved to be no less a personage than Manabozho, looked up and saw him. After regarding him with attention, "Who are you,little man," said Manabozho. "I have a mind to kill you." The little hero of the shell replied, "If you were to try to kill me you could not do it."

When he returned home he told his sister that they must separate. "I must go away," said he, "it is my fate. You too," he added, "must go away soon. Tell me where you would wish to dwell." She said, "I would like to go to the place of the breaking of daylight. I have always loved the east. The earliest glimpses of light are from that quarter, and it is, to my mind, the most beautiful part of the heavens. After I get there, my brother, whenever you see the clouds in that direction of various colors, you may think that your sister is painting her face."

"And I," said he, "my sister, shall live on the mountains and rocks. There I can see you at the earliest hour, and there the streams of water are clear, and the air pure. And I shall ever be called PUCK WUDJ ININEE, or the little wild man of the mountains."

"But," he resumed, "before we part forever, I must go and try to find some Manitoes." He left her, and travelled over the surface of the globe, and then went far down into the earth. He had been treated well wherever he went. At last he found a giant Manito, who had a large kettle which was forever boiling. The giant regarded him with a stern look, and then took him up in his hand, and threw him unceremoniously into the kettle. But by the protection of his personal spirit, he was shielded from harm, and with much ado got out of it and escaped. He returned to his sister, and related his rovings and misadventures. He finished his story by addressing her thus: "My sister,there is a Manito, at each of the four corners of the earth.* There is also one above them, far in the sky; and last," continued he, "there is another, and wicked one, who lives deep down in the earth. We must now separate. When the winds blow from the four corners of the earth you must then go. They will carry you to the place you wish. I go to the rocks and mountains, where my kindred will ever delight to dwell." He then took his ball stick, and commenced running up a high mountain, whooping as he went. Presently the winds blew, and, as he predicted, his sister was borne by them to the eastern sky, where she has ever since been, and her name is the Morning Star.

> Blow, winds, blow! my sister lingers
> For her dwelling in the sky,
> Where the morn, with rosy fingers,
> Shall her checks with vermil dye.
>
> There, my earliest views directed,
> Shall from her their color take,
> And her smiles, through clouds reflected,
> Guide me on, by wood or lake.
>
> While I range the highest mountains,
> Sport in valleys green and low,
> Or beside our Indian fountains
> Raise my tiny hip holla.

* The opinion that the earth is a square and level plain, and that the winds blow from its four corners, is a very ancient eastern opinion.

PEZHIU AND WABOSE,

OR

THE LYNX AND HARE.

A CHIPPEWA FABLE.

A LYNX almost famished, met a hare one day in the woods, in the winter season, when food was very scarce. The hare, however, stood up on a rock, and was safe from its enemy.

"Wabose," said the lynx, in a very kind manner, "come here, my little white one,* I wish to talk to you."

"Oh no," replied the hare, "I am afraid of you, and my mother told me never to go and talk to strangers."

"You are very pretty," answered the lynx, "and a very obedient child to your parents, but you must know that I am a relative of yours. I wish to send some word to your lodge. Come down and see me."

The hare was pleased to be called pretty, and when she heard that it was a relative, she jumped down from the place where she stood, and was immediately torn in pieces by the lynx.*

* Such is the meaning of WABOSE.
* Oneota.

PEBOAN AND SEEGWUN.

AN
ALLEGORY OF WINTER AND SPRING.

ODJIBWA.

AN old man was sitting in his lodge, by the side of a frozen stream. It was the close of winter, and his fire was almost out. He appeared very old and very desolate. His locks were white with age, and he trembled in every joint. Day after day passed in solitude, and he heard nothing but the sounds of the tempest, sweeping before it the new-fallen snow.

One day, as his fire was just dying, a handsome young man approached and entered his dwelling. His cheeks were red with the blood of youth, his eyes sparkled with animation, and a smile played upon his lips. He walked with a light and quick step. His forehead was bound with a wreath of sweet grass, in place of a warrior's frontlet, and he carried a bunch of flowers in his hand.

"Ah, my son," said the old man, "I am happy to see you. Come in. Come, tell me of your adventures, and what strange lands you have been to see. Let us pass the night together. I will tell you of my prowess and exploits, and what I can perform. You shall do the same, and we will amuse ourselves."

He then drew from his sack a curiously-wrought antique pipe, and having filled it with tobacco, rendered mild by an admixture of certain leaves, handed it to his guest. When this ceremony was concluded they began to speak.

"I blow my breath," said the old man, "and the streams stand still. The water becomes stiff and hard as clear stone."

"I breathe," said the young man, "and flowers spring up all over the plains."

"I shake my locks," retorted the old man, "and snow covers the land. The leaves fall from the trees at my command, and my breath blows them away. The birds get up from the water, and fly to a distant land. The animals hide themselves from

86

my breath, and the very ground becomes as hard as flint."

"I shake my ringlets," rejoined the young man, "and warm showers of soft rain fall upon the earth. The plants lift up their heads out of the earth, like the eyes of children glistening with delight. My voice recalls the birds. The warmth of my breath unlocks the streams. Music fills the groves wherever I walk, and all nature rejoices."

At length the sun began to rise. A gentle warmth came over the place. The tongue of the old man became silent. The robin and bluebird began to sing on the top of the lodge. The stream began to murmur by the door, and the fragrance of growing herbs and flowers came softly on the vernal breeze.

Daylight fully revealed to the young man the character of his entertainer. When he looked upon him, he had the icy visage of Peboan.* Streams began to flow from his eyes. As the sun increased, he grew less and less in stature, and anon had melted completely away. Nothing remained on the place of his lodge fire but the miskodeed,* a small white flower, with a pink border, which is one of the earliest species of northern plants.

* Winter.
* The Claytonia Virginica.

MON-DAW-MIN,

OR

THE ORIGIN OF INDIAN CORN.

ODJIBWA.

IN times past, a poor Indian was living with his wife and children in a beautiful part of the country. He was not only poor, but inexpert in procuring food for his family, and his children were all too young to give him assistance. Although poor, he was a man of a kind and contented disposition. He was always thankful to the Great Spirit for everything he received. The same disposition was inherited by his eldest son, who had now arrived at the proper age to undertake the ceremony of the Ke-ig-uish-im-o-win, or fast, to see what kind of a spirit would be his guide and guardian through life. Wunzh, for this was his name, had been an obedient boy from his infancy, and was of a pensive, thoughtful, and mild disposition, so that he was beloved by the whole family. As soon as the first indications of spring appeared, they built him the customary little lodge at a retired spot, some distance from their own, where he would not be disturbed during this solemn rite. In the mean time he prepared himself, and immediately went into it, and commenced his fast. The first few days, he amused himself, in the mornings, by walking in the woods and over the mountains, examining the early plants and flowers, and in this way prepared himself to enjoy his sleep, and, at the same time, stored his mind with pleasant ideas for his dreams. While he rambled through the woods, he felt a strong desire to know how the plants, herbs, and berries grew, without any aid from man, and why it was that some species were good to eat, and others possessed medicinal or poisonous juices. He recalled these thoughts to mind after he became too languid to walk about, and had confined himself strictly to the lodge; he wished he could dream of something that would prove a benefit to his father and family, and to all others. "True!"

he thought, "the Great Spirit made all things, and it is to him that we owe our lives. But could he not make it easier for us to get our food, than by hunting animals and taking fish? I must try to find out this in my visions."

On the third day he became weak and faint, and kept his bed. He fancied, while thus lying, that he saw a handsome young man coming down from the sky and advancing towards him. He was richly and gayly dressed, having on a great many garments of green and yellow colors, but differing in their deeper or lighter shades. He had a plume of waving feathers on his head, and all his motions were graceful.

"I am sent to you, my friend," said the celestial visitor, "by that Great Spirit who made all things in the sky and on the earth. He has seen and knows your motives in fasting. He sees that it is from a kind and benevolent wish to do good to your people, and to procure a benefit for them, and that you do not seek for strength in war or the praise of warriors. I am sent to instruct you, and show you how you can do your kindred good." He then told the young man to arise, and prepare to wrestle with him, as it was only by this means that he could hope to succeed in his wishes. Wunzh knew he was weak from fasting, but he felt his courage rising in his heart, and immediately got up, determined to die rather than fail. He commenced the trial, and after a protracted effort, was almost exhausted, when the beautiful stranger said, "My friend, it is enough for once; I will come again to try you;" and, smiling on him, he ascended in the air in the same direction from which he came. The next day the celestial visitor reappeared at the same hour and renewed the trial. Wunzh felt that his strength was even less than the day before, but the courage of his mind seemed to increase in proportion as his body became weaker. Seeing this, the stranger again spoke to him in the same words he used before, adding, "Tomorrow will be your last trial. Be strong, my friend, for this is the only way you can overcome me, and obtain the boon you seek." On the third day he again appeared at the same time and renewed the struggle. The poor youth was very faint in body, but grew stronger in mind at every contest, and was determined to prevail or perish in the attempt. He exerted his utmost powers, and after the contest had been continued the usual time, the stranger ceased his efforts and declared himself conquered. For the first time he entered the lodge, and sitting down beside the youth, he began to deliver his instructions to him, telling him in what manner he should proceed to take advantage of his victory.

"You have won your desires of the Great Spirit," said the stranger. "You have wrestled manfully. To-morrow will be the seventh day of your fasting. Your father will give you food to strengthen you, and as it is the last day of trial, you will prevail. I know this, and now tell you what you must do to benefit your family and your tribe. To-morrow," he repeated, "I shall meet you and wrestle with you for the last time; and, as soon as you have prevailed against me, you will strip off my garments and throw me down, clean the earth of roots and weeds, make it soft, and bury me in the spot. When you have done this, leave my body in the earth, and do not disturb it, but come occasionally to visit the place, to see whether I have come to life, and be careful never to let the grass or weeds grow on my grave. Once a month cover me with fresh earth. If you follow my instructions, you will accomplish your object of doing good to your fellow-creatures by teaching them the knowledge I now teach you." He then shook him by the hand and disappeared.

In the morning the youth's father came with some slight refreshments, saying, "My son, you have fasted long enough. If the Great Spirit will favor you, he will do it now. It is seven days since you have tasted food, and you must not sacrifice your life. The Master of Life does not require that." "My father," replied the youth, "wait till the sun goes down. I have a particular reason for extending my fast to that hour." "Very well," said the old man, "I shall wait till the hour arrives, and you feel inclined to eat."

At the usual hour of the day the sky-visitor returned, and the trial of strength was renewed. Although the youth had not availed himself of his father's offer of food, he felt that new strength had been given to him, and that exertion had renewed his strength and fortified his courage. He grasped his angelic antagonist with supernatural strength, threw him down, took from him his beautiful garments and plume, and finding him dead, immediately buried him on the spot, taking all the precautions he had been told of, and being very confident, at the same time, that his friend would again come to life. He then returned to his father's lodge, and partook sparingly of the meal that had been prepared for him. But he never for a moment forgot the grave of his friend. He carefully visited it throughout the spring, and weeded out the grass, and kept the

90

ground in a soft and pliant state. Very soon he saw the tops of the green plumes coming through the ground; and the more careful he was to obey his instructions in keeping the ground in order, the faster they grew. He was, however, careful to conceal the exploit from his father. Days and weeks had passed in this way. The summer was now drawing towards a close, when one day, after a long absence in hunting, Wunzh invited his father to follow him to the quiet and lonesome spot of his former fast. The lodge had been removed, and the weeds kept from growing on the circle where it stood, but in its place stood a tall and graceful plant, with bright-colored silken hair, surmounted with nodding plumes and stately leaves, and golden clusters on each side. "It is my friend," shouted the lad; "it is the friend of all mankind. It is *Mondawmin.** We need no longer rely on hunting alone; for, as long as this gift is cherished and taken care of, the ground itself will give us a living." He then pulled an ear. "See, my father," said he, "this is what I fasted for. The great Spirit has listened to my voice, and sent us something new,* and henceforth our people will not alone depend upon the chase or upon the waters."

He then communicated to his father the instructions given him by the stranger. He told him that the broad husks must be torn away, as he had pulled off the garments in his wrestling; and having done this, directed him how the ear must be held before the fire till the outer skin became brown, while all the milk was retained in the grain. The whole family then united in a feast on the newly-grown ears, expressing gratitude to the Merciful Spirit who gave it. So corn came into the world.

* The algic name for corn. The word is manifestly a trinary compound from *monedo*, spirit; *min*, a grain or berry; and *iaw*, the verb substantive.
* The Zea mays,it will be recollected, is indigenous to America, and was unknown in Europe before 1495.

NEZHIK-E-WA-WA-SUN,

OR

THE LONE LIGHTNING.

ODJIBWA.

A LITTLE orphan boy who had no one to care for him, was
once living with his uncle, who treated him very badly, making him do hard things and giving him very little to eat; so
that the boy pined away, he never grew much, and became,
through hard usage, very thin and light. At last the uncle
felt ashamed of this treatment, and determined to make
amends for it, by fattening him up, but his real object was,
to kill him by over-feeding. He told his wife to give the boy
plenty of bear's meat, and let him have the fat, which is
thought to be the best part. They were both very assiduous in
cramming him, and one day came near choking him to death,
by forcing the fat down his throat. The boy escaped and fled
from the lodge. He knew not where to go, but wandered about.
When night came on, he was afraid the wild beasts would eat
him, so he climbed up into the forks of a high pine tree, and
there he fell asleep in the branches, and had an aupoway, or
ominous dream.

A person appeared to him from the upper sky, and said, "My
poor little lad, I pity you, and the bad usage you have received
from your uncle has led me to visit you: follow me, and step
in my tracks." Immediately his sleep left him, and he rose up
and followed his guide, mounting up higher and higher into
the air, until he reached the upper sky. Here twelve arrows
were put into his hands, and he was told that there were a
great many manitoes in the northern sky, against whom he
must go to war, and try to waylay and shoot them. Accordingly he went to that part of the sky, and, at long intervals,
shot arrow after arrow, until he had expended eleven, in vain
attempt to kill the manitoes. At the flight of each arrow,
there was a long and solitary streak of lightning in the sky—

then all was clear again, and not a cloud or spot could be seen. The twelfth arrow he held a long time in his hands, and looked around keenly on every side to spy the manitoes he was after. But these manitoes were very cunning, and could change their form in a moment. All they feared was the boy's arrows, for these were magic arrows, which had been given to him by a good spirit, and had power to kill them, if aimed aright. At length, the boy drew up his last arrow, settled in his aim, and let fly, as he thought, into the very heart of the chief of the manitoes; but before the arrow reached him, the manito changed himself into a rock. Into this rock, the head of the arrow sank deep and stuck fast.

"Now your gifts are all expended," cried the enraged manito, "and I will make an example of your audacity and pride of heart, for lifting your bow against me"—and so saying, he transformed the boy into the Nezhik-e-wa wa sun, or Lone Lightning, which may be observed in the northern sky, to this day.

THE AK UK O JEESH,

OR

THE GROUNDHOG FAMILY.

AN ODJIBWA FABLE.

A FEMALE akukojeesh, or groundhog, with a numerous family of young ones, was burrowing in her wauzh, or hole in the ground, one long winter, in the north, when the young ones became impatient for spring. Every day the mother would go out and get roots and other things, which she brought in to them to eat; and she always told them to lie close and keep warm, and never to venture towards the mouth of the wauzh. But they became very impatient at last to see the light and the green woods. "Mother," said they, "is it not almost spring?" "No! no!" said she, in a cross humor, "keep still and wait patiently; it hails, it snows, it is cold—it is windy. Why should you wish to go out?" This she told them so often, and said it in such a bad temper, that they at last suspected some deception. One day she came in, after having been a long while absent, and fell asleep, with her mouth open. The little ones peeped in slily, and saw on her teeth the remains of the nice white bulbous roots of the mo-na-wing, or adder's tongue violet. They at once knew it was spring, and without disturbing the old one, who only wanted to keep them in till they were full grown, away they scampered, out of the hole, and dispersed themselves about the forest, and so the family were all scattered.

OPEECHEE,

OR

THE ORIGIN OF THE ROBIN.

FROM THE ODJIBWA.

AN old man had an only son named Opeechee, who had come to that age which is thought to be most proper to make the long and final fast, that is to secure through life a guardian genius or spirit. In the influence of this choice, it is well known, our people have relied for their prosperity in after life; it was, therefore, an event of deep importance.

The old man was ambitious that his son should surpass all others in whatever was deemed most wise and great among his tribe; and, to fulfil his wishes, he thought it necessary that he should fast a much longer time than any of those persons, renowned for their prowess or wisdom, whose fame he coveted. He therefore directed his son to prepare, with great ceremony, for the important event. After he had been in the sweating lodge and bath several times, he ordered him to lie down upon a clean mat, in a little lodge expressly prepared for him; telling him, at the same time, to endure his fast like a man, and that, at the expiration of *twelve* days, he should receive food and the blessing of his father.

The lad carefully observed this injunction, lying with perfect composure, with his face covered, awaiting those mystic visitations which were to seal his good or evil fortune. His father visited him regularly every morning, to encourage him to perseverance, expatiating at length on the honor and renown that would attend him through life if he accomplished the full term prescribed. To these admonitions and encouragements the boy never replied, but lay, without the least sign of discontent or murmuring, until the ninth day, when he addressed his father as follows:—

"My father, my dreams forebode evil. May I break my fast now, and at a more propitious time make a new fast?" The father answered—

"My son, you know not what you ask. If you get up now, all your glory will depart. Wait patiently a little longer. You have but three days yet to accomplish your desire. You know it is for your own good, and I encourage you to persevere."

The son assented; and, covering himself closer, he lay till the eleventh day, when he repeated his request. Very nearly the same answer was given him by his father, who added that the next day he would himself prepare his first meal, and bring it to him. The boy remained silent, but lay as motionless as a corpse. No one would have known he was living but by the gentle heaving of his breast.

The next morning, the father, elated at having gained his end, prepared a repast for his son, and hastened to set it before him. On coming to the door, he was surprised to hear his son talking to himself. He stooped to listen; and, looking through a small aperture, was more astonished when he beheld his son painted with vermilion over all his breast, and in the act of finishing his work by laying on the paint as far back on his shoulders as he could reach with his hands, saying, at the same time, to himself, "My father has destroyed my fortune as a man. He would not listen to my requests. He will be the loser. I shall be forever happy in my new state, for I have been obedient to my parent; he alone will be the sufferer, for my guardian spirit is a just one; though not propitious to me in the manner I desired, he has shown me pity in another way; he has given me another shape; and now I must go."

At this moment the old man broke in, exclaiming, "My son! my son! I pray you leave me not." But the young man, with the quickness of a bird, had flown to the top of the lodge, and perched himself on the highest pole, having been changed into a beautiful robin redbreast.

He looked down upon his father with pity beaming in his eyes, and addressed him as follows: "Regret not, my father, the change you behold. I shall be happier in my present state than I could have been as a man. I shall always be the friend of men, and keep near their dwellings. I shall ever be happy and contented; and although I could not gratify your wishes as a warrior, it will be my daily aim to make you amends for it as a harbinger of peace and joy. I will cheer you by my songs, and strive to inspire in others the joy and lightsomeness I feel in my present state. This will be some compensation to you for the loss of the glory you expected. I am now free from

96

the cares and pains of human life. My food is spontaneously furnished by the mountains and fields, and my pathway of life is in the bright air." Then stretching himself on his toes, as if delighted with the gift of wings, he carolled one of his sweetest songs, and flew away into a neighboring grove.*

* See Notes of the Pibbigwun.

SHINGEBISS.

AN

ALLEGORY OF SELF-RELIANCE.

FROM THE ODJIBWA.

THERE was once a Shingebiss, the name of the fall duck living alone, in a solitary lodge, on the shores of the deep bay of a lake, in the coldest winter weather. The ice had formed on the water, and he had but four logs of wood to keep his fire. Each of these would, however, burn a month, and as there were but four cold winter months, they were sufficient to carry him through till spring.

Shingebiss was hardy and fearless, and cared for no one. He would go out during the coldest day, and seek for places where flags and rushes grew through the ice, and plucking them up with his bill, would dive through the openings, in quest of fish. In this way he found plenty of food, while others were starving, and he went home daily to his lodge, dragging strings of fish after him, on the ice.

Kabebonicca* observed him, and felt a little piqued at his perseverance and good luck in defiance of the severest blasts of wind he could send from the northwest. "Why! this is a wonderful man," said he; "he does not mind the cold, and appears as happy and contented as if it were the month of June. I will try whether he cannot be mastered." He poured forth tenfold colder blasts, and drifts of snow, so that it was next to impossible to live in the open air. Still, the fire of Shingebiss did not go out: he wore but a single strip of leather around his body, and he was seen, in the worst weather, searching the shores for rushes, and carrying home fish.

"I shall go and visit him," said Kabebonicca, one day, as he saw Shingebiss dragging along a quantity of fish. And, accordingly, that very night, he went to the door of his lodge.

* A personification of the Northwest.

98

Meantime Shingebiss had cooked his fish, and finished his meal, and was lying, partly on his side, before the fire, singing his songs. After Kabebonicca had come to the door, and stood listening there, he sang as follows:—

Ka	Neej	Ka	Neej
Be	In	Be	In
Bon	In	Bon	In
Oc	Ee.	Oc	Ee.
Ca	We-ya!	Ca	We-ya!

The number of words, in this song, are few and simple, but they are made up from compounds which carry the whole of their original meanings, and are rather suggestive of the ideas floating in the mind than actual expressions of those ideas. Literally, he sings:—

Spirit of the Northwest—you are but my fellow man.

By being broken into syllables, to correspond with a simple chant, and by the power of intonation and repetition, with a chorus, these words are expanded into melodious utterance, if we may be allowed the term, and may be thus rendered:—

Windy god, I know your plan,
You are but my fellow man;
Blow you may your coldest breeze,
Shingebiss you cannot freeze.
Sweep the strongest wind you can,
Shingebiss is still your man;
Heigh! for life—and ho! for bliss,
Who so free as Shingebiss?

The hunter knew that Kabebonicca was at his door, for he felt his cold and strong breath; but he kept on singing his songs, and affected utter indifference. At length Kabebonicca entered, and took his seat on the opposite side of the lodge. But Shingebiss did not regard, or notice him. He got up, as if nobody were present, and taking his poker, pushed the log, which made his fire burn brighter, repeating, as he sat down again:—

You are but my fellow man.

Very soon the tears began to flow down Kabebonicca's cheeks, which increased so fast, that presently, he said to himself: "I cannot stand this—I must go out." He did so, and left Shingebiss to his songs; but resolved to freeze up all the flag orifices, and make the ice thick, so that he could not get any more fish. Still, Shingebiss, by dint of great diligence, found means to pull up new roots, and dive under for fish. At last, Kabebonicca was compelled to give up the contest. "He must be aided by some Monedo," said he. "I can neither freeze him nor starve him; he is a very singular being—I will let him alone."

THE STAR FAMILY,

OR
CELESTIAL SISTERS.

SHAWNEE.

WAUPEE, or the White Hawk, lived in a remote part of the forest, where animals and birds were abundant. Every day he returned from the chase with the reward of his toil, for he was one of the most skilful and celebrated hunters of his tribe. With a tall, manly form, and the fire of youth beaming from his eye, there was no forest too gloomy for him to penetrate, and no track made by the numerous kinds of birds and beasts which he could not follow.

One day he penetrated beyond any point which he had before

visited. He travelled through an open forest, which enabled him to see a great distance. At length he beheld a light breaking through the foliage, which made him sure that he was on the borders of a prairie. It was a wide plain covered with grass and flowers. After walking some time without a path, he suddenly came to a ring worn through the sod, as if it had been made by footsteps following a circle. But what excited his surprise was, that there was no path leading to or from it. Not the least trace of footsteps could be found, even in a crushed leaf or broken twig. He thought he would hide himself, and lie in wait to see what this circle meant. Presently he heard the faint sounds of music in the air. He looked up in the direction they came from, and saw a small object descending from above. At first it looked like a mere speck, but rapidly increased, and, as it came down, the music became plainer and sweeter. It assumed the form of a basket, and was filled with twelve sisters of the most lovely forms and enchanting beauty. As soon as the basket touched the ground, they leaped out, and began to dance round the magic ring, striking, as they did so, a shining ball as we strike the drum. Waupee gazed upon their graceful forms and motions from his place of concealment. He admired them all, but was most pleased with the youngest. Unable longer to restrain his admiration, he rushed out and endeavored to seize her. But the sisters, with the quickness of birds, the moment they described the form of a man, leaped back into the basket and were drawn up into the sky.

Regretting his ill luck and indiscretion, he gazed till he saw them disappear, and then said, "They are gone, and I shall see them no more." He returned to his solitary lodge, but found no relief to his mind. Next day he went back to the prairie, and took his station near the ring; but in order to deceive the sisters, he assumed the form of an opossum. He had not waited long, when he saw the wicker car descend, and heard the same sweet music. They commenced the same sportive dance, and seemed even more beautiful and graceful than before. He crept slowly towards the ring, but the instant the sisters saw him they were startled, and sprang into their car. It rose but a short distance, when one of the elder sisters spoke. "Perhaps," said she, "it is come to show us how the game is played by mortals." "Oh no!" the youngest replied; "quick, let us ascend." And all joining in a chant, they rose out of sight.

Waupee returned to his own form again, and walked sorrowfully back to his lodge. But the night seemed a very long one, and he went back betimes the next day. He reflected upon the sort of plan to follow to secure success. He found an old stump near by, in which there were a number of mice. He thought their small form would not create alarm, and accordingly assumed it. He brought the stump and sat it up near the ring. The sisters came down and resumed their sport. "But see," cried the younger sister, "that stump was not there before." She ran affrighted towards the car. They only smiled, and gathering round the stump, struck it in jest, when out ran the mice, and Waupee among the rest. They killed them all but one, which was pursued by the youngest sister; but just as she had raised her stick to kill it, the form of Waupee arose, and he clasped his prize in his arms. The other eleven sprang to their basket and were drawn up to the skies.

He exerted all his skill to please his bride and win her affections. He wiped the tears from her eyes. He related his adventures in the chase. He dwelt upon the charms of life on the earth. He was incessant in his attentions, and picked out the way for her to walk as he led her gently towards his lodge. He felt his heart glow with joy as she entered it, and from that moment he was one of the happiest of men. Winter and summer passed rapidly away, and their happiness was increased by the addition of a beautiful boy to their lodge. She was a daughter of one of the stars, and as the scenes of earth began to pall her sight, she sighed to revisit her father. But she was obliged to hide these feelings from her husband. She remembered the charm that would carry her up, and took occasion, while Waupee was engaged in the chase, to construct a wicker basket, which she kept concealed. In the meantime she collected such rarities from the earth as she thought would please her father, as well as the most dainty kinds of food. When all was in readiness, she went out one day, while Waupee was absent, to the charmed ring, taking her little son with her. As soon as they got into the car, she commenced her song and the basket rose. As the song was wafted by the wind, it caught her husband's ear. It was a voice which he well knew, and he instantly ran to the prairie. But he could not reach the ring before he saw his wife and child ascend. He lifted up his voice in loud appeals, but they were unavailing. The basket still went up. He watched it till it became a small speck, and finally it vanished in the sky. He then bent his head down to the ground, and was miserable.

Waupee bewailed his loss through a long winter and a long summer. But he found no relief. He mourned his wife's loss sorely, but his son's still more. In the meantime his wife had reached her home in the stars, and almost forgot, in the blissful employments there, that she had left a husband on the earth. She was reminded of this by the presence of her son, who, as he grew up, became anxious to visit the scene of his birth. His grandfather said to his daughter one day, "Go, my child, and take your son down to his father, and ask him to come up and live with us. But tell him to bring along a specimen of each kind of bird and animal he kills in the chase." She accordingly took the boy and descended. Waupee, who was ever near the enchanted spot, heard her voice as she came down the sky. His heart beat with impatience as he saw her form and that of his son, and they were soon clasped in his arms.

He heard the message of the Star, and began to hunt with the greatest activity, that he might collect the present. He spent whole nights, as well as days, in searching for every curious and beautiful bird or animal. He only preserved a tail, foot, or wing of each, to identify the species; and, when all was ready, they went to the circle and were carried up.

Great joy was manifested on their arrival at the starry plains. The Star Chief invited all his people to a feast, and, when they had assembled, he proclaimed aloud, that each one might take of the early gifts such as he liked best. A very strange confusion immediately arose. Some chose a foot, some a wing, some a tail, and some a claw. Those who selected tails or claws were changed into animals, and ran off; the others assumed the form of birds, and flew away. Waupee chose a white hawk's feather. His wife and son followed his example, when each one became a white hawk. Pleased with his transformation, and new vitality, the chief spread out gracefully his white wings, and followed by his wife and son, descended to the earth, where the species are still to be found.

OJEEG ANNUNG,*

OR

THE SUMMER-MAKER.

ODJIBWA.

THERE lived a celebrated hunter on the southern shores of Lake Superior, who was considered a Manito by some, for there was nothing but what he could accomplish. He lived off the path, in a wild, lonesome, place, with a wife whom he loved, and they were blessed with a son, who had attained his thirteenth year. The hunter's name was Ojeeg, or the Fisher, which is the name of an expert, sprightly little animal common to the region. He was so successful in the chase, that he seldom returned without bringing his wife and son a plentiful supply of venison, or other dainties of the woods. As hunting formed his constant occupation, his son began early to emulate his father in the same employment, and would take his bow and arrows, and exert his skill in trying to kill birds and squirrels. The greatest impediment he met with, was the coldness and severity of the climate. He often returned home, his little fingers benumbed with cold, and crying with vexation at his disappointment. Days, and months, and years passed away, but still the same perpetual depth of snow was seen, covering all the country as with a white cloak.

One day, after a fruitless trial of his forest skill, the little boy was returning homeward with a heavy heart, when he saw a small red squirrel gnawing the top of a pine bur. He had approached within a proper distance to shoot, when the squirrel sat up on its hind legs and thus addressed him:—

"My grandchild, put up your arrows, and listen to what I have to tell you." The boy complied rather reluctantly, when

---

* There is a group of stars in the Northern hemisphere which the Odjibwas call *Ojeeg Annung*, or the Fisher Stars. It is believed to be identical with the group of the Plough. They relate the following tale respecting it.

the squirrel continued: "My son, I see you pass frequently, with your fingers benumbed with cold, and crying with vexation for not having killed any birds. Now, if you will follow my advice, we will see if you cannot accomplish your wishes. If you will strictly pursue my advice, we will have perpetual summer, and you will then have the pleasure of killing as many birds as you please; and I will also have something to eat, as I am now myself on the point of starvation.

"Listen to me. As soon as you get home you must commence crying. You must throw away your bow and arrows in discontent. If your mother asks you what is the matter, you must not answer her, but continue crying and sobbing. If she offers you anything to eat, you must push it away with apparent discontent, and continue crying. In the evening, when your father returns from hunting, he will inquire of your mother what is the matter with you. She will answer that you came home crying, and would not so much as mention the cause to her. All this while you must not leave off sobbing. At last your father will say, 'My son, why is this unnecessary grief? Tell me the cause. You know I am a spirit, and that nothing is impossible for me to perform.' You must then answer him, and say that you are sorry to see the snow continually on the ground, and ask him if he could not cause it to melt, so that we might have perpetual summer. Say it in a supplicating way, and tell him this is the cause of your grief. Your father will reply, 'It is very hard to accomplish your request, but for your sake, and for my love for you, I will use my utmost endeavors.' He will tell you to be still, and cease crying. He will try to bring summer with all its loveliness. You must then be quiet, and eat that which is set before you."

The squirrel ceased. The boy promised obedience to his advice, and departed. When he reached home, he did as he had been instructed, and all was exactly fulfilled, as it had been predicted by the squirrel.

Ojeeg told him that it was a great undertaking. He must first make a feast, and invite some of his friends to accompany him on a journey. Next day he had a bear roasted whole. All who had been invited to the feast came punctually to the appointment. There were the Otter, Beaver, Lynx, Badger, and Wolverine. After the feast, they arranged it among themselves to set out on the contemplated journey in three days. When the time arrived, the Fisher took leave of his wife and son, as he foresaw that it was for the last time. He and his companions travelled in company day after day, meeting with nothing but the ordinary incidents. On the twentieth day they arrived at the foot of a high mountain, where they saw the tracks of some person who had recently killed an animal, which they knew by the blood that marked the way. The Fisher told his friends that they ought to follow the track, and see if they could not procure something to eat. They followed it for sometime; at last they arrived at a lodge, which had been hidden from their view by a hollow in the mountain. Ojeeg told his friends to be very sedate, and not to laugh on any account. The first object that they saw was a man standing at the door of the lodge, but of so deformed a shape that they could not possibly make out who or what sort of a man it could be. His head was enormously large; he had such a queer set of teeth, and no arms. They wondered how he could kill animals. But the secret was soon revealed. He was a great Manito. He invited them to pass the night, to which they consented.

He boiled his meat in a hollow vessel made of wood, and took it out of this singular kettle in some way unknown to his guests. He carefully gave each their portion to eat, but made so many odd movements that the Otter could not refrain from laughing, for he is the only one who is spoken of as a jester. The Manito looked at him with a terrible look, and then made a spring at him, and got on him to smother him, for that was his mode of killing animals. But the Otter, when he felt him on his neck, slipped his head back and made for the door, which he passed in safety; but went out with the curse of the Manito. The others passed the night, and they conversed on different subjects. The Manito told the Fisher that he would accomplish his object, but that it would probably cost him his life. He gave them his advice, directed them how to act, and described a certain road which they must follow, and they would thereby be led to the place of action.

They set off in the morning, and met their friend, the Otter, shivering with cold; but Ojeeg had taken care to bring along some of the meat that had been given him, which he presented to his friend. They pursued their way, and travelled twenty days more before they got to the place which the Manito had told them of. It was a most lofty mountain. They rested on its highest peak to fill their pipes and refresh themselves. Before smoking, they made the customary ceremony, pointing to the heavens, the four winds, the earth, and the zenith; in

107

the meantime, speaking in a loud voice, addressed the Great Spirit, hoping that their object would be accomplished. They then commenced smoking.

They gazed on the sky in silent admiration and astonishment, for they were on so elevated a point, that it appeared to be only a short distance above their heads. After they had finished smoking, they prepared themselves. Oleeg told the Otter to make the first attempt to try and make a hole in the sky. He consented with a grin. He made a leap, but fell down the hill stunned by the force of his fall; and the snow being moist, and falling on his back, he slid with velocity down the side of the mountain. When he found himself at the bottom, he thought to himself, it is the last time I make such another jump, so I will make the best of my way home. Then it was the turn of the Beaver, who made the attempt, but fell down senseless; then of the Lynx and Badger, who had no better success.

"Now," says Fisher to the Wolverine, "try your skill; your ancestors were celebrated for their activity, hardihood, and perseverance, and I depend on you for success. Now make the attempt." He did so, but also without success. He leaped the second time, but now they could see that the sky was giving way to their repeated attempts. Mustering strength, he made the third leap, and went in. The Fisher nimbly followed him.

They found themselves in a beautiful plain, extending as far as the eye could reach, covered with flowers of a thousand different hues and fragrance. Here and there were clusters of tall, shady trees, separated by innumerable streams of the purest water, which wound around their courses under the cooling shades, and filled the plain with countless beautiful lakes, whose banks and bosom were covered with water-fowl, basking and sporting in the sun. The trees were alive with birds of different plumage, warbling their sweet notes, and delighted with perpetual spring.

The Fisher and his friend beheld very long lodges, and the celestial inhabitants amusing themselves at a distance. Words cannot express the beauty and charms of the place. The lodges were empty of inhabitants, but they saw them lined with mocuks* of different sizes, filled with birds and fowls of different plumage. Ojeeg thought of his son, and immediately commenced cutting open the mocuks and letting out the birds,

* Baskets, or cages.

who descended in whole flocks through the opening which they had made. The warm air of those regions also rushed down through the opening, and spread its genial influence over the north.

When the celestial inhabitants saw the birds let loose, and the warm gales descending, they raised a shout like thunder, and ran for their lodges. But it was too late. Spring, summer, and autumn had gone; even perpetual summer had almost all gone; but they separated it with a blow, and only a part descended; but the ends were so mangled, that, wherever it prevails among th lower inhabitants, it is always sickly.*

When the Wolverine heard the noise, he made for the opening and safely descended. Not so the Fisher. Anxious to fulfil his son's wishes, he continued to break open the mocuks. He was, at last, obliged to run also, but the opening was now closed by the inhabitants. He ran with all his might over the plains of heaven, and, it would appear, took a northerly direction. He saw his pursuers so close that he had to climb the first large tree he came to. They commenced shooting at him with their arrows, but without effect, for all his body was invulnerable except the space of about an inch near the tip of his tail. At last one of the arrows hit the spot, for he had in this chase assumed the shape of the Fisher after whom he was named.

He looked down from the tree, and saw some among his assailants with the totems* of his ancestors. He claimed relationship, and told them to desist, which they only did at the approach of night. He then came down to try and find an opening in the celestial plain, by which he might descend to the earth. But he could find none. At last, becoming faint from the loss of blood from the wound on his tail, he laid himself down towards the north of the plain, and, stretching out his limbs, said, "I have fulfilled my promise to my son, though it has cost me my life; but I die satisfied in the idea that I have done so much good, not only for him, but for my fellow-beings. Hereafter I will be a sign to the inhabitants below for ages to come, who will venerate my name for having succeeded in procuring the varying seasons. They will now have from eight to ten moons without snow."

He was found dead next morning, but they left him as they

* The idea here indicated is among th peculiar notions of these tribes, and is grafted in the forms of their language, which will be pointed out in the progress of these researches.

* Family arms, or armorial mark.

CHILEELI,

OR
THE RED LOVER.

ODJIBWA.

MANY years ago there lived a warrior on the banks of Lake Superior, whose name was Wawanosh. He was the chief of an ancient family of his tribe, who had preserved the line of chieftainship unbroken from a remote time, and he consequently cherished a pride of ancestry. To the reputation of birth he added the advantages of a tall and commanding person, and the dazzling qualities of personal strength, courage, and activity. His bow was noted for its size, and the feats he had performed with it. His counsel was sought as much as his strength was feared, so that he came to be equally regarded as a hunter, a warrior, and a counsellor. He had now passed the meridian of his days, and the term AKKEE-WAIZEE, *i.e.*, one who has been long on the earth, was applied to him.

Such was Wawanosh, to whom the united voice of the nation awarded the first place in their esteem, and the highest authority in council. But distinction, it seems, is apt to engender haughtiness in the hunter state as well as civilized life. Pride was his ruling passion, and he clung with tenacity to the distinctions which he regarded as an inheritance.

Wawanosh had an only daughter, who had now lived to witness the budding of the leaves of the eighteenth spring. Her father was not more celebrated for his deeds of strength than she for her gentle virtues, her slendor form, her full beaming hazel eyes, and her dark and flowing hair.

"And through her cheek
The blush would make its way, and all but speak.
The sunborn blood suffused her neck, and threw
O'er her clear brown skin a lucid hue,
Like coral reddening through the darken'd wave,
Which draws the diver to the crimson cave."

111

Her hand was sought by a young man of humble parentage, who had no other merits to recommend him but such as might arise from a tall and commanding person, a manly step, and an eye beaming with the tropical fires of youth and love. These were sufficient to attract the favorable notice of the daughter, but were by no means satisfactory to the father, who sought an alliance more suitable to the rank and the high pretensions of his family.

"Listen to me young man," he replied to the trembling hunter, who had sought the interview, "and be attentive to my words. You ask me to bestow upon you my daughter, the chief solace of my age, and my choicest gift from the Master of Life. Others have asked of me this boon, who were as young, as active, and as ardent as yourself. Some of these persons have had better claims to become my son-in-law. Have you reflected upon the deeds which have raised me in authority, and made my name known to the enemies of my nation? Where is there a chief who is not proud to be considered the friend of Wawanosh? Where, in all the land, is there a hunter who has excelled Wawanosh? Where is there a warrior who can boast the taking of an equal number of scalps? Besides, have you not heard that my fathers came from the East, bearing the marks of chieftaincy?

"And what, young man, have *you* to boast? Have *you* ever met your enemies in the field of battle? Have *you* ever brought home a trophy of victory? Have *you* ever proved your fortitude by suffering protracted pain, enduring continued hunger, or sustaining great fatigue? Is your *name* known beyond the humble limits of your native village? Go, then, young man, and earn a name for yourself. It is none but the brave that can ever hope to claim an alliance with the house of Wawanosh. Think not my warrior blood shall mingle with the humble mark of the Awasees*—fit totem for fishermen!"

The intimidated lover departed, but he resolved to do a deed that should render him worthy of the daughter of Wawanosh, or die in the attempt. He called together several of his young companions and equals in years, and imparted to them his design of conducting an expedition against the enemy, and requested their assistance. Several embraced the proposal immediately; others were soon brought to acquiesce; and, before ten suns set, he saw himself at the head of a formidable

* Catfish.

112

party of young warriors, all eager, like himself, to distinguish themselves in battle. Each warrior was armed, according to the custom of the period, with a bow and a quiver of arrows, tipped with flint or jasper. He carried a sack or wallet, provided with a small quantity of parched and pounded corn, mixed with pemmican or maple sugar. He was furnished with a PUGGAMAUGUN, or war-club of hard wood, fastened to a girdle of deer skin, and a stone or copper knife. In addition to this, some carried the ancient *shemagun*, or lance, a smooth pole about a fathom in length, with a javelin of flint, firmly tied on with deer's sinews. Thus equipped, and each warrior painted in a manner to suit his fancy, and ornamented with appropriate feathers, they repaired to the spot appointed for the war-dance.

A level, grassy plain extended for nearly a mile from the lodge of Wawanosh along the lake shore. Lodges of bark were promiscuously interspersed over this green, and here and there a cluster of trees, or a solitary tall pine. A belt of yellow sand skirted the lake shore in front, and a tall, thick forest formed the background. In the centre of this plain stood a high shattered pine, with a clear space about, renowned as the scene of the war-dance time out of mind. Here the youths assembled, with their tall and graceful leader, distinguished by the feathers of the bald eagle, which he wore on his head. A bright fire of pine wood blazed upon the green. He led his men several times around this fire, with a measured and solemn·chant.* Then suddenly halting, the war-whoop was raised, and the dance immediately began. An old man, sitting at the head of the ring, beat time upon the drum, while several of the elder warriors shook their rattles, and "ever and anon" made the woods re-echo with their yells. Each warrior chanted alternately the verse of a song, of which the words generally embraced some prominent idea, often repeated.

> The eagles scream on high,
>   They whet their forked beaks:
> Raise—raise the battle cry,
>   'Tis fame our leader seeks.

Thus they continued the dance, till each had introduced his verse, with short intermissions, for two successive days and

* Notes of the Pibbigwun.

113

nights. Sometimes the village seer, who led the ceremony, would embrace the occasion of a pause to address them with words of encouragement, in a prophetic voice and air, suited to raise their voices.

In the dreamy hours of night
I beheld the bloody fight.
As reclined upon my bed,
Holy visions crowned my head;
High our guardian spirit bright
Stood above the dreadful fight;
Beaming eye and dazzling brand
Gleamed upon my chosen band,
While a black and awful shade
O'er the faithless foeman spread.
Soon they wavered, sunk, and fled,
Leaving wounded, dying, dead,
While my gallant warriors high
Waved their trophies in the sky.

At every recurrence of this kind, new energy was infused into the dance, and the warriors renewed their gesticulations, and stamped upon the ground as if they were trampling their enemies under their feet.

At length the prophet uttered his final prediction of success; and the warriors dropping off, one by one, from the fire, took their way to the place appointed for the rendezvous, on the confines of the enemy's country. Their leader was not among the last to depart, but he did not leave the village without seeking an interview with the daughter of Wawanosh. He disclosed to her his firm determination never to return, unless he could establish his name as a warrior. He told her of the pangs he had felt at the bitter reproaches of her father, and declared that his soul spurned the imputation of effeminacy and cowardice implied by his language. He averred that he could never be happy until he had proved to the whole tribe the strength of his heart, which is the Indian term for courage. He said that his dreams had not been propitious, but he should not cease to invoke the power of the Great Spirit. He repeated his protestations of inviolable attachment, which she returned, and, pledging vows of mutual fidelity, they parted.

That parting proved final. All she ever heard from her lover after this interview was brought by one of his successful

114

warriors, who said that he had distinguished himself by the most heroic bravery, but, at the close of the fight, he had received an arrow in his breast. The enemy fled, leaving many of their warriors dead on the field. On examining the wound, it was perceived to be beyond their power to cure. They carried him towards home a day's journey, but he languished and expired in the arms of his friends. From the moment the report was received, no smile was ever seen in the once happy lodge of Wawanosh. His daughter pined away by day and by night. Tears, sighs, and lamentation, were heard continually. Nothing could restore her lost serenity of mind. Persuasives and reproofs were alternately employed, but employed in vain. She would seek a sequestered spot, where she would sit under a shady tree, and sing her mournful laments for hours together. Passages of these are yet repeated by tradition.

It was not long before a small bird of beautiful plumage flew upon the tree under which she usually sat. This mysterious visitor, which, from its sweet and artless notes,is called Chileeli, seemed to respond in sympathy to her plaintive voice. It was a strange bird, such as had not before been observed. It came every day and remained chanting its notes till night-fall; and when it left its perch on the tree, it seemed, from the delicate play of the colors of its plumage, as if it had taken its hues from the rainbow. Her fond imagination soon led her to suppose it was the spirit of her lover, and her visits to the sequestered spot were repeated mere frequently. She passed much of her time in fasting and singing her plaintive songs. There she pined away, taking little nourishment, and constantly desiring to pass away to that land of expected bliss and freedom from care, where it is believed that the spirits of men will be again reunited, and tread over fields of flowery enjoyment. And when death came to her, it was not as the bearer of gloom and regrets, but as the herald of happiness. After her decease, the mysterious bird was never more seen, and it became a popular opinion that the mysterious visitor had flown away with her spirit.*

* Notes of the Pibbigwun.

SHEEM,

THE FORSAKEN BOY OR WOLF BROTHER.

AN ODJIBWA ALLEGORY OF FRATERNAL AFFECTION.

A SOLITARY lodge stood on the banks of a remote lake. It was near the hour of sunset. Silence reigned within and without. Not a sound was heard but the low breathing of the dying inmate and head of this poor family. His wife and three children surrounded his bed. Two of the latter were almost grown up: the other was a mere child. All their simple skill in medicine had been exhausted to no effect. They moved about the lodge in whispers, and were waiting the departure of the spirit. As one of the last acts of kindness, the skin door of the lodge had been thrown back to admit the fresh air. The poor man felt a momentary return of strength, and, raising himself a little, addressed his family.

"I leave you in a world of care, in which it has required all my strength and skill to supply you food, and protect you from the storms and cold of a severe climate. For you, my partner in life, I have less sorrow in parting, because I am persuaded you will not remain long behind me, and will therefore find the period of your sufferings shortened. But you, my children! my poor and forsaken children, who have just commenced the career of life, who will protect you from its evils? Listen to my words! Unkindness, ingratitude, and every wickedness is in the scene before you. It is for this cause that, years ago, I withdrew from my kindred and my tribe, to spend my days in this lonely spot. I have contented myself with the company of your mother and yourselves during seasons of very frequent scarcity and want, while your kindred, feasting in a scene where food is plenty, have caused the forests to echo with the shouts of successful war. I gave up these things for the enjoyment of peace. I wished to shield you from the bad examples you would inevitably have followed. I have seen you, thus far, grow up in innocence. If we have sometimes suffered bodily

116

want, we have escaped pain of mind.* We have been kept from scenes of rioting and bloodshed.

"My career is now at its close. I will shut my eyes in peace, if you, my children, will promise me to cherish each other. Let not your mother suffer during the few days that are left to her; and I charge you, on no account, to forsake your youngest brother. Of him I give you both my dying charge to take a tender care." He sank exhausted on his pallet. The family waited a moment, as if expecting to hear something further; but, when they came to his side, the spirit had taken its flight.

The mother and daughter gave vent to their feelings in lamentations. The elder son witnessed the scene in silence. He soon exerted himself to supply, with the bow and net, his father's place. Time, however, wore away heavily. Five moons had filled and waned, and the sixth was near its full, when the mother also died. In her last moments she pressed the fulfilment of their promise to their father, which the children readily renewed, because they were yet free from selfish motives.

The winter passed; and the spring, with its enlivening effects in a northern hemisphere, cheered the drooping spirits of the bereft little family. The girl, being the eldest, dictated to her brothers, and seemed to feel a tender and sisterly affection for the youngest, who was rather sickly and delicate. The other boy soon showed symptoms of restlessness and ambition, and addressed the sister as follows: "My sister, are we always to live as if there were no other human beings in the world? Must I deprive myself of the pleasure of associating with my own kind? I have determined this question for myself. I shall seek the villages of men, and you cannot prevent me."

The sister replied: "I do not say no, my brother, to what you desire. We are not prohibited the society of our fellow-mortals; but we are told to cherish each other, and to do nothing independent of each other. Neither pleasure nor pain ought, therefore, to separate us, especially from our younger brother, who being but a child, and weakly withal, is entitled to a double share of our affection. If we follow our separate gratifications, it will surely make us neglect him, whom we are bound by vows, both to our father and mother, to support."

* Wesugaindum, meaning pain or bitterness of mind, is a single expression in the original. It is a trinary compound.

The young man received this address in silence. He appeared daily to grow more restive and moody, and one day, taking his bow and arrows, left the lodge and never returned.

Affection nerved the sister's arm. She was not so ignorant of the forest arts as to let her brother want. For a long time she administered to his necessities, and supplied a mother's cares. At length, however, she began to be weary of solitude and of her charge. No one came to be a witness of her assiduity, or to let fall a single word in her native language. Years, which added to her strength and capability of directing the affairs of the household, brought with them the irrepressible desire of society, and made solitude irksome. At this point, selfishness gained the ascendency of her heart; for, in meditating a change in her mode of life, she lost sight of her younger brother, and left him to be provided for by contingencies.

One day, after collecting all the provisions she had been able to save for emergencies, after bringing a quantity of wood to the door, she said to her little brother: "My brother, you must not stray from the lodge. I am going to seek our elder brother. I shall be back soon." Then, taking her bundle, she set off in search of habitations. She soon found them, and was so much taken up with the pleasures and amusements of social life, that the thought of her brother was almost entirely obliterated. She accepted proposals of marriage; and, after that, thought still less of her hapless and abandoned relative.

Meantime her elder brother had also married, and lived on the shores of the same lake whose ample circuit contained the abandoned lodge of his father and his forsaken brother. The latter was soon brought to the pinching turn of his fate. As soon as he had eaten all the food left by his sister, he was obliged to pick berries and dig up roots. These were finally covered by the snow. Winter came on with all its rigors. He was obliged to quit the lodge in search of other food. Sometimes he passed the night in the clefts of old trees or caverns, and ate the refuse meals of the wolves. The latter, at last, became his only resource; and he became so fearless of these animals that he would sit close by them while they devoured their prey. The wolves, on the other hand, became so familiar with his face and form, that they were undisturbed by his approach; and, appearing to sympathize with him in his outcast condition, would always leave something for his repast. In this way he lived till spring. As soon as the lake was free from ice, he followed his new-found friends themselves to the shore. It happened, the same day, that his elder brother was fishing in his canoe, a considerable distance out in the lake, when he thought he heard the cries of a child on the shore, and wondered how any could exist on so bleak and barren a part of the coast. He listened again attentively, and distinctly heard the cry repeated. He made for shore as quick as possible, and, as he approached land, discovered and recognized his little brother, and heard him singing, in a plaintive voice—

> Neesia—neesia,
> Shyegwuh goosuh!
> Ni my een gwun iewh!
> Ni my een gwun iewh!
> Heo hwooh.
> My brother—my brother,
> Ah! see, I am turning into a wolf.*

At the termination of his song, which was drawn out with a peculiar cadence, he howled like a wolf. The elder brother was still more astonished, when, getting nearer shore, he perceived his poor brother partly transformed into that animal. He immediately leaped on shore, and strove to catch him in his arms, soothingly saying, "My brother, my brother, come to me." But the boy eluded his grasp, crying as he fled, "Neesia, neesia," & c., and howling in the intervals.

The elder brother, conscience stricken, and feeling his brotherly affection strongly return, with redoubled force exclaimed, in great anguish, "My brother! my brother! my brother!"

But, the nearer he approached, the more rapidly the transformation went on; the boy alternately singing and howling, and calling out the name, first of his brother, and then of his sister, till the change was completely accomplished, when he exclaimed, "I am a wolf!" and bounded out of sight.

* Notes of the Pibbigwun.

MISHEMOKWA,

OR

THE WAR WITH THE GIGANTIC BEAR WEARING THE PRE-
CIOUS PRIZE OF THE NECKLACE OF WAMPUM,

OR

THE ORIGIN OF THE SMALL BLACK BEAR.

AN OTTOWA LEGEND.

IN a remote part of the north lived a great magician called
IAMO, and his only sister, who had never seen a human being.
Seldom, if ever, had the man any cause to go from home; for, as
his wants demanded food, he had only to go a little distance
from the lodge, and there, in some particular spot, place his

arrows, with their barbs in the ground. Telling his sister where they had been placed, every morning she would go in search, and never fail of finding each struck through the heart of a deer. She had then only to drag them into the lodge and prepare their food. Thus she lived till she attained womanhood, when one day her brother said to her, "Sister, the time is near at hand when you will be ill. Listen to my advice. If you do not, it will probably be the cause of my death. Take the implements with which we kindle our fires. Go some distance from our lodge, and build a separate fire. When you are in want of food, I will tell you where to find it. You must cook for yourself, and I will for myself. When you are ill, do not attempt to come near the lodge, or bring any of the utensils you use. Be sure always to fasten to your belt the implements you need, for you do not know when the time will come. As for myself, I must do the best I can." His sister promised to obey him in all he had said.

Shortly after, her brother had cause to go from home. She was alone in her lodge, combing her hair. She had just untied the belt to which the implements were fastened, when suddenly the event, to which her brother had alluded, occurred. She ran out of the lodge, but in her haste forgot the belt. Afraid to return, she stood for sometime thinking. Finally she decided to enter the lodge and get it. For, thought she, my brother is not at home, I will stay but a moment to catch hold of it. She went back. Running in suddenly, she caught hold of it, and was coming out when her brother came in sight. He knew what was the matter. "Oh," he said, "did I not tell you to take care? But now you have killed me." She was going on her way, but her brother said to her, "What can you do there now? the accident has happened. Go in, and stay where you have always stayed. And what will become of you? You have killed me."

He then laid aside his hunting dress and accoutrements, and soon after both his feet began to inflame and turn black, so that he could not move. Still he directed his sister where to place the arrows, that she might always have food. The inflammation continued to increase, and had now reached his first rib; and he said, "Sister, my end is near. You must do as I tell you. You see my medicine-sack, and my war-club tied to it. It contains all my medicines, and my war-plumes, and my paints of all colors. As soon as the inflammation reaches my breast, you will take my war-club. It has a sharp point, and you will

121

cut off my head. When it is free from my body, take it, place its neck in the sack, which you must open at one end. Then hang it up in its former place. Do not forget my bow and arrows. One of the last you will take to procure food. The remainder tie to my sack, and then hang it up, so that I can look towards the door. Now and then I will speak to you, but not often." His sister again promised to obey.

In a little time his breast was affected. "Now," said he, "take the club and strike off my head." She was afraid, but he told her to muster courage. "*Strike,*" said he, and a smile was on his face. Mustering all her courage, she gave the blow and cut off the head. "Now," said the head, "place me where I told you." And fearfully she obeyed it in all its commands. Retaining its animation, it looked around the lodge as usual, and it would command its sister to go to such places as it thought would procure for her the flesh of different animals she needed. One day the head said, "The time is not distant when I shall be freed from this situation, but I shall have to undergo many sore evils. So the Superior Manito decrees, and I must bear all patiently." In this situation we must leave the head.

In a certain part of the country was a village inhabited by a numerous and warlike band of Indians. In this village was a family of ten young men—brothers. It was in the spring of the year that the youngest of these blackened his face and fasted. His dreams were propitious. Having ended his fast, he sent secretly for his brothers at night, so that none in the village could overhear or find out the direction they intended to go. Though their drum was heard, yet that was a common occurence. Having ended the usual formalities, he told them how favorable his dreams were, and that he had called them together to know if they would accompany him in a war excursion. They all answered they would. The third brother from the eldest, noted for his oddities, coming up with his war-club when his brother had ceased speaking, jumped up, "Yes," said he, "*I* will go, and this will be the way I will treat those we are going to fight;" and he struck the post in the centre of the lodge, and gave a yell. The others spoke to him, saying, "Slow, slow, Mudjikewis, when you are in other people's lodges." So he sat down. Then, in turn, they took the drum, and sang their songs, and closed with a feast. The youngest told them not to whisper their intention even to their wives, but secretly to prepare for their journey. They all promised obedience, and Mudjikewis was the first to say so.

The time for their departure drew near. Word was given to assemble on a certain night, when they would depart immediately. Mudjikewis was loud in his demands for his moccasins. Several times his wife asked him the reason. "Besides," said she, "you have a good pair on." "Quick, quick," he said, "since you must know, we are going on a war excursion. So be quick." He thus revealed the secret. That night they met and started. The snow was on the ground, and they travelled all night, lest others should follow them. When it was daylight, the leader took snow and made a ball of it; then tossing it into the air, he said, "It was in this way I saw snow fall in my dream, so that I could not be tracked." And he told them to keep close to each other for fear of losing themsleves, as the snow began to fall in very large flakes. Near as they walked, it was with difficulty they could see each other. The snow continued falling all that day and the following night. So it was impossible to track them.

They had now walked for several days, and Mudjikewis was always in the rear. One day, running suddenly forward, he gave the *Saw-saw-quan*,* and struck a tree with his war-club, which broke into pieces as if struck with lightning. "Brothers," said he, "this will be the way I will serve those whom we are going to fight." The leader answered, "Slow, slow, Mudjikewis. The one I lead you to is not to be thought of so lightly." Again he fell back and thought to himself, "What, what: Who can this be he is leading us to?" He felt fearful, and was silent. Day after day they travelled on, till they came to an extensive plain, on the borders of which human bones were bleaching in the sun. The leader spoke. "They are the bones of those who have gone before us. None has ever yet returned to tell the sad tale of their fate." Again Mudjikewis became restless, and, running forward, gave the accustomed yell. Advancing to a large rock which stood above the ground, he struck it, and it fell to pieces. "See, brothers," said he, "thus will I treat those whom we are going to fight." "Still, still," once more said the leader; "he to whom I am leading you is not to be compared to that rock."

Mudjikewis fell back quite thoughtful, saying to himself, "I wonder who this can be that he is going to attack." And he was afraid. Still they continued to see the remains of former warriors, who had been to the place where *they* were now

* War-cry.

123

going, some of whom had retreated as far back as the place where they first saw the bones, beyond which no one had ever escaped. At last they came to a piece of rising ground, from which they plainly distinguished, sleeping on a distant mountain, a mammoth bear.

The distance between them was great, but the size of the animal caused him plainly to be seen. "There," said the leader, "it is he to whom I am leading you; here our troubles only will commence, for he is a MISHEMOKWA* and a Manito. It is he who has that we prize so dearly (i. e., *wampum*), to obtain which, the warriors whose bones we saw sacrificed their lives. You must not be fearful. Be manly. We shall find him asleep." They advanced boldly till they came near, when they stopped to view him more closely. He was asleep. Then the leader went forward and touched the belt around the animal's neck. "This," he said, "is what we must get. It contains the wampum." They then requested the eldest to try and slip the belt over the bear's head, who appeared to be fast asleep, as he was not in the least disturbed by the attempt to obtain it. All their efforts were in vain, till it came to the one next the youngest. He tried, and the belt moved nearly over the monster's head, but he could get it no further. Then the youngest one and leader made his attempt, and succeeded. Placing it on the back of the oldest, he said, "Now we must run," and off they started. When one became fatigued with its weight, another would relieve him. Thus they ran till they had passed the bones of all former warriors, and were some distance beyond, when, looking back, they saw the monster slowly rising. He stood sometime before he missed his wampum. Soon they heard his tremendous howl, like distant thunder, slowly filling all the sky; and then they heard him speak and say, "Who can it be that has dared to steal my wampum? Earth is not so large but that I can find them." And he descended from the hill in pursuit. As if convulsed, the earth shook with every jump he made. Very soon he approached the party. They however kept the belt, exchanging it from one to another, and encouraging each other. But he gained on them fast. "Brothers," said the leader, "has never any one of you, when fasting, dreamed of some friendly spirit who would aid you as a guardian?" A dead silence followed. "Well," said he, "fasting, I dreamed of being in danger of instant death, when I saw a small lodge, with smoke curling

* A gigantic she bear wearing the sacred necklace of wampum.

124

from its top. An old man lived in it, and I dreamed he helped me. And may it be verified soon," he said, running forward and giving the peculiar yell, and a howl as if the sounds came from the depths of his stomach, and which is called *Checaudum*. Getting upon a piece of rising ground, behold! a lodge, with smoke curling from its top, appeared. This gave them all new strength, and they ran forward and entered it. The leader spoke to the old man who sat in the lodge saying, "*Nemesho*,* help us. We claim your protection, for the great bear will kill us." "Sit down and eat, my grandchildren," said the old man. "Who is a great Manito?" said he, "there is none but me; but let me look," and he opened the door of the lodge, when lo! at a little distance he saw the enraged animal coming on, with slow but powerful leaps. He closed the door. "Yes," said he, "*he* is indeed a great Manito. My grandchildren, you will be the cause of my losing my life. You asked my protection, and I granted it; so now come what may, I will protect you. When the bear arrives at the door, you must run out of the other end of the lodge." Then putting his hand to the side of the lodge where he sat, he brought out a bag, which he opened. Taking out two small black dogs, he placed them before him. "These are the ones I use when I fight," said he; and he commenced patting, with both hands, the sides of one of them, and they began to swell out, so that he soon filled the lodge by his bulk. And he had great strong teeth. When he attained his full size he growled, and from that moment, as from instinct, he jumped out at the door and met the bear, who in another leap would have reached the lodge. A terrible combat ensued. The skies rang with the howls of the fierce monsters. The remaining dog soon took the field. The brothers, at the onset, took the advice of the old man, and escaped through the opposite side of the lodge. They had not proceeded far before they heard the dying cry of one of the dogs, and soon after of the other. "Well," said the leader, "the old man will share their fate; so run, run, he will soon be after us." They started with fresh vigor, for they had received food from the old man; but very soon the bear came in sight, and again was fast gaining upon them. Again the leader asked the brothers if they could do nothing for their safety. All were silent. The leader, running forward, did as before. "I dreamed," he cried, "that, being in great trouble, an old man helped me who was a Manito. We shall soon see his

* My grandfather.

lodge." Taking courage, they still went on. After going a short distance they saw the lodge of the old Manito. They entered immediately and claimed his protection, telling him a Manito was after them. The old man, setting meat before them, said, "Eat. Who is a Manito? there is no Manito but me. There is none whom I fear." And the earth trembled as the monster advanced. The old man opened the door and saw him coming. He shut it slowly, and said, "Yes, my grandchildren, you have brought trouble upon me." Procuring his medicine sack, he took out his small war-clubs of black stone, and told the young men to run through the other side of the lodge. As he handled the clubs they became very large, and the old man stepped out just as the bear reached the door. Then striking him with one of the clubs, it broke in pieces. The bear stumbled. Renewing the attempt with the other war-club, that also was broken, but the bear fell senseless. Each blow the old man gave him sounded like a clap of thunder, and the howls of the bear ran along till they filled the heavens.

The young men had now ran some distance, when they looked back. They could see that the bear was recovering from the blows. First he moved his paws, and soon they saw him rise on his feet. The old man shared the fate of the first, for they now heard his cries as he was torn in pieces. Again the monster was in pursuit, and fast overtaking them. Not yet discouraged, the young men kept on their way; but the bear was now so close, that the leader once more applied to his brothers, but they could do nothing. "Well," said he, "my dreams will soon be exhausted. After this I have but one more." He advanced, invoking his guardian spirit to aid him. "Once," said he, "I dreamed that, being sorely pressed, I came to a large lake, on the shore of which was a canoe, partly out of water, having ten paddles all in readiness. Do not fear," he cried, "we shall soon get to it." And so it was, even as he had said. Coming to the lake, they saw the canoe with ten paddles, and immediately they embarked. Scarcely had they reached the centre of the lake when they saw the bear arrive at its borders. Lifting himself on his hind legs, he looked all around. Then he waded into the water; then losing his footing, he turned back, and commenced making the circuit of the lake. Meanwhile, the party remained stationary in the centre to watch his movements. He travelled around, till at last he came to the place from whence he started. Then he commenced drinking up the water, and they saw the current fast setting in towards his open mouth. The leader encouraged them to paddle hard for the opposite shore. When only a short distance from land, the current had increased so much, that they were drawn back by it, and all their efforts to reach it were vain.

Then the leader again spoke, telling them to meet their fates manfully. "Now is the time, Mudjikewis," said he, "to show your prowess. Take courage, and sit in the bow of the canoe; and when it approaches his mouth, try what effect your club will have on his head." He obeyed, and stood ready to give the blow; while the leader, who steered, directed the canoe for the open mouth of the monster.

Rapidly advancing, they were just about to enter his mouth, when Mudjikewis struck him a tremendous blow on the head, and gave the saw-saw-quan. The bear's limbs doubled under him, and he fell stunned by the blow. But before Mudjikewis could renew it the monster disgorged all the water he had drank, with a force which sent the canoe with great velocity to the opposite shore. Instantly leaving the canoe, again they fled, and on they went till they were completely exhausted. The earth again shook, and soon they saw the monster hard after them. Their spirits drooped, and they felt discouraged. The leader exerted himself, by actions and words, to cheer them up; and once more he asked them if they thought of nothing, or could do nothng for their rescue; and, as before all were silent. "Then," he said, "this is the last time I can apply to my guardian spirit. Now if we do not succeed, our fates are decided." He ran forward, invoking his spirit with great earnestness, and gave the yell. "We shall soon arrive," said he to his brothers, "to the place where my last guardian spirit dwells. In him I place great confidence. Do not, do not be afraid, or your limbs will be fear-bound. We shall soon reach his lodge. Run, run," he cried.

They were now in sight of the lodge of Iamo, the magician of the undying head—of that great magician whose life had been the forfeit of the kind of necromantic leprosy caused by the careless steps of the fatal curse of uncleanliness in his sister. This lodge was the sacred spot of expected relief to which they had been fleeing, from the furious rage of the giant Bear, who had been robbed of her precious boon, the *magissauniqua*. For it had been the design of many previous war parties to obtain this boon.

In the meantime, the undying head of Iamo had remained in

the medicine sack, suspended on the sides of his wigwam, where his sister had placed it, with its mystic charms, and feathers, and arrows. This head retained all life and vitality, keeping its eyes open, and directing its sister, in order to procure food, where to place the magic arrows, and speaking at long intervals. One day the sister saw the eyes of the head brighten, as if through pleasure. At last it spoke. "Oh! sister," it said, "in what a pitiful situation you have been the cause of placing me. Soon, very soon, a party of young men will arrive and apply to me for aid; but, alas! how can I give what I *would* have done with so much pleasure. Nevertheless, take two arrows, and place them where you have been in the habit of placing the others, and have meat prepared and cooked before they arrive. When you hear them coming and calling on my name, go out and say, 'Alas! it is long ago that an accident befell him; I was the cause of it.' If they still come near, ask them in and set meat before them. And now you must follow my directions strictly. When the bear is near, go out and meet him. You will take my medicine sack, bows and arrows, and my head. You must then untie the sack, and spread out before you my paints of all colors, my war eagle feathers, my tufts of dried hair, and whatever else it contains. As the bear approaches, you will take all these articles, one by one, and say to him, 'This is my deceased brother's paint,' and so on with all the other articles, throwing each of them as far from you as you can. The virtues contained in them will cause him to totter; and, to complete destruction, you will take my head, and that too you will cast as far off as you can, crying aloud, 'See, this is my deceased brother's head.' He will then fall senseless. By this time the young men will have eaten, and you will call them to your assistance. You must then cut the carcass into pieces, yes, into *small* pieces, and scatter them to the four winds; for, unless you do this, he will again revive." She promised that all should be done as he said. She had only time to prepare the meat, when the voice of the leader was heard calling upon Iamo for aid. The woman went out and invited them in as her brother had directed. But the war party, being closely pursued, came promptly up to the lodge. She invited them in, and placed the meat before them. While they were eating they heard the bear approaching. Untying the medicine sack and taking the head, she had all in readiness for his approach. When he came up, she did as she had been told. "Behold, Mishemokwa," she cried, "this is the meda sack of

Iamo. These are war eagle's feathers of Iamo (casting them aside). These are magic arrows of Iamo (casting them down). These are the sacred paints and magic charms of Iamo. These are dried tufts of the hair of furious beasts. And this (swinging it with all her might) is his undying head." The monster began to totter, as she cast one thing after the other on the ground, but still recovering strength, came close up to the woman till she flung the head. As it rolled along the ground, the blood, excited by the feelings of the head in this terrible scene, gushed from the nose and mouth. The bear, tottering, soon fell with a tremendous noise. Then she cried for help, and the young men came rushing out, having partially regained their strength and spirits.

Mudjikewis, stepping up, gave a yell, and struck the monster a blow upon the head. This he repeated till it seemed like a mass of brains; while the others, as quick as possible, cut him into very small pieces, which they than scattered in every direction. While thus employed, happening to look around where they had thrown the meat, wonderful to behold! they saw, starting up and running off in every direction, small black bears, such as are seen at the present day. The country was soon overspread with these black animals. And it was from this monster that the present race of bears, the mukwahs, derived their origin.

Having thus overcome their pursuer, they returned to the lodge. In the meantime, the woman, gathering the implements she had scattered, and the head, placed them again in the sack. But the head did not speak again.

The war party were now triumphant, but they did not know what use to make of their triumph. Having spent so much time, and traversed so vast a country in their flight, the young men gave up the idea of ever returning to their own country, and game being plenty, they determined to remain where they now were, and make this their home. One day they moved off some distance from the lodge for the purpose of hunting, having left the wampum captured with the woman. They were very successful, and amused themselves, as all young men do when alone, by talking and jesting with each other. One of them spoke and said, "We have all this sport to ourselves; let us go and ask our sister if she will not let us bring the head to this place, as it is still alive. It may be pleased to hear us talk and be in our company. In the meantime, we will take food to our sister." They went, and requested the head. She told them to take it, and they took it to their hunting-grounds, and tried to amuse it, but only at times did they see its eyes beam with pleasure. One day, while busy in their encampment, they were unexpectedly attacked by unknown Indians. The skirmish was long contested and bloody. Many of their foes were slain, but still they were thirty to one. The young men fought desperately till they were all killed. The attacking party then retreated to a height of ground, to muster their men, and to count the number of missing and slain. One of their young men had strayed away, and, in endeavoring to overtake them, came to the place where the undying head was hung up. Seeing that alone retain animation, he eyed it for sometime with fear and surprise. However, he took it down and opened the sack, and was much pleased to see the beautiful feathers, one of which he placed on his head.

Starting off, it waved gracefully over him till he reached his party, when he threw down the head and sack, and told them how he had found it, and that the sack was full of paints and feathers. They all looked at the head and made sport of it. Numbers of the young men took up the paint and painted themselves, and one of the party took the head by the hair and said, "Look, you ugly thing, and see your paints on the faces of warriors." But the feathers were so beautiful, that numbers of them also placed *them* on their heads. Then again they used all kinds of indignity to the head, for which they were in turn repaid by the death of those who had used the feathers. Then the chief commanded them to throw all away except the head. "We will see," said he, "when we get home, what we can do to it. We will try to make it shut its eyes."

When they reached their homes they took it to the council lodge, and hung it up before the fire, fastening it with raw hide soaked, which would shrink and become tightened by the action of the fire. "We will then see," they said, "if we cannot make it shut its eyes."

Meanwhile, for several days, the sister of Iamo had been waiting for the young men to bring back the head; till at last, getting impatient, she went in search of it. The young men she found lying within short distances of each other, dead, and covered with wounds. Various other bodies lay scattered in different directions around them. She searched for the head and sack, but they were nowhere to be found. She raised her voice and wept, and blackened her face. Then she walked in different directions, till she came to the place from whence the head had been taken. There she found the magic bow and arrows, where the young men, ignorant of their qualities, had left them. She thought to herself that she would find her brother's head, and came to a piece of rising ground, and there saw some of his paints and feathers. These she carefully put up, and hung upon the branch of a tree till her return.

At dusk she arrived at the first lodge of the enemy, in a very extensive village. Here she used a charm, common among Indians when they wish to meet with a kind reception. On applying to the old man and woman of the lodge, she was kindly received. She made known her errand. The old man promised to aid her, and told her that the head was hung up before the council fire, and that the chiefs of the village, with their young men, kept watch over it continually. The former are considered as Manitoes. She said she only wished to see it, and would be satisfied if she could only get to the door of the lodge. She knew she had not sufficient power to take it by force. "Come with me," said the Indian, "I will take you there." They went, and they took their seats near the door. The council lodge was filled with warriors, amusing themselves with games, and constantly keeping up a fire to smoke the head, as they said, to make dry meat. They saw the eyes move, and not knowing what to make of it, one spoke and said, "Ha! ha! it is beginning to feel the effects of the smoke." The sister looked up from the door, and as her eyes met those of her brother, tears rolled down the cheeks of the undying head. "Well," said the chief, "I thought we would make you do something at last. Look! look at it—shedding tears," said he to those around him; and they all laughed and passed their jokes upon it. The chief, looking around and observing the woman, after sometime said to the old man who came with her, "Who have you got there? I have never seen that woman before in our village." "Yes," replied the man, "you have seen her; she is a relation of mine, and seldom goes out. She stays in my lodge, and asked me to allow her to come with me to this place." In the centre of the lodge sat one of those vain young men who are always forward, and fond of boasting and displaying themselves before others. "Why," said he, "I have seen her often, and it is to his lodge I go almost every night to court her." All the others laughed and continued their games. The young man did not know he was telling a lie to the woman's advantage, who by that means escaped scrutiny.

She returned to the old man's lodge, and immediately set out for her own country. Coming to the spot where the bodies of her adopted brothers lay, she placed them together, their feet toward *the east.* Then taking an axe which she had, she cast it up into the air, crying out, "Brothers, get up from under it, or it will fall on you." This she repeated three times, and the third time the brothers all arose and stood on their feet.

Mudjikewis commenced rubbing his eyes and stretching himself. "Why," said he, "I have overslept myself." "No, indeed," said one of the others, "do you not know we were all killed, and that is our sister who has brought us to life?" The young men took the bodies of their enemies and *burned* them. Soon after, the woman went to procure wives for them, in a distant country, they knew not where; but she returned with ten young females, which she gave to the young men, beginning with the eldest. Mudjikewis stepped to and fro, uneasy lest he should not get the one he liked. But he was not disappointed, for she fell to his lot. And they were well matched, for she was a female magician. They then all moved into a very large lodge, and their sister Iamoqua told them that the women must now take turns in going to her brother's head every night, trying to untie it. They all said they would do so with pleasure. The eldest made the first attempt, and with a rushing noise she fled through the air.

Towards daylight she returned. She had been unsuccessful, as she succeeded in untying only one of the knots. All took their turns regularly, and each one succeeded in untying only one knot each time. But when the youngest went, she commenced the work as soon as she reached the lodge; although it had always been occupied, still the Indians never could see any one, for they all possessed invisibility. For ten nights now, the smoke had not ascended, but filled the lodge and drove them out. This last night they were all driven out, and the young woman carried off the head.

The young people and the sister heard the young woman coming high through the air, and they heard her saying, "Prepare the body of our brother." And as soon as they heard it, they went to a small lodge where the black body of Iamo lay. His sister commenced cutting the neck part, from which the head had been severed. She cut so deep as to cause it to bleed; and the others who were present, by rubbing the body and applying medicines, expelled the blackness. In the meantime, the one who brought it, by cutting the neck of the head, caused that also to bleed.

132

As soon as she arrived, they placed that close to the body, and by the aid of medicines and various other means, succeeded in restoring Iamo to all his former beauty and manliness. All rejoiced in the happy termination of their troubles, and they had spent some time joyfully together, when Iamo said, "Now I will divide the wampum;" and getting the belt which contained it, he commenced with the eldest, giving it in equal proportions. But the youngest got the most splendid and beautiful, as the bottom of the belt held the richest and rarest.

They were told that, since they had all once died, and were restored to life, they were no longer mortals, but *spirits*, and they were assigned different stations in the invisible world. Only Mudjikewis's place was, however, named. He was to direct the *west wind*, hence generally called Kabeyun, the father of Manabozho, there to remain forever. They were commanded, as they had it in their power, to do good to the inhabitants of the earth; and forgetting their sufferings in procuring the wampum, to give all things with a liberal hand. And they were also commanded that it should also be held by them *sacred*; those grains or shells of the pale hue to be emblematic of peace, while those of the darker hue would lead to evil and to war.

The spirits, then, amid songs and shouts, took their flight to their respective abodes on high; while Iamo, with his sister Iamoqua, descended into the depths below.

THE RED SWAN.

THREE brothers were left destitute, by the death of their parents, at an early age. The eldest was not yet able to provide fully for their support, but did all he could in hunting, and with his aid, and the stock of provisions left by their father, they were preserved and kept alive, rather, it seems, by miraculous interposition, than the adequacy of their own exertions. For the father had been a hermit,* having removed far away from the body of the tribe, so that when he and his wife died they left their children without neighbors and friends, and the lads had no idea that there was a human being near them. They did not even know who their parents had been, for the eldest was too young, at the time of their death, to remember

* Pai-gwud-aw-diz-zid.

it. Forlorn as they were, they did not, however, give up to despondency, but made use of every exertion they could, and in process of time, learned the art of hunting and killing animals. The eldest soon became an expert hunter, and was very successful in procuring food. He was noted for his skill in killing buffalo, elk, and moose, and he instructed his brothers in the arts of the forest as soon as they became old enough to follow him. After they had become able to hunt and take care of themselves, the elder proposed to leave them, and go in search of habitations, promising to return as soon as he could procure them wives. In this project he was overruled by his brothers, who said they could not part with him. Maujeekewis, the second eldest, was loud in his disapproval, saying, "What will you do with *those you propose to get*—we have lived so long without them, and we can still do without them." His words prevailed, and the three brothers continued together for a time.

One day they agreed to kill each, a male of those kind of animals each was most expert in hunting, for the purpose of making quivers from their skins. They did so, and immediately commenced making arrows to fill their quivers, that they might be prepared for any emergency. Soon after, they hunted on a wager, to see who should come in first with game, and prepare it so as to regale the others. They were to shoot no other animal, but such as each was in the habit of killing. They set out different ways; Odjibwa, the youngest, had not gone far before he saw a bear, an animal he was not to kill, by the agreement. He followed him close, and drove an arrow through him, which brought him to the ground. Although contrary to the bet, he immediately commenced skinning him, when suddenly something red tinged all the air around him. He rubbed his eyes, thinking he was perhaps deceived, but without effect, for the red hue continued. At length he heard a strange noise at a distance. It first appeared like a human voice, but after following the sound for some distance, he reached the shores of a lake, and soon saw the object he was looking for. At a distance out in the lake, sat a most beautiful Red Swan, whose plumage glittered in the sun, and who would now and then make the same noise he had heard. He was within long bow shot, and pulling the arrow from the bow-string up to his ear, took deliberate aim and shot. The arrow took no effect; and he shot and shot again till his quiver was empty. Still the swan remained, moving around and around, stretching its long neck and dipping its bill into the water, as if heedless of the arrows shot at it. Odjibwa ran home, and got all his own and his brothers' arrows, and shot them all away. He then stood and gazed at the beautiful bird. While standing, he remembered his brothers' saying that in their deceased father's medicine sack were three magic arrows. Off he started, his anxiety to kill the swan overcoming all scruples. At any other time, he would have deemed it sacrilege to open his father's medicine sack, but now he hastily seized the three arrows and ran back, leaving the other contents of the sack scattered over the lodge. The swan was still there. He shot the first arrow with great precision, and came very near to it. The second came still closer; as he took the last arrow, he felt his arm firmer, and drawing it up with vigor, saw it pass through the neck of the swan a little above the breast. Still it did not prevent the bird from flying off, which it did, however, at first slowly, flapping its wings and rising gradually into the air, and then flying off toward the sinking of the sun.* Odjibwa was disappointed; he knew that his brothers would be displeased with him; he rushed into the water and rescued the two magic arrows, the third was carried off by the swan; but he thought that it could not fly very far with it, and let the consequences be what they might, he was bent on following it.

Off he started on the run; he was noted for speed, for he would shoot an arrow, and then run so fast that the arrow always fell behind him. I can run fast, he thought, and I can get up with the swan sometime or other. He thus ran over hills and prairies, toward the west, till near night, and was only going to take one more run, and then seek a place to sleep for the night, when suddenly he heard noises at a distance, which he knew were from people; for some were cutting trees, and the strokes of their axes echoed through the woods. When he emerged from the forest, the sun was just falling below the horizon, and he felt pleased to find a place to sleep in, and get something to eat, as he had left home without a mouthful. All these circumstances could not damp his ardor for the accomplishment of his object, and he felt that if he only persevered, he would succeed. At a distance, on a rising piece of ground, he could see an extensive town. He went toward it, but soon heard the watchman, MUDJEE-KOKOKOHO, who was placed on some height to overlook the place, and give notice of the approach

* Pungish-e-moo, falling or sinking to a position of repose.

of friends or foes—crying out, "We are visited;" and a loud holla indicated that they all heard it. The young man advanced, and was pointed by the watchman to the lodge of the chief, "It is there you must go in,". he said, and left him. "Come in, come in," said the chief, "take a seat there," pointing to the side where his daughter sat. "It is there you must sit." Soon they gave him something to eat, and very few questions were asked him, being a stranger. It was only when he spoke, that the others answered him. "Daughter," said the chief, after dark, "take our son-in-law's moccasins, and see if they be torn; if so, mend them for him, and bring in his bundle." The young man thought it strange that he should be so warmly received, and married instantly, without his wishing it, although the young girl was pretty. It was sometime before she would take his moccasins, which he had taken off. It displeased him to see her so reluctant to do so, and when she did reach them, he snatched them out of her hand and hung them up himself. He laid down and thought of the swan, and made up his mind to be off by dawn. He awoke early, and spoke to the young woman, but she gave no answer. He slightly touched her. "What do you want?" she said, and turned her back toward him. "Tell me," he said, "what time the swan passed. I am following it, and come out and point the direction." "Do you think you can catch up to it?" she said. "Yes," he answered. "Naubesah" (foolishness), she said. She, however, went out and pointed in the direction he should go. The young man went slowly till the sun arose, when he commenced travelling at his accustomed speed. He passed the day in running, and when night came, he was unexpectedly pleased to find himself near another town; and when at a distance, he heard the watchman crying out, "We are visited;" and soon the men of the village stood out to see the stranger. He was again told to enter the lodge of the chief, and his reception was, in every respect, the same as he met the previous night; only that the young woman was more beautiful, and received him very kindly, but although urged to stay, his mind was fixed on the object of his journey. Before daylight he asked the young woman what time the Red Swan passed, and to point out the way. She did so, and said it passed yesterday when the sun was between midday and *pungishemoo*—its falling place. He again set out rather slowly, but when the sun had arisen he tried his speed by shooting an arrow ahead, and running after it; but it fell behind him. Nothing remarkable happened in the course of

137

the day, and he went on leisurely. Toward night, he came to the lodge of an old man. Sometime after dark he saw a light emitted from a small low lodge. He went up to it very slyly, and peeping through the door, saw an old man alone, warming his back before the fire, with his head down on his breast. He thought the old man did not know that he was standing near the door, but in this he was disappointed; for so soon as he looked in, "Walk in, Nosis,"* he said, "take a seat opposite to me, and take off your things and dry them, for you must be fatigued; and I will prepare you something to eat." Odjibwa did as he was requested. The old man, whom he perceived to be a magician, then said: "My kettle with water stands near the fire;" and immediately a small earthen or a kind of metallic pot with legs appeared by the fire. He then took one grain of corn, also one whortleberry, and put them in the pot. As the young man was very hungry, he thought that his chance for a supper was but small. Not a word or a look, however, revealed his feelings. The pot soon boiled, when the old man spoke, commanding it to stand some distance from the fire; "Nosis," said he, "feed yourself," and he handed him a dish and ladle made out of the same metal as the pot. The young man helped himself to all that was in the pot; he felt ashamed to think of his having done so, but before he could speak, the old man said, "Nosis, eat, eat;" and soon after he again said, "Help yourself from the pot." Odjibwa was surprised on looking into it to see it full; he kept on taking *all out*, and as soon as it was done, it was again filled, till he had amply satisfied his hunger. The magician then spoke, and the pot occupied its accustomed place in one part of the lodge. The young man then leisurely reclined back, and listened to the predictions of his entertainer, who told him to keep on, and he would obtain his object. "To tell you more," said he, "I am not permitted; but go on as you have commenced, and you will not be disappointed; tomorrow you will again reach one of my fellow old men; but the one you will see after him will tell you all, and the manner in which you will proceed to accomplish your journey. Often has this Red Swan passed, and those who have followed it have never returned: but you must be firm in your resolution, and be prepared for all events." "So will it be," answered Odjibwa, and they both laid down to sleep. Early in the morning, the old man had his magic kettle prepared, so that his guest should eat

* My grandchild.

138

before leaving. When leaving, the old man gave him his parting advice.

Odjibwa set out in better spirits than he had done since leaving home. Night again found him in company with an old man, who received him kindly, and directed him on his way in the morning. He travelled with a light heart, expecting to meet the one who was to give him directions how to proceed to get the Red Swan. Toward nightfall, he reached the third old man's lodge. Before coming to the door, he heard him saying, "Nosis, come in," and going in immediately, he felt quite at home. The old man prepared him something to eat, acting as the other magicians had done, and his kettle was of the same dimensions and material. The old man waited till he had done eating, when he commenced addressing him. "Young man, the errand you are on is very difficult. Numbers of young men have passed with the same purpose, but never returned. Be careful, and if your guardian spirits are powerful, you may succeed. This Red Swan you are following, is the daughter of a magician, who has plenty of everything, but he values his daughter but little less than wampum. He wore a cap of wampum, which was attached to his scalp; but powerful Indians—warriors of a distant chief, came and told him, that their chief's daughter was on the brink of the grave, and she herself requested his scalp of wampum to effect a cure. 'If I can only see it, I will recover,' she said, and it was for this reason they came, and after long urging the magician, he at last consented to part with it, only from the idea of restoring the young woman to health; although when he took it off, it left his head bare and bloody. Several years have passed since, and it has not healed. The warriors' coming for it, was only a cheat, and they now are constantly making sport of it, dancing it about from village to village; and on every insult it receives, the old man groans from pain. Those Indians are too powerful for the magician, and numbers have sacrificed themselves to recover it for him, but without success. The Red Swan has enticed many a young man, as she has done you, in order to get them to procure it, and whoever is the fortunate one that succeeds, will receive the Red Swan as his reward. In the morning you will proceed on your way, and toward evening you will come to the magician's lodge, but before you enter you will hear his groans; he will immediately ask you in, and you will see no one but himself; he will make inquiries of you, as regards your dreams, and the powers of your guardian spirits;

he will then ask you to attempt the recovery of his scalp; he will show you the direction, and if you feel inclined, as I dare say you do, go forward, my son, with a strong heart, persevere, and I have a presentiment you will succeed." The young man answered, "I will try." Early next morning, after having eaten from the magic kettle, he started off on his journey. Toward evening he came to the lodge as he was told, and soon heard the groans of the magician. "Come in," he said, even before the young man reached the door. On entering he saw his head all bloody, and he was groaning most terribly. "Sit down, sit down," he said, "while I prepare you something to eat," at the same time doing as the other magicians had done, in preparing food—"You see," he said, "how poor I am; I have to attend to all my wants." He said this to conceal the fact that the Red Swan was there, but Odjibwa perceived that the lodge was partitioned, and he heard a rustling noise, now and then, in that quarter, which satisfied him that it was occupied. After having taken his leggings and moccasins off, and eaten, the old magician commenced telling him how he had lost his scalp—the insults it was receiving—the pain he was suffering in consequence—his wishes to regain it—the unsuccessful attempts that had already been made, and the numbers and power of those who detained it; stated the best and most probable way of getting it; touching the young man on his pride and ambition, by the proposed adventure, and last, he spoke of such things as would make an Indian rich. He would interrupt his discourse by now and then groaning, and saying, "Oh, how shamefully they are treating it." Odjibwa listened with solemn attention. The old man then asked him about his dreams—his dreams (or as *he saw when asleep**) at the particular time he had fasted and blackened his face to procure guardian spirits.

The young man then told him one dream; the magician groaned; "No, that is not it," he said. The young man told him another. He groaned again; "That is not it," he said. The young man told him of two or three others. The magician groaned at each recital, and said, rather peevishly, "No, those are not them." The young man then thought to himself, Who are you? you may groan as much as you please; I am inclined not to tell you any more dreams. The magician then spoke in rather a supplicating tone. "Have you no more dreams of another

---

* Enaw-baundum.

140

kind?" "Yes," said the young man, and told him one. "That is it, that is it," he cried; "you will cause me to live. That was what I was wishing you to say;" and he rejoiced greatly. "Will you then go and see if you cannot procure my scalp?" "Yes," said the young man, "I will go; and the day after to-morrow,* when you hear the cries of the Kakak,+ you will know, by this sign, that I am successful, and you must prepare your head, and lean it out through the door, so that the moment I arrive, I may place your scalp on." "Yes, yes," said the magician; "as you say, it will be done." Early next morning, he set out on his perilous adventure, and about the time that the sun hangs toward home, (afternoon) he heard the shouts of a great many people. He was in a wood at the time, and saw, as he thought, only a few men; but the further he went, the more numerous they appeared. On emerging into a plain, their heads appeared like the hanging leaves for number. In the centre he perceived a post, and something waving on it, which was the scalp. Now and then the air was rent with the *Sau-sau-quan*, for they were dancing the war dance around it. Before he could be perceived, he turned himself into a No-noskau-see (hummingbird), and flew toward the scalp.

As he passed some of those who were standing by, he flew close to their ears, making the humming noise which this bird does when it flies. They jumped on one side, and asked each other what it could be. By this time he had nearly reached the scalp, but fearing he should be perceived while untying it, he changed himself into a Me-sau-be-wau-aun (the down of anything that floats lightly on the air), and then floated slowly and lightly on to the scalp. He untied it, and moved off slowly, as the weight was almost too great. It was as much as he could do to keep it up, and prevent the Indians from snatching it away. The moment they saw it was moving, they filled the air with their cries of "It is taken from us; it is taken from us." He continued moving a few feet above them: the rush and hum of the people was like the dead beating surges after a storm. He soon gained on them, and they gave up the pursuit. After going a little further he changed himself into a Kakak, and flew off with his prize, making that peculiar noise which this bird makes.

In the meantime, the magician had followed his instructions,

* The Indian expression is, Awuss-Waubung—the day beyond to-morrow.
* A species of hawk.

141

placing his head outside of the lodge, as soon as he heard the cry of the Kakak, and soon after he heard the rustling of its wings. In a moment Odjibwa stood before him. He immediately gave the magician a severe blow on the head with the wampum scalp: his limbs extended and quivered in agony from the effects of the blow: the scalp adhered, and the young man walked in and sat down, feeling perfectly at home. The magician was so long in recovering from the stunning blow, that the young man feared he had killed him. He was however pleased to see him show signs of life; he first commenced moving, and soon sat up. But how surprised was Odjibwa to see, not an aged man, far in years and decrepitude, but one of the handsomest young men he ever saw stand up before him.

"Thank you, my *friend*," he said; "you see that your kindness and bravery have restored me to my former shape. It was so ordained, and you have now accomplished the victory." The young magician urged the stay of his deliverer for a few days; and they soon formed a warm attachment for each other. The magician never alluded to the Red Swan in their conversations.

At last, the day arrived when Odjibwa made preparations to return. The young magician amply repaid him for his kindness and bravery, by various kinds of wampum, robes, and all such things as he had need of to make him an influential man. But though the young man's curiosity was at its height about the Red Swan, he controlled his feelings, and never so much as even hinted of her; feeling that he would surrender a point of propriety in so doing; while the one he had rendered such service to, whose hospitality he was now enjoying, and who had richly rewarded him, had never so much as even mentioned anything about her, but studiously concealed her.

Odjibwa's pack for travelling was ready, and he was taking his farewell smoke, when the young magician thus addressed him: "Friend, you know for what cause you came thus far. You have accomplished your object, and conferred a lasting obligation on me. Your perseverance shall not go unrewarded; and if you undertake other things with the same spirit you have this, you will never fail to accomplish them. My duty renders it necessary for me to remain where I am, although I should feel happy to go with you. I have given you all you will need as long as you live; but I see you feel backward to speak about the Red Swan. I vowed that whoever procured me my scalp, should be rewarded by possessing the Red Swan." He then spoke, and knocked on the partition. The door immediately opened, and the Red Swan met his eager gaze. She was a most beautiful female, and as she stood majestically before him, it would be impossible to describe her charms, for she looked as if she did not belong to earth. "Take her," the young magician said; "she is my sister, treat her well; she is worthy of you, and what you have done for me merits more. She is ready to go with you to your kindred and friends, and has been so ever since your arrival, and my good wishes go with you both." She then looked very kindly on her husband, who now bid farewell to his friend indeed, and accompanied by the object of his wishes, he commenced retracing his footsteps.

They travelled slowly, and after two or three days reached the lodge of the third old man, who had fed him from his small magic pot. He was very kind, and said, "You see what your perseverance has procured you; do so always and you will succeed in all things you undertake."

On the following morning when they were going to start, he pulled from the side of the lodge a bag, which he presented to the young man, saying, "Nosis, I give you this; it contains a present for you; and I hope you will live happily till old age." They then bid farewell to him and proceeded on.

They soon reached the second old man's lodge. Their reception there was the same as at the first; he also gave them a present, with the old man's wishes that they would be happy. They went on and reached the first town, which the young man had passed in his pursuit. The watchman gave notice, and he was shown into the chief's lodge. "Sit down there, son-in-law," said the chief, pointing to a place near his daughter. "And you also," he said to the Red Swan.

The young woman of the lodge was busy in making something, but she tried to show her indifference about what was taking place, for she did not even raise her head to see who was come. Soon the chief said, "Let someone bring in the bundle of our son-in-law." When it was brought in, the young man opened one of the bags, which he had received from one of the old men; it contained wampum, robes, and various other articles; he presented them to his father-in-law, and all expressed their surprise at the value and richness of the gift. The chief's daughter then only stole a glance at the present, then at Odjibwa and his beautiful wife; she stopped working, and remained silent and thoughtful all the evening. They conversed about his adventures; after this the chief told him that he should take his daughter along with him in the morning;

143

the young man said "Yes." The chief then spoke out, saying, "Daughter, be ready to go with him in the morning."

There was a Maujeekewis in the lodge, who thought to have got the young woman to wife; he jumped up, saying, "Who is he (meaning the young man), that he should take her for a few presents. I will kill him," and he raised a knife which he had in his hand. But he only waited till someone held him back, and then sat down, for he was too great a coward to do as he had threatened. Early they took their departure, amid the greetings of their new friends, and toward evening reached the other town. The watchman gave the signal, and numbers of men, women, and children stood out to see them. They were again shown into the chief's lodge, who welcomed them by saying, "Son-in-law, you are welcome," and requested him to take a seat by his daughter; and the two women did the same.

After the usual formalities of smoking and eating, the chief requested the young man to relate his travels in the hearing of all the inmates of the lodge, and those who came to see. They looked with admiration and astonishment at the Red Swan, for she was so beautiful. Odjibwa gave them his whole history. The chief then told him that his brothers had been to their town in search of him, but had returned, and given up all hopes of ever seeing him again. He concluded by saying that since he had been so fortunate and so manly, he should take his daughter with him; "for although your brothers," said he, "were here, they were too timid to enter any of our lodges, and merely inquired for you and returned. You will take my daughter, treat her well, and that will bind us more closely together."

It is always the case in towns, that someone in it is foolish or clownish. It happened to be so here; for a Maujeekewis was in the lodge; and after the young man had given his father-in-law presents, as he did to the first, this Maujeekewis jumped up in a passion, saying, "Who is the stranger, that he should have her? I want her myself." The chief told him to be quiet, and not to disturb or quarrel with one who was enjoying their hospitality. "No, no," he boisterously cried, and made an attempt to strike the stranger. Odjibwa was above fearing his threats, and paid no attention to him. He cried the louder, "I will have her; I will have her." In an instant he was laid flat on the ground from a blow of a war club given by the chief. After he came to himself, the chief upbraided him for his foolishness, and told him to go out and tell stories to the old women.

144

Their arrangements were then made, and the stranger invited a number of families to go and visit their hunting grounds, as there was plenty of game. They consented, and in the morning a large party were assembled to accompany the young man; and the chief with a large party of warriors escorted them a long distance. When ready to return the chief made a speech, and invoked the blessing of the great good Spirit on his son-in-law and party.

After a number of days' travel, Odjibwa and his party came in sight of his home. The party rested while he went alone in advance to see his brothers. When he entered the lodge he found it all dirty and covered with ashes: on one side was his eldest brother, with his face blackened, and sitting amid ashes, crying aloud. On the other side was Maujeekewis, his other brother; his face was also blackened, but his head was covered with feathers and swan's down; he looked so odd, that the young man could not keep from laughing, for he appeared and pretended to be so absorbed with grief that he did not notice his brother's arrival. The eldest jumped up and shook hands with him, and kissed him, and felt very happy to see him again.

Odjibwa, after seeing all things put to rights, told them that he had brought each of them a wife. When Maujeekewis heard about the wife, he jumped up and said, "Why is it just now that you have come?" and made for the door and peeped out to see the woman. He then commenced jumping and laughing, saying, "Women! women!" That was the only reception he gave his brother. Odjibwa then told them to wash themselves and prepare, for he would go and fetch them in. Maujeekewis jumped and washed himself, but would every now and then go and peep out to see the women. When they came near, he said, "I will have this one, and that one;" he did not exactly know which—he would go and sit down for an instant, and then go and peep and laugh; he acted like a madman.

As soon as order was restored, and all seated, Odjibwa presented one of the women to his eldest brother, saying, "These women were given to me; I now give one to each; I intended so from the first." Maujeekewis spoke, and said, "I think three wives would have been *enough* for you." The young man led one to Maujeekewis, saying, "My brother, here is one for you, and live happily." Maujeekewis hung down his head as if he was ashamed, but would every now and then steal a glance at his wife, and also at the other women. By and by he turned toward his wife, and acted as if he had been married for years. "Wife," he said, "I will go and hunt," and off he started.

All lived peaceably for sometime, and their town prospered, the inhabitants increased, and everything was abundant among them. One day dissatisfaction was manifested in the conduct of the two elder brothers, on account of Odjibwa's having taken their deceased father's magic arrows: they upbraided and urged him to procure others if he could. Their object was to get him away, so that one of them might afterward get his wife. One day, after listening to them, he told them he would go. Maujeekewis and himself went together into a sweating lodge to purify themselves. Even there, although it was held sacred, Maujeekewis upbraided him for the arrows. He told him again he would go; and next day, true to his word, he left them. After travelling a long way he came to an opening in the earth, and descending, it led him to the abode of departed spirits. The country appeared beautiful, the extent of it was lost in the distance: he saw animals of various kinds in abundance. The first he came near to were buffalo; his surprise was great when these animals addressed him as human beings. They asked him what he came for, how he descended, why he was so bold as to visit the abode of the dead. He told them he was in search of magic arrows to appease his brothers. "Very well," said the leader of the buffaloes, whose whole form was nothing but bone. "Yes, we know it," and he and his followers moved off a little space as if they were afraid of him. "You have come," resumed the Buffalo Spirit, "to a place where a living man has never before been. You will return immediately to your tribe, for your brothers are trying to dishonor your wife; and you will live to a very old age, and live and die happily; you can go no further in these abodes of ours." Odjibwa looked, as he thought to the west, and saw a bright light, as if the sun was shining in its splendor, but he saw no sun. "What light is that I see yonder?" he asked. The all-boned buffalo answered, "It is the place where those who were good dwell." "And that dark cloud?" Odjibwa again asked. "Mud-jee-izzhi-wabezewin," (wickedness) answered the buffalo. He asked no more questions, and, with the aid of his guardian spirits, again stood on this earth and saw the sun giving light as usual, and breathed the pure air. All else he saw in the abodes of the dead, and his travels and actions previous to his return, are unknown. After wandering a long time in quest of information to make his people happy, he one

146

evening drew near to his village or town; passing all the other lodges and coming to his own, he heard his brothers at high words with each other; they were quarrelling for the possession of his wife. She had, however, remained constant, and mourned the absence and probable loss of her husband; but she had mourned him with the dignity of virtue. The noble youth listened till he was satisfied of the base principles of his brothers. He then entered the lodge, with the stern air and conscious dignity of a brave and honest man. He spoke not a word, but placing the magic arrows to his bow, drew them to their length and laid the brothers dead at his feet. Thus ended the contest between the hermit's sons, and a firm and happy union was consummated between ODJIBWA, or him of the primitive or intonated voice, and the Red Swan.

TAU-WAU-CHEE-HEZKAW,

OR

THE WHITE FEATHER.

A DACOTAH LEGEND.

THERE was an old man living in the centre of a forest, with
his grandson, whom he had taken when quite an infant. The
child had no parents, brothers, or sisters; they had all been
destroyed by six large giants, and he had been informed that
he had no other relative living besides his grandfather. The
band to whom he belonged had put up their children on a
wager in a race against those of the giants, and had thus lost
them. There was an old tradition in the band, that it would
produce a great man, who would wear a white feather, and

who would astonish everyone with his skill and feats of bravery.

The grandfather, as soon as the child could play about, gave him a bow and arrows to amuse himself. He went into the edge of the woods one day, and saw a rabbit; but not knowing what it was, he ran home and described it to his grandfather. He told him what it was, that its flesh was good to eat, and that if he would shoot one of his arrows into its body, he would kill it. He did so, and brought the little animal home, which he asked his grandfather to boil, that they might feast on it. He humored the boy in this, and encouraged him to go on in acquiring the knowledge of hunting, until he could kill deer and larger animals; and he became, as he grew up, an expert hunter. As they lived alone, and away from other Indians, his curiosity was excited to know what was passing in the world. One day he came to the edge of a prairie, where he saw ashes like those at his grandfather's lodge, and lodge-poles left standing. He returned and inquired whether his grandfather put up the poles and made the fire. He was answered no, nor did he believe that he had seen anything of the kind. It was all imagination.

Another day he went out to see what there was curious; and, on entering the woods, he heard a voice calling out to him, "Come here, you destined wearer of the White Feather. You do not yet wear it, but you are worthy of it. Return home and take a short nap. You will dream of hearing a voice, which will tell you to rise and smoke. You will see in your dream a pipe, smoking sack, and a large white feather. When you awake you will find these articles. Put the feather on your head, and you will become a great hunter, a great warrior, and a great man, capable of doing anything. As a proof that you will become a great hunter, when you smoke, the smoke will turn into pigeons." The voice then informed him who he was, and disclosed the true character of his grandfather, who had imposed upon him. The voice-spirit then gave him a *vine*, and told him he was of an age to revenge the injuries of his relations. 'When you meet your enemy," continued the spirit, "you will run a race with him. He will not see the vine, because it is enchanted. While you are running, you will throw it over his head and entangle him, so that you will win the race."

Long ere this speech was ended, he had turned to the quarter from which the voice proceeded, and was astonished to behold a man, for as yet he had never seen any man besides his grandfather, whose object it was to keep him in ignorance. But the circumstance that gave him the most surprise was, that this man, who had the looks of great age, was composed of *wood* from his breast downward, and appeared to be fixed in the earth.

He returned home, slept, heard the voice, awoke, and found the promised articles. His grandfather was greatly surprised to find him with a white feather on his forehead, and to see flocks of pigeons flying out of his lodge. He then recollected what had been predicted, and began to weep at the prospect of losing his charge.

Invested with these honors, the young man departed the next morning to seek his enemies and gratify his revenge. The giants lived in a very high lodge in the middle of a wood. He travelled on till he came to this lodge, where he found that his coming had been made known by *the little spirits who carry the news.* The giants came out, an gave a cry of joy as they saw him coming. When he approached nearer, they began to make sport of him, saying, "Here comes the little man with the white feather, who is to achieve such wonders." They, however, spoke very fair to him when he came up, saying he was a brave man, and would do brave things. This they said to encourage, and the more surely to deceive him. He, however, understood the object.

He went fearlessly up to the lodge. They told him to commence the race with the smallest of their number. The point to which they were to run was a peeled tree towards the rising sun, and then back to the starting-place, which was marked by a CHAUNKAHPEE, or war-club, made of iron. This club was the stake, and whoever won it was to use it in beating the other's brains out. If he beat the first giant, he was to try the second, and so on until they had all measured speed with him. He won the first race by a dexterous use of the vine, and immediately dispatched his competitor, and cut off his head. Next morning he ran with the second giant, whom he also outran, killed, and decapitated. He proceeded in this way for five successive mornings, always conquering by the use of his vine, cutting off the heads of the vanquished. The survivor acknowledged his power, but prepared secretly to deceive him. He wished him to leave the heads he had cut off, as he believed he could again reunite them with the bodies, by means of one of their *medicines.* White Feather insisted, however, in carrying all the heads to his grandfather. One more contest was to

150

be tried, which would decide the victory; but, before going to the giant's lodge on the sixth morning, he met his old counselor in the woods, who was stationary. He told him that he was about to be deceived. That he had never known any other sex but his own; but that, as he went on his way to the lodge, he would meet the most beautiful woman in the world. He must pay no attention to her, but, on meeting her, he must wish himself changed into a male elk. The transformation would take place immediately, when he must go to feeding and not regard her.

He proceeded towards the lodge, met the female, and became an elk. She reproached him for having turned himself into an elk on seeing her; said she had travelled a great distance for the purpose of seeing him, and becoming his wife. Now this woman was the sixth giant, who had assumed this disguise; but Tau-Wau-Chee-Hezkaw remained in ignorance of it. Her reproaches and her beauty affected him so much, that he wished himself a man again, and he at once resumed his natural shape. They sat down together, and he began to caress her, and make love to her. He finally ventured to lay his head on her lap, and went to sleep. She pushed his head aside at first, for the purpose of trying if he was really asleep; and when she was satisfied he was, she took her axe and broke his back. She then assumed her natural shape, which was in the form of the sixth giant, and afterwards changed him into a dog, in which degraded form he followed his enemy to the lodge. He took the white feather from his brow, and wore it as a trophy on his own head.

There was an Indian village at some distance, in which there lived two girls, who were rival sisters, the daughters of a chief. They were fasting to acquire power for the purpose of enticing the wearer of the white feather to visit their village. They each secretly hoped to engage his affections. Each one built herself a lodge at a short distance from the village. The giant knowing this, and having now obtained the valued plume, went immediately to visit them. As he approached, the girls saw and recognized the feather. The eldest sister prepared her lodge with great care and parade, so as to attract the eye. The younger, supposing that he was a man of sense, and would not be enticed by mere parade, touched nothing in her lodge, but left it as it ordinarily was. The eldest went out to meet him, and invited him in. He accepted her invitation, and made her his wife. The younger invited the enchanted dog into her

151

lodge, and made him a good bed, and treated him with as much attention as if he were her husband.

The giant, supposing that whoever possessed the white feather possessed also all its virtues, went out upon the prairie to hunt, but returned unsuccessful. The dog went out the same day a hunting upon the banks of a river. He drew a stone out of the water, which immediately became a beaver. The next day the giant followed the dog, and hiding behind a tree, saw the manner in which the dog went into the river and drew out a stone, which at once turned into a beaver. As soon as the dog left the place, the giant went to the river, and observing the same manner, drew out a stone, and had the satisfaction of seeing it transformed into a beaver. Tying it to his belt, he carried it home, and, as is customary, threw it down at the door of the lodge before he entered. After being seated a short time, he told his wife to bring in his belt or hunting girdle. She did so, and returned with it, with nothing tied to it but a *stone*.

The next day, the dog, finding his method of catching beavers had been discovered, went to a wood at some distance, and broke off a charred limb from a burned tree, which instantly became a bear. The giant, who had again watched him, did the same, and carried a bear home; but his wife, when she came to go out for it, found nothing but a black stick tied to his belt.

The giant's wife determined she would go to her father, and tell him what a valuable husband she had, who furnished her lodge with abundance. She set out while her husband went to hunt. As soon as they had departed, the dog made signs to his mistress to sweat him after the manner of the Indians. She accordingly made a lodge just large enough for him to creep in. She then put in heated stones, and poured on water. After this had been continued the usual time, he came out a very handsome young man, but had not the power of speech.

Meantime, the elder daughter had reached her father's, and told him of the manner in which her sister supported a dog, treating him as her husband, and of the singular skill this animal had in hunting. The old man, suspecting there was some magic in it, sent a deputation of young men and women to ask her to come to him, and bring her dog along. When this deputation arrived, they were surprised to find, in the place of the dog, so fine a young man. They both accompanied the messengers to the father, who was no less astonished. He assembled all the old and wise men of the nation to see the exploits which, it was reported, the young man could perform.

The giant was among the number. He took his pipe and filled it, and passed it to the Indians, to see if anything would happen when they smoked. It was passed around to the dog, who made a sign to hand it to the giant first, which was done, but nothing affected. He then took it himself. He made a sign to them to put the white feather upon his head. This was done, and immediately he regained his speech. He then commenced smoking, and behold! immense flocks of white and blue pigeons rushed from the smoke.

The chief demanded of him his history, which he faithfully recounted. When it was finished, the chief ordered that the giant should be transformed into a dog, and turned into the middle of the village, where the boys should pelt him to death with clubs. This sentence was executed.

The chief then ordered, on the request of the White Feather, that all the young men should employ themselves four days in making arrows. He also asked for a buffalo robe. This robe he cut into thin shreds, and sowed in the prairie. At the end of the four days he invited them to gather together all their arrows, and accompany him to a buffalo hunt. They found that these shreds of skin had grown into a very large herd of buffalo. They killed as many as they pleased, and enjoyed a grand festival, in honor of his triumph over the giants.

Having accomplished their labor, the White Feather got his wife to ask her father's permission to go with him on a visit to his grandfather. He replied to this solicitation, that a woman must follow her husband into whatever quarter of the world he may choose to go.

The young men then placed the white feather in his frontlet, and, taking his war-club in his hand, led the way into the forest, followed by his faithful wife.

PAUGUK,

AND

THE MYTHOLOGICAL INTERPRETATION OF HIAWATHA.

IN a class of languages, where the personification of ideas, or sentiments, frequently compensates for the paucity of expression, it could hardly be expected that death should be omitted. The soul, or spirit, deemed to be an invisible essence, is deonominated *Ochichaug*; this is the term translators employ for the Holy Ghost. There is believed to be the spirit of a vital and personal animus, distinct from this, to which they apply the term Jeebi or *Ghost*. Death, or the mythos of the condition of the human frame, deprived of even the semblance of blood, and muscle, and life, is represented by the word Pauguk. Pauguk is a horrible phantom of human bones, without bones, without muscular tissue of voice, the appearance of which presages speedy dissolution. Of all the myths of the Indians, this is the most gloomy and fearful.

In strict accordance, however, with aboriginal tastes and notions, Pauguk is represented as a hunter. He is armed with a bow and arrows, or a pug-gamagan, or war-club. Instead of objects of the chase, men, women, and children are substituted as the objects of pursuit. To see him is indicative of death. Some accounts represent him as covered with a thin transparent skin, with the sockets of his eyes filled with balls of fire.

Pauguk never speaks. Unlike the *Jeebi* or ghost, his limbs never assume the rotundity of life. Neither is he confounded in form with the numerous class of Monedoes, or of demons. He does not possess the power of metamorphosis, or of transforming himself into the shapes of animals. Unvaried in repulsiveness, he is ever an object of fear; but unlike every other kind or class of creation of the Indian mind, Pauguk never disguises himself, or affects the cunning of concealment—never effects to be what he is not.

Manabozho alone had power to invoke him unharmed.

154

When he had expended all his arts to overcome Paup-Puk-Keewiss, who could at will transform himself, directly or indirectly, into any class or species of the animal creation, going often, as he did, as a jeebi, from one carcass into another, at last, at the final conflict at the rock, he dispatched him with the real power of death, after summoning the elements of thunder and lightning to his aid. And when thus deprived of all sublunary power, the enraged Great Hare, Manito (such seems the meaning of Manabozho), changed the dead carcass of his enemy into the great *caniew*, or war eagle. Nothing had given Manabozho half the trouble and vexation of the flighty, defying, changeable and mischievous Paup-Puk-Keewiss, who eluded him by jumping from one end of the continent to the other. He had killed the great power of evil in the prince of serpents, who had destroyed Chebizbos his grandson—he had survived the flood produced by the great Serpent, and overcome, in combat, the mysterious power held by the Pearl, or sea shell Feather, and the Mishemokwa, or great Bear with the wampum necklace, but Paup-Puk-Keewiss put him to the exercise of his reserved powers of death and annihilation. And it is by this act that we perceive that Hiawatha, or Manabozho, was a divinity. Manabozho had been a hunter, a fisherman, a warrior, a suppliant, a poor man, a starveling, a laughing stock and a mere beggar; he now shows himself a god, and as such we must regard him as the prime Indian myth.

This myth, the more it is examined, the more extensive does it appear to be incorporated in some shape in the Indian mythology. If interpreted agreeably to the metaphysical symbols of the old world, it would appear to be distilled from the same oriental symbolical crucible, which produced an Osiris and a Typhon—for the American Typhon is represented by the Mishikinabik, or serpent, and the American Osiris by a Hiawatha, Manabozho, Micabo, or great Hare-God, or Ghost.

This myth, as it is recognized under the name of Hiawatha by the Iroquois, is without the misadventures over which, in the person of Manabozho, the Algonquins laugh so heartily, and the particular recitals of which, as given in prior pages, afford so much amusement to their lodge circles. According to the Iroquois version, Tarenyawagon was deputed by the Master of Life, who is also called the Holder of Heaven, to the earth, the better to prepare it for the residence of man, and to teach the tribes the knowledge necessary to their condition, as well as to rid the land of giants and monsters. Having accomplished this benevolent labor, he laid aside his heavenly character and name, assuming that of Hiawatha; took a wife, and settled in a beautiful part of the country. Hiawatha having set himself down to live as one of them, it was his care to hold up, at all times, the best examples of prudential wisdom. All things, hard or wondrous, were possible for him to do, as in the case of the hero of the Algonquin legend, and he had, like him, a magic canoe to sail up and down the waters wherever he wished.

Hiawatha, after he had performed the higher functions appertaining to his character, settled down in the Iroquois country, and was universally regarded as a sage. He instructed the tribes how to repel savage invaders, who were in the habit of scourging the country, and was ever ready to give them wise counsels. The chief things of these good counsels to the tribes were to attend to their proper vocation, as hunters and fishermen, to cultivate corn, and to cease dissensions and bickerings among themselves. He finally instructed them to form a general league and confederacy against their common enemies. These maxims were enforced at a general council of the Iroquois tribe, held at Onondaga, which place became the seat of their council fire, and first government. This normal council of Iroquois sages resulted in placing the tribes in their assembled, not tribal capacity, under the care of a moderator, or chief magistrate of the assembled cantons, called Atatarho.*

Tradition recites many particulars of the acts of Hiawatha. It is preserved in their recitals, that after his mission was virtually ended, or, rather, drawing to a close, how he proceeded, in great state, to the council, in his magic canoe, taking with him his favorite daughter. With her he landed on the shore of the lake of Onondaga, and was proceeding to the elevated grounds appointed for the council, when a remarkable phenomenon appeared in the heavens, which seemed, in its symbolical import, to say to Hiawatha: "Thy work is near its close." A white bird, the bird of Heaven, appeared to come as a special messenger to him and to his daughter, appearing as a small speck high in the higher atmosphere. As it de-

* Cusic tells us there were thirteen of these magistrates before America was discovered. Here mythology takes the shape of historical tradition.

scended and revealed its character, its flight was attended with the greatest swiftness and force, and with no little of the impetuosity of a stroke of lightning. To the dismay of all, it struck the daughter of Hiawatha with such force as to drive her remains into the earth, completely annihilating her. The bird itself was annihilated in annihilating Hiawatha's daughter. All that remained of it were its scattered white plumes, purely white as silver clouds, and these plumes the warriors eagerly gathered as the chief tokens, to be worn on their heads as symbols of their bravery in war—a custom maintined to this day. Hiawatha stood aghast. He did not know how to interpret the terrible token. He deeply mourned his daughter's fate; for a long time he was inconsolable, and sat with his head down. But, in the end, and by persuasion, he roused himself from his reverie. His thoughts revolved on his original mission to the Indian tribes. The Great Spirit perhaps tells me, he said to himself, that my work here below is finished, and I must return to him. For awhile, he had not heeded the invitations to attend the largely gathered council which waited for him, but as soon as his grief would enable him to attend, he roused himself for the task. After tasting food, he assumed his usual manly dignity of character, and assumed the oritorical attitude. Waiting till the other speakers had finished, he addressed his last counsels to the listening tribes. By his wisdom and eloquent appeal, he entranced them. By this valedictory address, replete with political wisdom, he closed his career. Having done this, he announced the termination of his mission; then, entering his magic canoe, he began to rise in the air—sweet strains of music were heard to arise as he mounted, and these could be heard till he was carried up beyond human sight.

IENA, THE WANDERER,

OR

MAGIC BUNDLE.

A CHIPPEWA ALLEGORY.

There was once a poor man called Iena,* who was in the habit of wandering about from place to place, forlorn, without relations and almost helpless. One day, as he went on a hunting excursion, he hung up his bundle on the branch of a tree, to relieve himself from the burden of carrying it, and then went in quest of game. On returning to the spot in the evening, he was surprised to find a small but neat lodge built in the place where he had left his bundle; and on looking in, he beheld a beautiful female sitting in the lodge, with his blanket lying beside her. During the day he had been fortunate in killing a deer, which he had laid down at the lodge door. But, to his surprise, the woman, in her attempt to bring it in, broke both her legs. He looked at her with astonishment, and thought to himself, "I supposed I was blessed, but I find my mistake. Gweengweeshee,"* said he, "I will leave my game with you, that you may feast on it."

He then took up his bundle and departed. After walking some time he came to another tree, on which he suspended his bundle as before, and went in search of game. Success again rewarded his efforts, and he returned bringing a deer, but found, as before, that a lodge had sprung up in the place where he had suspended his bundle. He looked in, and saw, as before, a beautiful female sitting alone, with his bundle by her side. She arose, and came out to bring in the deer, which he had deposited at the door, and he immediately went into the lodge and sat by the fire, as he felt fatigued with the day's labors. Wondering, at last, at the delay of the woman, he arose, and

* From Ienawdizzi, a wanderer.
* The night-hawk.

peeping through the door of the lodge, beheld her eating all the fat of the deer. He exclaimed, "I thought I was blessed, but I find I am mistaken." Then addressing the woman, "Poor Wabizhas,"* said he, "feast on the game that I have brought." He again took up his bundle and departed, and as usual, hung it up on the branch of a tree, and wandered off in quest of game. In the evening he returned with his customary good luck, bringing in a fine deer, and again found a lodge occupying the place of his bundle. He gazed through an aperture in the side of the lodge, and saw a beautiful woman sitting alone, with a bundle by her side. As soon as he entered the lodge, she arose with alacrity, brought in the carcass, cut it up and hung up the meat to dry. After this, she prepared a portion of it for the supper of the weary hunter. The man thought to himself, "Now I am certainly blessed." He continued his practice of hunting every day, and the woman, on his return, always readily took care of the meat, and prepared his meals for him. One thing, however, astonished him; he had never, as yet, seen her eat anything, and kindly said to her, "Why do you not eat?" She replied, "I have food of my own, which I eat."

On the fourth day he brought home with him a branch of uzadi* as a cane, which he placed, with his game, at the door of the lodge. His wife, as usual, went out to prepare and bring in the meat. While thus engaged, he heard her laughing to herself, and saying, "This is very acceptable." The man, in peeping out to see the cause of her joy, saw her, with astonishment, eating the bark of the poplar cane in the same manner that beavers gnaw. He then exclaimed, "Ho, ho! Ho, ho! this is Amik;"* and ever afterward he was careful at evening to bring in a bough of the poplar or the red willow, when she would exclaim, "Oh, this is very acceptable; this is a change, for one gets tired eating white fish always (meaning the poplar); but the carp (meaning the red willow) is a pleasant change."

On the whole, Iena was much pleased with his wife for her neatness and attention to the things in the lodge, and he lived a contented and happy man. Being industrious, she made him beautiful bags from the bark of trees, and dressed the skins

* A marten.
* The common poplar, or P. tremuloides.
* The beaver.

of the animals he killed in the most skillful manner. When spring opened, they found themselves blessed with two children, one of them resembling the father and the other the mother. One day the father made a bow and arrows for the child that resembled him, who was a son, saying, "My son, you will use these arrows to shoot at the little beavers when they begin to swim about the rivers." The mother, as soon as she heard this, was highly displeased; and taking her children, unknown to her husband, left the lodge in the night. A small river ran near the lodge, which the woman approached with her children. She built a dam across the stream, erected a lodge of earth, and lived after the manner of the beavers.

When the hunter awoke, he found himself alone in his lodge, and his wife and children absent. He immediately made diligent search after them, and at last discovered their retreat on the river. He approached the place of their habitation, and throwing himself prostrate on the top of the lodge, exclaimed, "Shingisshenaun tshee neeboyaun."* The woman allowed the children to go close to their father, but not to touch him; for, as soon as they came very near, she would draw them away again, and in this manner she continued to torment him a long time. The husband lay in this situation until he was almost starved, when a young female approached him, and thus accosted him: "Look here; why are you keeping yourself in misery, and thus starving yourself? Eat this," reaching him a little mokuk containing fresh raspberries which she had just gathered. As soon as the beaveress, his former wife, beheld this, she began to abuse the young woman, and said to her, "Why do you wish to show any kindness to that *animal* that has but two legs? you will soon repent it." She also made sport of the young woman, saying, "Look at her; she has a long nose, and she is just like a bear." The young woman, who was all the time a bear in disguise, hearing herself thus reproached, broke down the dam of the beaver, let the water run out, and nearly killed the beaver herself. Then turning to the man, she thus addressed him: "Follow me; I will be kind to you. Follow me closely. You must be courageous, for there are three persons who are desirous of marrying me, and will oppose you. Be careful of yourself. Follow me nimbly, and, just as we approach the lodge, put your feet in the prints of mine, for I have eight sisters who will do their utmost to divert your

* Here I will lie until I die.

160

attention and make you lose the way. Look neither to the right nor the left, but enter the lodge just as I do, and take your seat where I do." As they proceeded they came in sight of a large lodge, when he did as he had been directed, stepping in her tracks. As they entered the lodge the eight sisters clamorously addressed him. "Oh, Ogidahkumigo* has lost his way." and each one invited him to take his seat with her, desiring to draw him from their sister. The old people also addressed him as he entered, and said, "Oh, make room for our son-in-law." The man, however, took his seat by the side of his protectress, and was not farther importuned.

ODANAMEKUMIGO* if I was jealous." He then drew up his bow and drove his arrow into the stone. Seeing this, the bears turned around, and with their eyes fixed on him, stepped backward and left the lodge, which highly delighted the woman. She exulted to think that her husband had conquered them.

Finally, one of the old folks made a cry, and said, "Come, come! there must be a gathering of provisions for the winter." So they all took their *cossoes*, or bark dishes, and departed to gather acorns for the winter. As they departed, the old man said to his daughter, "Tell Ogidahkumigo to go to the place where your sisters have gone and let him select one of them, so that, through her aid, he may have some food for himself during the winter; but be sure to caution him to be very careful, when he is taking the skin from the animal, that he does not cut the flesh." No sooner had the man heard this message, than he selected one of his sisters-in-law; and when he was taking the skin from her, for she was all the while an enchanted female bear, although careful, he cut her a little upon one of her arms, when she jumped up, assumed her natural form, and ran home. The man also went home, and found her with her arm bound up, and quite unwell.

A second cry was then made by the master of the lodge: "Come come! seek for winter quarters;" and they all got ready to separate for the season. By this time the man had two children, one resembling himself and the other his wife. When the cry was made, the little boy who resembled his father was in such a hurry in putting on his moccasins, that he misplaced

* This term means a man that lives on the surface of the earth, as contra-distinguished from beings living under ground.

* He who lives in the city underground.

161

them, putting the moccasin of the right foot upon the left. And this is the reason why the foot of the bear is turned in.

They proceeded to seek their winter quarters, the wife going before to point the way. She always selected the *thickest* part of the forest, where the child resembling the father found it difficult to get along; and he never failed to cry out and complain. Iena then went in advance, and sought the open plain, whereupon the child resembling the mother would cry out and complain, because she disliked an *open* path. As they were encamping, the woman said to her husband, "Go and break branches for the lodge for the night." He did so; but when she looked at the *manner* in which her husband broke the branches, she was very much offended, for he broke them *upward* instead of *downward.* "It is not only very awkward," said she, "but we will be found out; for the Ogidahkumigoes* will see where we have passed by the branches we have broken:" to avoid this, they agreed to change their route, and were finally well established in their winter quarters. The wife had sufficient food for her child, and would now and then give the dry berries she had gathered in the summer to her husband.

One day, as spring drew on, she said to her husband, "I must boil you some meat," meaning her own paws, which bears suck in the month of April. She had all along told him, during the winter, that she meant to resume her real shape of a female bear, and to give herself up to the Ogidahkumigoes, to be killed by them, and that the time of their coming was near at hand. It came to pass, soon afterward, that a hunter discovered her retreat. She told her husband to move aside, "for," she added, "I am now giving myself up." The hunter fired and killed her.

Iena then came out from his hiding-place, and went home with the hunter. As they went, he instructed him what he must hereafter do when he killed bears. "You must," said he, "never cut the flesh in taking off the skin, nor hang up the feet with the flesh when drying it. But you must take the head and feet, and decorate them handsomely, and place tobacco on the head, for these animals are very fond of this article, and on the *fourth day* they come to life again."

* People who live above ground.

162

MISHOSHA,

OR

THE MAGICIAN OF LAKE SUPERIOR.

IN an early age of the world, when there were fewer inhabitants than there now are, there lived an Indian, in a remote place, who had a wife and two chidren. They seldom saw anyone out of the circle of their own lodge. Animals were abundant in so secluded a situation, and the man found no difficulty in supplying his family with food.

In this way they lived in peace and happiness, which might have continued if the hunter had not found cause to suspect his wife. She secretly cherished an attachment for a young man whom she accidentally met one day in the woods. She even planned the death of her husband for his sake, for she knew if she did not kill her husband, her husband, the moment he detected her crime, would kill her.

The husband, however, eluded her project by his readiness and decision. He narrowly watched her movements. One day he secretly followed her footsteps into the forest, and having concealed himself behind a tree, he soon beheld a tall young man approach and lead away his wife. His arrows were in his hands, but he did not use them. He thought he would kill her the moment she returned.

Meantime, he went home and sat down to think. At last he came to the determination of quitting her forever, thinking that her own conscience would punish her sufficiently, and relying on her maternal feelings to take care of the two children, who were boys, he immediately took up his arms and departed.

When the wife returned she was disappointed in not finding her husband, for she had now concerted her plan, and intended to have dispatched him. She waited several days, thinking he might have been led away by the chase, but finding he did not return, she suspected the true cause. Leaving her two children in the lodge, she told them she was going a short distance and would return. She then fled to her paramour and came back no more.

The children, thus abandoned, soon made way with the food left in the lodge, and were compelled to quit it in search of more. The eldest boy, who was of an intrepid temper, was strongly attached to his brother, frequently carrying him when he became weary, and gathering all the wild fruit he saw. They wandered deeper and deeper into the forest, losing all traces of their former habitation, until they were completely lost in its mazes.

The eldest boy had a knife, with which he made a bow and arrows, and was thus enabled to kill a few birds for himself and brother. In this manner they continued to pass on, from one piece of forest to another, not knowing whither they were going. At length they saw an opening through the woods, and were shortly afterward delighted to find themselves on the borders of a large lake. Here the elder brother busied himself in picking the seed pods of the wild rose, which he reserved as food. In the meantime, the younger brother amused himself by shooting arrows in the sand, one of which happened to fall into the lake. PANIGWUN,* the elder brother, not willing to

* The end wing feather.

lose the arrow, waded in the water to reach it. Just as he was about to grasp the arrow, a canoe passed up to him with great rapidity. An old man, sitting in the centre, seized the affrighted youth and placed him in the canoe. In vain the boy addressed him—"My grandfather (a term of respect for old people), pray take my little brother also. Alone, I cannot go with you; he will starve if I leave him." Mishosha (the old man) only laughed at him. Then uttering the charm, CHEMAUN POLL, and giving his canoe a slap, it glided through the water with inconceivable swiftness. In a few moments they reached the habitation of the magician, standing on an island in the centre of the lake. Here he lived with his two daughters, who managed the affairs of his household. Leading the young man up to the lodge, he addressed his eldest daughter. "Here," said he, "my daughter I have brought a young man to be your husband." Husband! thought the young woman; rather another victim of your bad arts, and your insatiate enmity to the human race. But she made no reply, seeming thereby to acquiesce in her father's will.

The young man thought he saw surprise depicted in the eyes of the daughter, during the scene of this introduction, and determined to watch events narrowly. In the evening he overheard the two daughters in conversation. "There," said the eldest daughter, "I told you he would not be satisfied with his last sacrifice. He has brought another victim, under the pretence of providing me a husband. Husband, indeed! the poor youth will be in some horrible predicament before another sun has set. When shall we be spared the scenes of vice and wickedness which are daily taking place before our eyes?"

Panigwun took the first opportunity of acquainting the daughters how he had been carried off, and been compelled to leave his little brother on the shore. They told him to wait until their father was asleep, then to get up and take his canoe, and using the charm he had obtained, it would carry him quickly to his brother. That he could carry him food, prepare a lodge for him, and be back before daybreak. He did, in every respect, as he had been directed—the canoe obeyed the charm, and carried him safely over, and after providing for the subsistence of his brother, he told him that in a short time he should come for him. Then returning to the enchanted island, he resumed his place in the lodge, before the magician awoke. Once, during the night, Mishosha awoke, and not seeing his

165

destined son-in-law, asked his daughter what had become of him. Shè replied that he had merely stepped out, and would be back soon. This satisfied him. In the morning, finding the young man in the lodge, his suspicions were completely lulled. "I see, my daughter," said he, "you have told the truth."

As soon as the sun arose, Mishosha thus addressed the young man. "Come, my son, I have a mind to gather gulls' eggs. I know an island where there are great quantities, and I wish your aid in getting them." The young man saw no reasonable excuse; and getting into the canoe, the magician gave it a slap, and uttering a command, they were in an instant at the island. They found the shores strown with gulls' eggs, and the island full of birds of this species. "Go, my son," said the old man, "and gather the eggs, while I remain in the canoe."

But Panigwun had no sooner got ashore, than Mishosha pushed his canoe a little from the land, and exclaimed— "Listen, ye gulls! you have long expected an offering from me. I now give you a victim. Fly down and devour him." Then striking his canoe, he left the young man to his fate.

The birds immediately came in clouds around their victim, darkening the air with their numbers. But the youth seizing the first that came near him, and drawing his knife, cut off its head. He immediately skinned the bird and hung the feathers as a trophy on his breast. "Thus," he exclaimed, "will I treat every one of you who approaches me. Forbear, therefore, and listen to my words. It is not for you to eat human flesh. You have been given by the Great Spirit as food for man. Neither is it in the power of that old magician to do you any good. Take me on your backs and carry me to his lodge, and you shall see that I am not ungrateful." The gulls obeyed; collecting in a cloud for him to rest upon, and quickly flew to the lodge, where they arrived before the magician. The daughters were surprised at his return, but Mishosha, on entering the lodge, conducted himself as if nothing extraordinary had taken place.

The next day he again addressed the youth: "Come, my son," said he, "I will take you to an island covered with the most beautiful stones and pebbles, looking like silver. I wish you to assist me in gathering some of them. They will make handsome ornaments, and possess great medicinal virtues." Entering the canoe, the magician made use of his charm, and they were carried in a few moments to a solitary bay in an island, where there was a smooth sandy beach. The young man went ashore as usual, and began to search. "A little further, a little further," cried the old man. "Upon that rock you will get some fine ones." Then pushing his canoe from land— "Come, thou great king of fishes," cried the old man; "you have long expected an offering from me. Come, and eat the stranger whom I have just put ashore on your island." So saying, he commanded his canoe to return, and it ws soon out of sight.

Immediately a monstrous fish thrust his long snout from the water, crawling partially on the beach, and opening wide his jaws to receive his victim. "When!" exclaimed the young man, drawing his knife and putting himself in a threatening attitude, "when did you ever taste human flesh? Have a care of yourself. You were given by the Great Spirit to man, and if you, or any of your tribe eat human flesh you will fall sick and die. Listen not to the words of that wicked man, but carry me back to his island, in return for which I will present you a piece of red cloth." The fish complied, raising his back out of the water, to allow the young man to get on. Then taking his way through the lake, he landed his charge safely on the island before the return of the magician. The daughters were still more surprised to see that he had escaped the arts of their father the second time. But the old man on his return maintained his taciturnity and self-composure. He could not, however, help saying to himself—"What manner of boy is this, who is ever escaping from my power? But his spirit shall not save him. I will entrap him to-morrow. Ha, ha, ha!"

Next day the magician addressed the young man as follows: "Come, my son," said he, "you must go with me to procure some young eagles. I wish to tame them. I have discovered an island where they are in great abundance." When they had reached the island, Mishosha led him inland until they came to the foot of a tall pine, upon which the nests were. "Now, my son," said he, "climb up this tree and bring down the birds." The young man obeyed. When he had with great difficulty got near the nest, "Now," exclaimed the magician, addressing the tree, "stretch yourself up and be very tall." The tree rose up at the command. "Listen, ye eagles," continued the old man, "you have long expected a gift from me. I now present you this boy, who has had the presumption to molest your young. Stretch forth your claws and seize him." So saying, he left the young man to his fate, and returned.

But the intrepid youth, drawing his knife, and cutting off

167

the head of the first eagle that menaced him, raised his voice and exclaimed, "Thus will I deal with all who come near me. What right have you, ye ravenous birds, who were made to feed on beasts, to eat human flesh? Is it because that cowardly old canoe-man has bid you do so? He is an old woman. He can neither do you good nor harm. See, I have already slain one of your number. Respect my bravery, and carry me back that I may show you how I shall treat you."

The eagles, pleased with his spirit, assented, and clustering thick around him formed a seat with their backs, and flew toward the enchanted island. As they crossed the water they passed over the magician, lying half asleep in his canoe.

The return of the young man was hailed with joy by the daughters, who now plainly saw that he was under the guidance of a strong spirit. But the ire of the old man was excited, although he kept his temper under subjection. He taxed his wits for some new mode of ridding himself of the youth, who had so successfully baffled his skill. He next invited him to go a hunting.

Taking his canoe, they proceeded to an island and built a lodge to shelter themselves during the night. In the meanwhile the magician caused a deep fall of snow, with a storm of wind and severe cold. According to custom, the young man pulled off his moccasins and leggings, and hung them before the fire to dry. After he had gone to sleep, the magician, watching his opportunity, got up, and taking one moccasin and one legging, threw them into the fire. He then went to sleep. In the morning, stretching himself as he arose and uttering an exclamation of surprise, "My son," said he, "what has become of your moccasin and legging? I believe this is the moon in which fire attracts, and I fear they have been drawn in." The young man suspected the true cause of his loss, and rightly attributed it to a design of the magician to freeze him to death on the march. But he maintained the strictest silence, and drawing his conaus over his head, thus communed with himself: "I have full faith in the Manito who has preserved me thus far, I do not fear that he will forsake me in this cruel emergency. Great is his power, and I invoke it now that he may enable me to prevail over this wicked enemy of mankind."

He then drew on the remaining moccasin and legging, and taking a dead coal from the fireplace, invoked his spirit to give it efficacy, and blackened his foot and leg as far as the lost garment usually reached. He then got up and announced himself ready for the march. In vain Mishosha led him through snows and over morasses, hoping to see the lad sink at every moment. But in this he was disappointed, and for the first time they returned home together.

Taking courage from this success, the young man now determined to try his own power, having previously consulted with the daughters. They all agreed that the life the old man led was detestable, and that whoever would rid the whole of him, would entitle himself to the thanks of the human race.

On the following day the young man thus addressed his hoary captor: "My grandfather, I have often gone with you on perilous excursions, and never murmured. I must now request that you will accompany me. I wish to visit my little brother, and to bring him home with me." They accordingly went on a visit to the mainland, and found the little lad in the spot where he had been left. After taking him into the canoe, the young man again addressed the magician: "My grandfather, will you go and cut me a few of those red willows on the bank, I wish to prepare some smoking mixture." "Certainly, my son," replied the old man; "what you wish is not very hard. Ha, ha, ha! do you think me too old to get up there?" No sooner was Mishosha ashore, than the young man, placing himself in the proper position struck the canoe with his hand, and pronouncing the charm, N'CHIMAUN POLL, the canoe immediately flew through the water on its return to the island. It was evening when the two brothers arrived, and carried the canoe ashore. But the elder daughter informed the young man that unless he sat up and watched the canoe, and kept his hand upon it, such was the power of their father, it would slip off and return to him. Panigwun watched faithfully till near the dawn of day, when he could no longer resist the drowsiness which oppressed him, and he fell into a short doze. In the meantime, the canoe slipped off and sought its master, who soon returned in high glee. "Ha, ha, ha! my son," said he; you thought to play me a trick. It was very clever. But you see I am too old for you."

A short time after, the youth again addressed the magician. "My grandfather, I wish to try my skill in hunting. It is said there is plenty of game on an island not far off, and I have to request that you will take me there in your canoe." They accordingly went to the island and spent the day in hunting. Night coming on they put up a temporary lodge. When the magician had sunk into a profound sleep, the young man got up, and taking one of Mishosha's leggings and moccasins from the place where they hung, threw them into the fire, thus retaliating the artifice before played upon himself. He had discovered that the foot and leg were the only vulnerable parts of the magician's body. Having committed these articles to the fire, he besought his Manito that he would raise a great storm of snow, wind, and hail, and then laid himself down beside the old man. Consternation was depicted on the countenance of the latter, when he awoke in the morning and found his moccasin and legging missing. "I believe, my grandfather," said the young man, "that this is the moon in which fire attracts, and I fear your foot and leg garments have been drawn in." Then rising and bidding the old man follow him, he began the morning's hunt, frequently turning to see how Mishosha kept up. He saw him faltering at every step, and almost benumbed with cold, but encouraged him to follow, saying, we shall soon get through and reach the shore; although he tookpains, at the same time, to lead him in roundabout ways, so as to let the frost take complete effect. At length the old man reached the brink of the island where the woods are succeeded by a border of smooth sand. But he could go no farther; his legs became stiff and refused motion, and he found himself fixed to the spot. But he still kept stretching out his arms and swinging his body to and fro. Every moment he found the numbness creeping higher. He felt his legs growing downward like roots, the feathers of his head turned to leaves, and in a few seconds he stood a tall and stiff sycamore, leaning toward the water.

Panigwun leaped into the canoe, and pronouncing the charm, was soon transported to the island, where he related his victory to the daughters. They applauded the deed, agreed to put on mortal shapes, become wives to the two young men, and forever quit the enchanted island. And passing immediately over to the main land, they lived lives of happiness and peace.

PEETA KWAY,

THE FOAM-WOMAN.

AN OTTOWA LEGEND.

THERE once lived a woman called Monedo Kway* on the sand mountains called "the Sleeping Bear," of Lake Michigan, who had a daughter as beautiful as she was modest and discreet. Everybody spoke of the beauty of this daughter. She was so handsome that her mother feared she would be carried off, and to prevent it she put her in a box on the lake, which was tied by a long string to a stake on the shore. Every morning the mother pulled the box ashore, and combed her daughter's long, shining hair, gave her food, and then put her out again on the lake.

One day a handsome young man chanced to come to the spot at the moment she was receiving her morning's attentions from her mother. He was struck with her beauty, and immediately went home and told his feelings to his uncle, who was a great chief and a powerful magician. "My nephew," replied the old man, "go to the mother's lodge, and sit down in a modest manner, without saying a word. You need not ask her the question. But whatever *you think* she will understand, and what *she thinks* in answer you will also understand." The young man did so. He sat down, with his head dropped in a thoughtful manner, without uttering a word. He then thought, "I wish she would give me her daughter." Very soon he understood the mother's thoughts in reply. "Give you my daughter?" thought she; "*you!* No, indeed, my daughter shall never marry *you.*" The young man went away and reported the result to his uncle. "Woman without good sense;" said he, "who is she keeping her daughter for? Does she think she will marry the Mudjikewis?* Proud heart! we will try her magic skill, and

* Female spirit or prophetess.
* A term indicative of the heir or successor to the first place in power.

see whether she can withstand our power." The pride and haughtiness of the mother was talked of by the spirits living on that part of the lake. They met together and determined to exert their power in humbling her. For this purpose they resolved to raise a great storm on the lake. The water began to toss and roar, and the tempest became so severe, that the string broke, and the box floated off through the straits down Lake Huron, and struck against the sandy shores at its outlet. The place where it struck was near the lodge of a superannuated old spirit called Ishkwon Daimeka, or the keeper of the gate of the lakes. He opened the box and let out the beautiful daughter, took her into his lodge, and married her.

When the mother found that her daughter had been blown off by the storm, she raised very loud cries and lamented exceedingly. This she continued to do for a long time, and would not be comforted. At length, after two or three years, the spirits had pity on her, and determined to raise another storm and bring her back. It was even a greater storm than the first; and when it began to wash away the ground and encroach on the lodge of Ishkwon Daimeka, she leaped into the box, and the waves carried her back to the very spot of her mother's lodge on the shore. Monedo Equa was overjoyed; but when she opened the box, she found that her daughter's beauty had almost all departed. However, she loved her still because she was her daughter, and now thought of the young man who had made her the offer of marriage. She sent a formal message to him, but he had altered his mind, for he knew that she had been the wife of another: "I marry your daughter?" said he; "*your* daughter! No, indeed! I shall never marry her."

The storm that brought her back was so strong and powerful, that it tore away a large part of the shore of the lake, and swept off Ishkwon Daimeka's lodge, the fragments of which, lodging in the straits, formed those beautiful islands which are scattered in the St. Clair and Detroit rivers. The old man himself was drowned, and his bones are buried under them. They heard him singing his songs of lamentation as he was driven off on a portion of his lodge; as if he had been called to testify his bravery and sing his war song at the stake.

> I ride the waters like the winds;
> No storms can blench my heart.

PAH-HAH-UNDOOTAH,

THE RED HEAD.

A DACOTAH LEGEND.

As spring approaches, the Indians return from their wintering grounds to their villages, engage in feasting, soon exhaust their stock of provisions, and begin to suffer for the want of food. Such of the hunters as are of an active and enterprising cast of character, take the occasion to separate from the mass of the population, and remove to some neighboring locality in the forest, which promises the means of subsistence during this season of general lassitude and enjoyment.

Among the families who thus separated themselves, on a certain occasion, there was a man called ODSHEDOPH WAU-CHEENTONGAH, or the Child of Strong Desires, who had a wife and one son. After a day's travel he reached an ample wood with his family, which was thought to be a suitable place to encamp. The wife fixed the lodge, while the husband went out to hunt. Early in the evening he returned with a deer. Being tired and thirsty he asked his son to go to the river for some water. The son replied that it was dark and he was afraid. He urged him to go, saying that his mother, as well as himself, was tired, and the distance to the water was very short. But no persuasion was of any avail. He refused to go. "Ah, my son," said the father, at last, "if you are afraid to go to the river, you will never kill the Red Head."

The boy was deeply mortified by this observation. It seemed to call up all his latent energies. He mused in silence. He refused to eat, and made no reply when spoken to.

The next day he asked his mother to dress the skin of the deer, and make it into moccasins for him, while he busied himself in preparing a bow and arrows. As soon as these things were done, he left the lodge one morning at sunrise, without saying a word to his father or mother. He fired one of his arrows into the air, which fell westward. He took that

173

course, and at night coming to the spot where the arrow had fallen, was rejoiced to find it piercing the heart of a deer. He refreshed himself with a meal of the venison, and the next morning fired another arrow. After travelling all day, he found it also in another deer. In this manner he fired four arrows, and every evening found that he had killed a deer. What was very singular, however, was, that he left the arrows sticking in the carcasses, and passed on without withdrawing them. In consequence of this, he had no arrow for the fifth day, and was in great distress at night for the want of food. At last he threw himself upon the ground in despair, concluding that he might as well perish there as go further. But he had not lain long before he heard a hollow, rumbling noise, in the ground beneath him. He sprang up, and discovered at a distance the figure of a human being, walking with a stick. He looked attentively and saw that the figure was walking in a wide beaten path, in a prairie, leading from a lodge to a lake. To his surprise, this lodge was at no great distance. He approached a little nearer and concealed himself. He soon discovered that the figure was no other than that of the terrible witch, WOK-ON-KAHTOHN-ZOOEYAH-PEE-KAH-HAITCHEE, or the little old woman who makes war. Her path to the lake was perfectly smooth and solid, and the noise our adventurer had heard, was caused by the striking of her walking staff upon the ground. The top of this staff was decorated with a string of the toes and bills of birds of every kind, who at every stroke of the stick, fluttered and sung their various notes in concert.

She entered her lodge and laid off her mantle, which was entirely composed of the scalps of women. Before folding it, she shook it several times, and at every shake the scalps uttered loud shouts of laughter, in which the old hag joined. Nothing could have frightened him more than this horrific exhibition. After laying by the cloak she came directly to him. She informed him that she had known him from the time he left his father's lodge, and watched his movements. She told him not to fear or despair, for she would be his friend and protector. She invited him into her lodge, and gave him a supper. During the repast, she inquired of him his motives for visiting her. He related his history, stated the manner in which he had been disgraced, and the difficulties he labored under. She cheered him with the assurance of her friendship, and told him he would be a brave man yet.

She then commenced the exercise of her power upon him.

His hair being very short, she took a large leaden comb, and after drawing it through his hair several times, it became of a handsome feminine length. She then proceeded to dress him as a female, furnishing him with the necessary garments, and decorated his face with paints of the most beautiful dye. She gave him a bowl of shining metal. She directed him to put in his girdle a blade of scented sword-grass, and to proceed the next morning to the banks of the lake, which was no other than that over which the Red Head reigned. Now PAH-HAH-UNDOOTAH, or the Red Head, was a most powerful sorcerer and the terror of all the country, living upon an island in the centre of the lake.

She informed him that there would be many Indians on the island, who, as soon as they saw him use the shining bowl to drink with, would come and solicit him to be their wife, and to take him over to the island. These offers he was to refuse, and say that he had come a great distance to be the wife of the Red Head, and that if the chief could not come for her in his own canoe, she should return to her village. She said that as soon as the Red Head heard of this, he would come for her in his own canoe, in which she must embark. On reaching the island he must consent to be his wife, and in the evening induce him to take a walk out of the village, when he was to take the first opportunity to cut off his head with the blade of grass. She also gave him general advice how he was to conduct himself to sustain his assumed character of a woman. His fear would scarcely permit him to accede to this plan, but the recollection of his father's words and looks decided him.

Early in the morning, he left the witch's lodge, and took the hard beaten path to the banks of the lake. He reached the water at a point directly opposite the Red Head's village. It was a beautiful day. The heavens were clear, and the sun shone out in the greatest effulgence. He had not been long there, having sauntered along the beach, when he displayed the glittering bowl, by dipping water from the lake. Very soon a number of canoes came off from the island. The men admired his dress, and were charmed with his beauty, and a great number made proposals of marriage. These he promptly declined, agreeably to the concerted plan. When the facts were reported to the Red Head, he ordered his canoe to be put in the water by his chosen men, and crossed over to see this wonderful girl. As he came near the shore, he saw that the ribs of the sorcerer's canoe were formed of living rattlesnakes, whose heads pointed outward to guard him from enemies. Our adventurer had no sooner stepped into the canoe than they began to hiss and rattle, which put him in a great fright. But the magician spoke to them, after which they became pacified and quiet, and all at once they were at the landing upon the island. The marriage immediately took place, and the bride made presents of various valuables which had been furnished by the old witch.

As they were sitting in the lodge surrounded by friends and relatives, the mother of the Red Head regarded the face of her new daughter-in-law for a long time with fixed attention. From this scrutiny she was convinced that this singular and hasty marriage augured no good to her son. She drew her husband aside and disclosed to him her suspicions: "This can be no female," said she; "the figure and manners, the countenance, and more especially the expression of the eyes, are, beyond a doubt, those of a man." Her husband immediately rejected her suspicions, and rebuked her severely for the indignity offered to her daughter-in-law. He became so angry, that seizing the first thing that came to hand, which happened to be his pipe stem, he beat her unmercifully. This act requiring to be explained to the spectators, the mock bride immediately rose up, and assuming an air of offended dignity, told the Red Head that after receiving so gross an insult from his relatives he could not think of remaining with him as his wife, but should forthwith return to his village and friends. He left the lodge followed by the Red Head, and walked until he came upon the beach of the island, near the spot where they had first landed. Red Head entreated him to remain. He pressed him by every motive which he thought might have weight, but they were all rejected. During this conference they had seated themselves upon the ground, and Red Head, in great affliction, reclined his head upon his fancied wife's lap. This was the opportunity ardently sought for, and it was improved to the best advantage. Every means was taken to lull him to sleep, and partly by a soothing manner, and partly by a seeming compliance with his request, the object was at last attained. Red Head fell into a sound sleep. Our aspirant for the glory of a brave man then drew his blade of grass, and drawing it once across the neck of the Red Head completely severed the head from the body.

He immediately stripped off his dress, seized the bleeding head, and plunging into the lake, swam safely over to the main

176

shore. He had scarcely reached it, when, looking back, he saw amid the darkness the torches of persons come out in search of the new-married couple. He listened till they had found the headless body, and he heard their piercing shrieks of sorrow, as he took his way to the lodge of his kind adviser.

She received him with rejoicing. She admired his prudence, and told him his bravery could never be questioned again. Lifting up the head, she said he need only have brought the scalp. She cut off a small piece for herself, and told him he might now return with the head, which would be evidence of an achievement that would cause the Indians to respect him. On your way home, she said, you will meet with but one difficulty. MAUNKAH KEESH WOCCAUNG, or the spirit of the Earth, requires an offering from those who perform extraordinary achievements. As you walk along in a prairie, there will be an earthquake. The earth will open and divide the prairie in the middle. Take this partridge and throw it into the opening, and instantly spring over it. All this happened precisely as it had been foretold. He cast the partridge into the crevice and leapt over it. He then proceeded without obstruction to a place near his village, where he secreted his trophy. On entering the village he found his parents had returned from the place of their spring encampment, and were in great sorrow for their son, whom they supposed to be lost. One and another of the young men had presented themselves to the disconsolate parents, and said, "Look up, I am your son." Having been often deceived in this manner, when their own son actually presented himself, they sat with their heads down, and with-their eyes nearly blinded with weeping. It was sometime before they could be prevailed upon to bestow a glance upon him. It was still longer before they recognized him for their son; when he recounted his adventures they believed him mad. The young men laughed at him. He left the lodge and soon returned with his trophy. It was soon recognized. All doubts of the reality of his adventures now vanished. He was greeted with joy and placed among the first warriors of the nation. He finally became a chief, and his family were ever after respected and esteemed.

THE WHITE STONE CANOE.

THERE was once a very beautiful young girl, who died suddenly on the day she was to have been married to a handsome young man. He was also brave, but his heart was not proof against this loss. From the hour she was buried, there was no more joy or peace for him. He went often to visit the spot where the women had buried her, and sat musing there, when, it was thought, by some of his friends, he would have done better to try to amuse himself in the chase, or by diverting his thoughts in the war-path. But war and hunting had both lost their charms for him. His heart was already dead within him. He pushed aside both his war-club and his bow and arrows.

He had heard the old people say, that there was a path that led to the land of souls, and he determined to follow it. He accordingly set out, one morning, after having completed his preparations for the journey. At first he hardly knew which way to go. He was only guided by the tradition that he must go south. For awhile he could see no change in the face of the country. Forests, and hills, and valleys, and streams had the same looks which they wore in his native place. There was snow on the ground, when he set out, and it was sometimes seen to be piled and matted on the thick trees and bushes. At length it began to diminish, and finally disappeared. The forest assumed a more cheerful appearance, and the leaves put forth their buds, and before he was aware of the completeness of the change, he found himself surrounded by spring. He had left behind him the land of snow and ice. The air became mild; the dark clouds of winter had rolled away from the sky; a pure field of blue was above him, and as he went he saw flowers beside his path, and heard the songs of birds. By these signs he knew that he was going the right way, for they agreed with the traditions of his tribe. At length he spied a path. It led him through a grove, then up a long and elevated ridge, on the very top of which he came to a lodge. At the door stood an old man, with white hair, whose eyes, though deeply sunk, had a fiery brilliancy. He had a long robe of skins thrown loosely

around his shoulders, and a staff in his hands. It was Chebia-
bos.

The young Chippewa began to tell his story; but the vener-
able chief arrested him, before he had proceeded to speak ten
words. "I have expected you," he replied, "and had just risen
to bid you welcome to my abode. She whom you seek, passed
here but a few days since, and being fatigued with her journey,
rested herself here. Enter my lodge and be seated, and I will
then satisfy your inquiries, and give you directions for your
journey from this point." Having done this, they both issued
forth to the lodge door. "You see yonder gulf," said he, "and the
wide stretching blue plains beyond. It is the land of souls.
You stand upon its borders, and my lodge is the gate of en-
trance. But you cannot take your body along. Leave it here
with your bow and arrows, your bundle, and your dog. You
will find them safe on your return." So saying, he re-entered
the lodge, and the freed traveller bounded forward, as if his
feet had suddenly been endowed with the power of wings. But
all things retained their natural colors and shapes. The woods
and leaves, and streams and lakes, were only more bright and
comely than he had ever witnessed. Animals bounded across
his path, with a freedom and a confidence which seemed to tell
him, there was no blood shed here. Birds of beautiful plumage
inhabited the groves, and sported in the waters. There was but
one thing, in which he saw a very unusual effect. He noticed
that his passage was not stopped by trees or other objects. He
appeared to walk directly through them. They were, in fact,
but the souls or shadows of material trees. He became sensible
that he was in a land of shadows. When he had travelled half
a day's journey, through a country which was continually
becoming more attractive, he came to the banks of a broad
lake, in the centre of which was a large and beautiful island.
He found a canoe of shining white stone, tied to the shore. He
was now sure that he had come the right path, for the aged
man had told him of this. There were also shining paddles. He
immediately entered the canoe, and took the paddles in his
hands, when to his joy and surprise, on turning round, he
beheld the object of his search in another canoe, exactly its
counterpart in everything. She had exactly imitated his
motions, and they were side by side. They at once pushed out
from shore and began to cross the lake. Its waves seemed to be
rising, and at a distance looked ready to swallow them up; but
just as they entered the whitened edge of them they seemed to

melt away, as if they were but the images of waves. But no sooner was one wreath of foam passed, than another, more threatening still rose up. Thus they were in perpetual fear; and what added to it, was the *clearness of the water*, through which they could see heaps of beings who had perished before, and whose bones lay strewed on the bottom of the lake. The Master of Life had, however, decreed to let them pass, for the actions of neither of them had been bad. But they saw many others struggling and sinking in the waves. Old men and young men, males and females of all ages and ranks, were there; some passed, and some sank. It was only the little children whose canoes seemed to meet no waves. At length, every difficulty was gone, as in a moment, and they both leaped out on the happy island. They felt that the very air was food. It strengthened and nourished them. They wandered together over the blissful fields, where everything was formed to please the eye and the ear. There were no tempests—there was no ice, no chilly winds—no one shivered for the want of warm clothes: no one suffered for hunger—no one mourned the dead. They saw no graves. They heard of no wars. There was no hunting of animals; for the air itself was their food. Gladly would the young warrior have remained there forever, but he was obliged to go back for his body. He did not see the Master of Life, but he heard his voice in a soft breeze. "Go back," said this voice, "to the land from whence you come. Your time has not yet come. The duties for which I made you, and which you are to perform, are not yet finished. Return to your people and accomplish the duties of a good man. You will be the ruler of your tribe for many days. The rules you must observe will be told you by my messenger, who keeps the gate. When he surrenders back your body, he will tell you what to do. Listen to him, and you shall afterwards rejoin the spirit, which you must now leave behind. She is accepted, and will be ever here, as young and as happy as she was when I first called her from the land of snows." When this voice ceased, the narrator awoke. It was the fancy work of a dream, and he was still in the bitter land of snows, and hunger, and tears.

ONAIAZO, THE SKY-WALKER.

A LEGEND OF A VISIT TO THE SUN.

AN OTTOWA MYTH.

A LONG time ago, there lived an aged Odjibwa and his wife, on the shores of Lake Huron. They had an only son, a very beautiful boy, whose name was O-na-wut-a-qut-o, or he that catches the clouds. The family were of the totem of the beaver. The parents were very proud of him, and thought to make him a celebrated man, but when he reached the proper age, he would not submit to the We-koon-de-win, or fast. When this time arrived, they gave him charcoal, instead of his breakfast, but he would not blacken his face. If they denied him food, he would seek for birds' eggs, along the shores, or pick up the heads of fish that had been cast away, and broil them. One day, they took away violently the food he had thus prepared, and cast him some coals in place of it. This act brought him to a decision. He took the coals and blackened his face, and went out of the lodge. He did not return, but slept without; and during the night, he had a dream. He dreamed that he saw a very beautiful female come down from the clouds and stand by his side. "O-no-wut-a-qut-o," said she, "I am come for you—step in my tracks." The young man did so, and presently felt himself ascending above the tops of the trees—he mounted up, step by step, into the air, and through the clouds. His guide, at length, passed through an orifice, and he, following her, found himself standing on a beautiful plain.

A path led to a splendid lodge. He followed her into it. It was large, and divided into two parts. On one end he saw bows and arrows, clubs and spears, and various warlike implements tipped with silver. On the other end were things exclusively belonging to females. This was the home of his fair guide, and he saw that she had, on the frame, a broad rich belt, of many colors, which she was weaving. She said to him: "My brother is coming and I must hide you." Putting him in one

181

corner, she spread the belt over him. Presently the brother came in, very richly dressed, and shining as if he had points of silver all over him. He took down from the wall a splendid pipe, together with his sack of a-pa-ko-ze-gun, or smoking mixture. When he had finished regaling himself in this way, and laid his pipe aside, he said to his sister: "Nemissa" (which is, my elder sister), "when will you quit these practices? Do you forget that the Greatest of the Spirits had commanded that you should not take away the child from below? Perhaps you suppose that you have concealed O-no-wut-a-qut-o, but do I not know of his coming? If you would not offend me, send him back immediately." But this address did not alter her purpose. She would not send him back. Finding that she was purposed in her mind, he then spoke to the young lad, and called him from his hiding-place. "Come out of your conceal-ment," said he, "and walk about and amuse yourself. You will grow hungry if you remain there." He then presented him a bow and arrows, and a pipe of red stone, richly ornamented. This was taken as the word of consent to his marriage; so the two were considered husband and wife from that time.

O-no-wut-a-qut-o found everything exceedingly fair and beautiful around him, but he found no inhabitants except her brother. There were flowers on the plains. There were bright and sparkling streams. There were green valleys and pleas-ant trees. There were gay birds and beautiful animals, but they were not such as he had been accustomed to see. There was also day and night, as on the earth; but he observed that every morning the brother regularly left the lodge, and re-mained absent all day; and every evening the sister departed, though it was commonly but for a part of the night.

His curiosity was aroused to solve this mystery. He obtained the brother's consent to accompany him in one of his daily journeys. They travelled over a smooth plain, without bound-aries, until O-no-wut-a-qut-o felt the gnawings of appetite, and asked his companion if there were no game. "Patience! my brother," said he, "we shall soon reach the spot where I eat my dinner, and you will then see how I am provided." After walk-ing on a long time, they came to a place which was spread over with fine mats, where they sat down to refresh themselves. There was, at this place, a hole through the sky; and O-no-wut-a-qut-o, looked down, at the bidding of his companion, upon the earth. He saw below the great lakes, and the villages of the Indians. In one place, he saw a war party stealing on the camp of their enemies. In another, he saw feasting and dancing. On a green plain, young men were engaged at ball. Along a stream, women were employed in gathering the a-puk-wa for mats.

"Do you see," said the brother, "that group of children playing beside a lodge? Observe that beautiful and active boy," said he, at the same time darting something at him, from his hand. The child immediately fell, and was carried into the lodge.

They looked again, and saw the people gathering about the lodge. They heard the she-she-gwun, of the meeta, and the song he sung, asking that the child's life might be spared. To this request, the companion of O-no-wut-a-qut-o made answer: "Send me up the sacrifice of a white dog." Immediately a feast was ordered by the parents of the chid, the white dog was killed, his carcass was roasted, and all the wise men and medicine men of the village assembled to witness the ceremony. "There are many below," continued the voice of the brother, "whom you call great in medical skill, but it is because their ears are open, and they listen to my voice, that they are able to succeed. When I have struck one with sickness, they direct the people to look to me; and when they send me the offering I ask, I remove my hand from off them, and they are well." After he had said this, they saw the sacrifice parcelled out in dishes, for those who were at the feast. The master of the feast then said, "We send this to thee, great Manito," and immediately the roasted animal came up. Thus their dinner was supplied, and after they had eaten, they returned to the lodge by another way.

After this manner they lived for sometime; but the place became wearisome at last. O-no-wut-a-qut-o thought of his friends, and wished to go back to them. He had not forgotten his native village, and his father's lodge; and he asked leave of his wife to return. At length she consented. "Since you are better pleased ," she replied, "with the cares and the ills, and the poverty of the world, than with the peaceful delights of the sky, and its boundless prairies, go! I give you permission, and since I have brought you hither, I will conduct you back; but, remember, you are still my husband, I hold a chain in my hand by which I can draw you back whenever I will. My power over you is not, in any manner, diminished. Beware, therefore, how you venture to take a wife among the people below. Should you ever do so, it is then that you shall feel the force of my displeasure."

As she said this, her eyes sparkled—she raised herself slightly on her toes, and stretched herself up, with a majestic air; and at that moment, O-no-wut-a qut-o awoke from his dream. He found himself on the ground, near his father's lodge, at the very spot where he had laid himself down to fast. Instead of the bright beings of a higher world, he found himself surrounded by his parents and relatives. His mother told him he had been absent a year. The change was so great, that he remained for sometime moody and abstracted, but by degrees he recovered his spirits. He began to doubt the reality of all he had heard and seen above. At last, he forgot the admonitions of his spouse, and married a beautiful young woman of his own tribe. But within four days, she was a corpse. Even this fearful admonition was lost, and he repeated the offence by a second marriage. Soon afterwards, he went out of the lodge, one night, but never returned. It was believed that his Sun-wife had recalled him to the region of the clouds, where, the tradition asserts, he still dwells, and walks on the daily rounds, which he once witnessed.

BOSH-KWA-DOSH,

OR

THE MASTODON.

THERE was once a man who found himself alone in the world. He knew not whence he came, nor who were his parents, and he wandered about from place to place, in search of something. At last he became wearied and fell asleep. He dreamed that he heard a voice saying, "Nosis," that is, my grandchild. When he awoke, he actually heard the word repeated, and looking around, he saw a tiny little animal hardly big enough to be seen on the plain. While doubting whether the voice could come from such a diminutive source, the little animal said to him, "My grandson, you will call me Bosh-kwa-dosh. Why are you so desolate? Listen to me, and you shall find friends and be happy. You must take me up and bind me to your body, and never put me aside, and success in life shall attend you." He obeyed the voice, sewing up the little animal in the folds of a string, or narrow belt, which he tied around his body, at his navel. He then set out in search of someone like himself, or other object. He walked a long time in the woods without seeing man or animal. He seemed all alone in the world. At length he came to a place where a stump was cut, and on going over a hill he descried a large town in a plain. A wide road led through the middle of it; but what seemed strange was, that on one side there were no inhabitants in the lodges, while the other side was thickly inhabited. He walked boldly into the town.

The inhabitants came out and said: "Why here is the being we have heard so much of—here is Anish-in-a-ba. See his eyes, and his teeth in a half circle—see the Wyaukenawbedaid! See his bowels, how they are formed;"—for it seems they could look through him. The king's son, the Mudjekewis, was particularly kind to him, and calling him brother-in-law, commanded that he should be taken to his father's lodge and received with attention. The king gave him one of his daughters. These

185

people (who are supposed to be human, but whose rank in the scale of being is left equivocal) passed much of their time in play and sports and trials of various kinds. When some time had passed, and he become refreshed and rested, he was invited to join in these sports. The first test which they put him to, was the trial of frost. At some distance was a large body of frozen water, and the trial consisted in lying down naked on the ice, and seeing who could endure the longest. He went out with two young men, who began, by pulling off their garments, and lying down on their faces. He did likewise, only keeping on the narrow magic belt with the tiny little animal sewed in it; for he felt that in this alone was to be his reliance and preservation. His competitors laughed and tittered during the early part of the night, and amused themselves by thoughts of his fate. Once they called out to him, but he made no reply. He felt a manifest warmth given out by his belt. About midnight, finding they were still, he called out to them, in return, "What!" said he, "are you benumbed already? I am but just beginning to feel a little cold." All was silence. He, however, kept his position till early day break, when he got up and went to them. They were both quite dead, and frozen so hard, that the flesh had bursted out under their finger nails, and their teeth stood out. As he looked more closely, what was his surprise to find them both transformed into buffalo cows. He tied them together, and carried them towards the village. As he came in sight, those who had wished his death were disappointed, but the Mudjekewis, who was really his friend, rejoiced. "See!" said he, "but one person approaches—it is my brother-in-law." He then threw down the carcasses in triumph, but it was found that by their death he had restored two inhabitants to the before empty lodges, and he afterwards perceived that every one of these beings, whom he killed, had the like effect, so that the depopulated part of the village soon became filled with people.

The next test they put him to, was the trial of speed. He was challenged to the race ground, and began his career with one whom he thought to be a man; but everything was enchanted here, for he soon discovered that his competitor was a large black bear. The animal outran him, tore up the ground, and sported before him, and put out its large claws as if to frighten him. He thought of his little guardian spirit in the belt, and wishing to have the swiftness of the Kakake, *i. e.* sparrowhawk, he found himself rising from the ground, and with the speed of this bird he outwent his rival, and won the race, while the bear came up exhausted and lolling out his tongue. His friend the Mudjekewis stood ready, with his war-club, at the goal, and the moment the bear camp up, dispatched him. He then turned to the assembly, who had wished his friend and brother's death, and after reproaching them, he lifted up his club and began to slay them on every side. They fell in heaps on all sides; but it was plain to be seen, the moment they fell, that they were not men, but animals—foxes, wolves, tigers, lynxes, and other kinds, lay thick around the Mudjekewis.

Still the villagers were not satisfied. They thought the trial of frost had not been fairly accomplished, and wished it repeated. He agreed to repeat it, but being fatigued with the race, he undid his guardian belt, and laying it under his head, fell asleep. When he awoke, he felt refreshed, and feeling strong in his own strength, he went forward to renew the trial on the ice, but quite forgot the belt, nor did it at all occur to him when he awoke, or when he lay down to repeat the trial. About midnight his limbs became stiff, the blood soon ceased to circulate, and he was found in the morning a stiff corpse. The victors took him up and carried him to the village, where the loudest tumult of victorious joy was made, and they cut his body into a thousand pieces, that each one might eat a piece.

The Mudjekewis bemoaned his fate, but his wife was inconsolable. She lay in a state of partial distraction, in the lodge. As she lay here, she thought she heard someone groaning. It was repeated through the night, and in the morning she carefully scanned the place, and running her fingers through the grass, she discovered the secret belt, on the spot where her husband had last reposed. "Aubishin!" cried the belt—that is, untie me, or unloose me. Looking carefully, she found the small seam which inclosed the tiny little animal. It cried out the more earnestly, "Aubishin!" and when she had carefully ripped the seams, she beheld, to her surprise, a minute, naked little beast, smaller than the smallest new-born mouse, without any vestige of hair, except at the tip of its tail; it could crawl a few inches, but reposed from fatigue. It then went forward again. At each movement it would *pupowee,* that is to say, shake itself like a dog, and at each shake it became larger. This it continued until it acquired the strength and size of a middle sized dog, when it ran off.

The mysterious dog ran to the lodges, about the village, looking for the bones of his friend, which he carried to a secret

187

place, and as fast as he found them arranged all in their natural order. At length he had formed all the skeleton complete, except the heel bone of one foot. It so happened that two sisters were out of camp, according to custom, at the time the body was cut up, and this heel was sent out to them. The dog hunted every lodge, and being satisfied that it was not to be found in the camp, he sought it outside of it, and found the lodge of the two sisters. The younger sister was pleased to see him, and admired and patted the pretty dog, but the elder sat mumbling the very heel-bone he was seeking, and was surly and sour, and repelled the dog, although he looked most wistfully up in her face, while she sucked the bone from one side of her mouth to the other. At last she held it in such a manner that it made her cheek stick out, when the dog, by a quick spring, seized the cheek, and tore cheek and bone away and fled.

He now completed the skeleton, and placing himself before it, uttered a hollow, low, long-drawn-out howl, when the bones came compactly together. He then modulated his howl, when the bones knit together and became tense. The third howl brought sinews upon them, and the fourth, flesh. He then turned his head upwards, looking into the sky, and gave a howl, which caused everyone in the village to startle, and the the ground itself to tremble, at which the breath entered into his body, and he first breathed and then arose. "Hy kow!" I have overslept myself, he exclaimed; "I will be too late for the trial." "Trial!" said Bosh-kwa-dosh, "I told you never to let me be separate from your body, you have neglected this. You were defeated, and your frozen body cut into a thousand pieces, and scattered over the village; but my skill has restored you. Now I will declare myself to you, and show who and what I am!"

He then began to PUPOWEE, or shake himself, and at every shake, he grew. His body became heavy and massy, his legs thick and long, with big clumsy ends, or feet. He still shook himself, and rose and swelled. A long snout grew from his head, and two great shining teeth out of his mouth. His skin remained as it was, naked, and only a tuft of hair grew on his tail. He rose up as high as the trees. He was enormous. "I should fill the earth," said he, "were I to exert my utmost power, and all there is on the earth would not satisfy me to eat. Neither could it fatten me or do me good. I should want more. The Great Spirit created me to show his power when there were nothing but animals on the earth. But were all animals as large as myself, there would not be grass enough for food. But the earth was made for man, and not for beasts. I give some of those great gifts which I possess. All the animals shall be your food, and you are no longer to flee before them, and be their sport and food." So saying, he walked off with heavy steps and with fierce looks, at which all the little animals trembled.

THE SUN-CATCHER,

OR

BOY WHO SET A SNARE FOR THE SUN.

A MYTH OF THE ORIGIN OF THE DORMOUSE.

FROM THE ODJIBWA.

AT the time when the animals reigned in the earth, they had killed all but a girl, and her little brother, and these two were living in fear and seclusion. The boy was a perfect pigmy, and never grew beyond the stature of a small infant, but the girl increased with her years, so that the labor of providing food and lodging devolved wholly on her. She went out daily to get wood for their lodge-fire, and took her little brother along that no accident might happen to him; for he was too little to leave alone. A big bird might have flown away with him. She made him a bow and arrows, and said to him one day, "I will leave you behind where I have been chopping—you must hide yourself, and you will soon see the Gitshee-gitshee-gaun-ia-see-ug, or snow birds, come and pick the worms out of the wood, where I have been chopping" (for it was in the winter). "Shoot one of them and bring it home." He obeyed her, and tried his best to kill one, but came home unsuccessful. She told him he must not despair, but try again the next day. She accordingly left him at the place she got wood, and returned. Towards nightfall, she heard his little footsteps on the snow, and he came in exultingly, and threw down one of the birds which he had killed. "My sister," said he, "I wish you to skin it and stretch the skin, and when I have killed more, I will have a coat made out of them." "But what shall we do with the body?" said she, for as yet men had not begun to eat animal food, but lived on vegetables alone. "Cut it in two," he answered, "and season our pottage with one half of it at a time." She did so. The boy, who was of a very small stature, continued his efforts, and succeeded in killing ten birds, out of the skins

190

of which his sister made him a little coat.

"Sister," said he one day, "are we all alone in the world? Is there nobody else living?" She told him that those they feared and who had destroyed their relatives lived in a certain quarter, and that he must by no means go in that direction. This only served to inflame his curiosity and raise his ambition, and he soon after took his bow and arrows and went in that direction. After walking a long time and meeting nothing, he became tired, and lay down on a knoll, where the sun had melted the snow. He fell fast asleep; and while sleeping, the sun beat so hot upon him, that it singed and drew up his bird-skin coat, so that when he awoke and stretched himself, he felt bound in it, as it were. He looked down and saw the damage done to his coat. He flew into a passion, and upbraided the sun, and vowed vengeance against it. "Do not think you are too high," said he, "I shall revenge myself."

On coming home, he related his disaster to his sister, and lamented bitterly the spoiling of his coat. He would not eat. He lay down as one that fasts, and did not stir, or move his position for ten days, though she tried all she could to arouse him. At the end of ten days, he turned over, and then lay ten days on the other side. When he got up, he told his sister to make him a snare, for he meant to catch the sun. She said she had nothing; but finally recollected a little piece of dried deer's sinew, that her father had left, which she soon made into a string suitable for a noose. But the moment she showed it to him, he told her it would not do, and bid her get something else. She said she had nothing—nothing at all. At last she thought of her hair, and pulling some of it out of her head, made a string. But he instantly said it would not answer, and bid her, pettishly, and with authority, make him a noose. She told him there was nothing to make it of, and went out of the lodge. She said to herself, when she had got without the lodge, and while she was all alone, "neow obewy indapin." From my body, some will I take. This she did, and twisting them into a tiny cord, she handed it to her brother. The moment he saw this curious braid, he was delighted. "This will do," he said, and immediately put it to his mouth and began pulling it through his lips; and as fast as he drew it changed it into a red metal cord, which he wound around his body and shoulders, till he had a large quantity. He then prepared himself, and set out a little after midnight, that he might catch the sun before it rose. He fixed his snare on a spot just where the sun would strike the land, as it rose above the earth's disk; and sure enough, he caught the sun, so that it was held fast in the cord, and did not rise.

The animals who ruled the earth were immediately put into a great commotion. They had no light. They called a council to debate upon the matter, and to appoint someone to go and cut the cord—for this was a very hazardous enterprise, as the rays of the sun would burn whoever came so near to them. At last the dormouse undertook it—for at this time the dormouse was the largest animal in the world. When it stood up it looked like a mountain. When it got to the place where the sun was snared, its back began to smoke and burn with the intensity of the heat, and the top of its carcass was reduced to enormous heaps of ashes. It succeeded, however, in cutting the cord with its teeth, and freeing the sun, but it was reduced to a very small size, and has remained so ever since. Men call it the Kug-e-been-gwa-kwa—the blind woman.

WA-WA-BE-ZO-WIN,

OR

THE SWING ON THE PICTURED ROCKS OF LAKE SUPERIOR.

A TRADITION OF THE ODJIBWAS.

THERE was an old hag of a woman living with her daughter-in-law, and son, and a little orphan boy, whom she was bringing up. When her son-in-law came home from hunting, it was his custom to bring his wife the moose's lip, the kidney of the bear, or some other choice bits of different animals. These she would cook crisp, so as to make a sound with her teeth in eating them. This kind attention of the hunter to his wife at last excited the envy of the old woman. She wished to have the same luxuries, and in order to get them she finally resolved to make way with her son's wife. One day, she asked her to leave her infant son to the care of the orphan boy, and come out and swing with her. She took her to the shore of a lake, where there was a high range of rocks overhanging the water. Upon the top of this rock, she erected a swing. She then undressed, and fastened a piece of leather around her body, and commenced swinging, going over the precipice at every swing. She continued it but a short time, when she told her daughter to do the same. The daughter obeyed. She undressed, and tying the leather string as she was directed, began swinging. When the swing had got in full motion and well a going, so that it went clear beyond the precipice at every sweep, the old woman slyly cut the cords and let her daughter drop into the lake. She then put on her daughter's clothing, and thus disguised went home in the dusk of the evening and counterfeited her appearance and duties. She found the child crying, and gave it the breast, but it would not draw. The orphan boy asked her where its mother was. She answered, "She is still swinging." He said, "I shall go and look for her." "No!" said she, "you must not—what should you go for?" When the husband came in, in the evening, he gave the coveted morsel to his supposed wife. He missed his mother-in-law, but said nothing. She eagerly ate the dainty, and tried to keep the child still. The husband looked rather astonished to see his wife studiously averting her face, and asked her why the child cried so. She said, she did not know—that it would not draw.

In the meantime, the orphan boy went to the lake shores, and found no one. He mentioned his suspicions, and while the old woman was out getting wood, he told him all he had heard or seen. The man then painted his face black, and placed his spear upside down in the earth, and requested the Great Spirit to send lightning, thunder, and rain, in the hope that the body of his wife might arise from the water. He then began to fast, and told the boy to take the child and play on the lake shore.

We must now go back to the swing. After the wife had plunged into the lake, she found herself taken hold of by a water-tiger, whose tail twisted itself round her body, and drew her to the bottom. There she found a fine lodge, and all things ready for her reception, and she became the wife of the water-tiger. Whilst the children were playing along the shore, and the boy was casting pebbles into the lake, he saw a gull coming from its centre, and flying towards the shore, and when on shore, the bird immediately assumed the human shape. When he looked again, he recognized the lost mother. She had a leather belt around her loins, and another belt of white metal, which was, in reality, the tail of the water-tiger, her husband. She suckled the babe, and said to the boy— "Come here with him, whenever he cries, and I will nurse him."

The boy carried the child home, and told these things to the father. When the child again cried, the father went also with the boy to the lake shore, and hid himself in a clump of trees. Soon the appearance of a gull was seen, with a long shining belt, or chain, and as soon as it came to the shore, it assumed the mother's shape, and she began to suckle the child. The husband had brought along his spear, and seeing the shining chain, he boldly struck it and broke the links apart. He then took his wife and child home, with the orphan boy. When they entered the lodge, the old woman looked up, but it was a look of despair; she instantly dropped her head. A rustling was heard in the lodge, and the next moment she leaped up and flew out of the lodge, and was never heard of more.

MUKAKEE MINDEMOEA,

OR

THE TOAD-WOMAN.

AN ODJIBWA LEGEND.

GREAT good luck once happened to a young woman who was living all alone in the woods, with nobody near her but her little dog, for, to her surprise, she found fresh meat every morning at her door. She felt very anxious to know who it was that supplied her, and watching one morning, very early, she saw a handsome young man deposit the meat. After his being seen by her, he became her husband, and she had a son by him. One day, not long after this, the man did not return at evening, as usual, from hunting. She waited till late at night, but all in vain. Next day she swung her baby to sleep in its tikenagun, or cradle, and then said to her dog: "Take care of your brother whilst I am gone, and when he cries, halloo for me." The cradle was made of the finest wampum, and all its bandages and decorations were of the same costly material. After a short time, the woman heard the cry of her faithful dog, and running home as fast as she could, she found her child gone and the dog too. But on looking round, she saw pieces of the wampum of her child's cradle bit off by the dog, who strove to retain the child and prevent his being carried off by an old woman called Mukakee Mindemoea, or the Toad-Woman. The mother followed at full speed, and occasionally came to lodges inhabited by old women, who told her at what time the thief had passed; they also gave her shoes, that she might follow on. There were a number of these old women, who seemed as if they were all prophetesses. Each of them would say to her, that when she arrived in pursuit of her stolen child at the next lodge, she must set the toes of the moccasins they had loaned her pointing homewards, and they would return of themselves. She would get others from her entertainers further on, who would also give her directions how to proceed to recover her son. She thus followed in the pursuit, from valley to valley, and stream to stream, for months and years; when she came, at length, to the lodge of the last of the friendly old Nocoes, or grandmothers, as they were called, who gave her final instructions how to proceed. She told her she was near the place where her son was, and directed her to build a lodge of shingoob, or cedar boughs, near the old Toad-Woman's lodge, and to make a little bark dish and squeeze her milk into it. "Then," she said, "your first child (meaning the dog) will come and find you out." She did accordingly, and in a short time she heard her son, now grown, going out to hunt, with his dog, calling out to him, "Monedo Pewaubik (that is, Steel or Spirit Iron), Twee! Twee!" She then set ready the dish and filled it with her milk. The dog soon scented it and came into the lodge; she placed it before him. "See, my child," said she, addressing him, "the food you used to have from me, your mother." The dog went and told his young master that he had found his *real* mother; and informed him that the old woman, whom he *called* his mother, was not his mother, that she had stolen him when an infant in his cradle, and that he had himself followed her in hopes of getting him back. The young man and his dog then went on their hunting excursion, and brought

back a great quantity of meat of all kinds. He said to his pretended mother, as he laid it down, "Send some to the stranger
that has arrived lately." The old hag ansnwered, "No! why
should I send to her—the Sheegowish."* He insisted; and she
at last consented to take something,throwing it in at the door,
with the remark, "My son gives you, or feeds you this." But
it was of such an offensive nature that she threw it immediately out after her.

After this the young man paid the stranger a visit, at her
lodge of cedar boughs, and partook of her dish of milk. She
then told him she was his real mother, and that he had been
stolen away from her by the detestable Toad-Woman, who was
a witch. He was not quite convinced. She said to him, "Feign
yourself sick, when you go home, and when the Toad-Woman
asks what ails you, say that you want to see your cradle; for your
cradle was of wampum,'and your faithful brother, the dog, bit
a piece off to try and detain you, which I picked up, as I followed in your track. They were real wampum, white and blue,
shining and beautiful." She then showed him the pieces. He
went home and did as his real mother bid him. "Mother,"
said he, "why am I so different in my looks from the rest of
your children?" "Oh," said she, "it was a very bright clear
blue sky when you were born; that is the reason." When the
Toad-Woman saw he was ill, she asked what she could do for
him. He said nothing would do him good, but the sight of his
cradle. She ran immediately and goat a cedar cradle; but he
said "That is not my cradle." She went and got one of her own
children's cradles (for she had four), but he turned his head
and said, "That is not mine." She then produced the real
cradle, and he saw it was the same, in substance, with the
pieces the other had shown him; and he was convinced, for he
could even see the marks of the dog's teeth upon it.

He soon got well, and went out hunting, and killed a fat bear.
He and his dog-brother then stripped a tall pine of all its
branches, and stuck the carcass on the top, taking the usual
sign of his having killed an animal—the tongue. He told the
Toad-Woman where he had left it, saying, "It is very far, even
to the end of the earth." She answered, "It is not so far but I
can get it;" so off she set. As soon as she was gone, the young
man and his dog killed the Toad-Woman's children, and

* A term conpounded from *sheegowiss*, a widow, and *mowigh*, something
nasty.

staked them on each side of the door, with a piece of fat in their mouths, and then went to his real mother and hastened her departure with them. The Toad-Woman spent a long time in finding the bear, and had much ado in climbing the tree to get down the carcass. As she got near home, she saw the children looking out, apparently, with the fat in their mouths, and was angry at them, saying, "Why do you destroy the pomatum of your brother?" But her fury was great indeed, when she saw they were killed and impaled. She ran after the fugitives as fast as she could, and was near overtaking them, when the young man said, "We are pressed hard, but let this stay her progress," throwing his fire steel behind him, which caused the Toad-Woman to slip and fall repeatedly. But still she pursued and gained on them, when he threw behind him his flint, which again retarded her, for it made her slip and stumble, so that her knees were bleeding; but she continued to follow on, and was gaining ground, when the young man said, "Let the Oshau shaw go min un (snake berry) spring up to detain her," and immediately these berries spread like scarlet all over the path for a long distance, which she could not avoid stooping down to pick and eat. Still she went on, and was again advancing on them, when the young man as last said to the dog, "Brother, chew her into mummy, for she plagues us." So the dog, turning round, seized her and tore her to pieces, and they escaped.

nay, even frightened him; he hesitated a few moments. Was it better for him to remain in his camp, or seek another at some distance? While in this incertitude, he remembered his juggling, or rather his dream. He thought that his only aim in undertaking his journey was to see the Master of Life. This restored him to his senses. He thought it probable that one of those three roads led to the place which he wished to visit. He therefore resolved upon remaining in his camp until the morrow, when he would, at random, take one of them. His curiosity, however, scarcely allowed him time to take his meal; he left his encampment and fire, and took the widest of the paths. He followed it until the middle of the day without seeing anything to impede his progress; but, as he was resting a little to take breath, he suddenly perceived a large fire coming from underground. It excited his curiosity; he went towards it to see what it might be; but, as the fire appeared to increase as he drew nearer, he was so overcome with fear, that he turned back and took the widest of the other two paths. Having followed it for the same space of time as he had the first, he perceived a similar spectacle. His fright, which had been lulled by the change of road, awoke him, and he was obliged to take the third path, in which he walked a whole day without seeing anything. All at once, a mountain of a marvelous whiteness burst upon his sight. This filled him with astonishment; nevertheless, he took courage and advanced to examine it. Having arrived at the foot, he saw no signs of a road. He became very sad, not knowing how to continue his journey. In this conjuncture, he looked on all sides and perceived a female seated upon the mountain; her beauty was dazzling, and the whiteness of her garments surpassed that of snow. The woman said to him in his own language, "You appear surprised to find no longer a path to reach your wishes. I know that you have for a long time longed to see and speak to the Master of Life; and that you have undertaken this journey purposely to see him. The way which leads to his abode is upon this mountain. To ascend it, you must undress yourself completely, and leave all your accoutrements and clothing at the foot. No person shall injure them. You will then go and wash yourself in the river which I am now showing you, and afterward ascend the mountain."

The Indian obeyed punctually the woman's words; but one difficulty remained. How could he arrive at the top of the mountain, which was steep, without a path, and as smooth as glass? He asked the woman how he was to accomplish it. She replied, that if he really wished to see the Master of Life, he must, in mounting, only use his left hand and foot. This appeared almost impossible to the Indian. Encouraged, however, by the female, he commenced ascending, and succeeded after much trouble. When at the top, he was astonished to see no person, the woman having disappeared. He found himself alone, and without a guide. Three unknown villages were in sight; they were constructed on a different plan from his own, much handsomer, and more regular. After a few moments' reflection, he took his way towards the handsomest. When about half way from the top of the mountain, he recollected that he was naked, and was afraid to proceed; but a voice told him to advance, and have no apprehensions; that, as he had washed himself, he might walk in confidence. He proceeded without hesitation to a place which appeared to be the gate of the village, and stopped until someone came to open it. While he was considering the exterior of the village, the gate opened, and the Indian saw coming towards him a handsome man dressed all in white, who took him by the hand, and said he was going to satisfy his wishes by leading him to the presence of the Master of Life.

The Indian suffered himself to be conducted, and they arrived at a place of unequalled beauty. The Indian was lost in admiration. He there saw the Master of Life, who took him by the hand, and gave him for a seat a hat bordered with gold. The Indian, afraid of spoiling the hat, hesitated to sit down; but, being again ordered to do so, he obeyed without reply.

The Indian being seated, God said to him, "I am the Master of Life, whom thou wishest to see, and to whom thou wishes to speak. Listen to that which I will tell thee for thyself and for all the Indians. I am the Maker of Heaven and earth, the trees, lakes, rivers, men, and all that thou seest or hast seen on the earth or in the heavens; and because I love you, you must do my will; you must also avoid that which I hate; I hate you to drink as you do, until you lose your reason; I wish you not to fight one another; you take two wives, or run after other people's wives; you do wrong; I hate such conduct; you should have but one wife, and keep her until death. When you go to war, you juggle, you sing the medicine song, thinking you speak to me; you deceive yourselves; it is to the Manito that you speak; he is a wicked spirit who induces you to evil, and for want of knowing me, you listen to him.

201

"The land on which you are, I have made for you, not for others: wherefore do you suffer the whites to dwell upon your lands? Can you not do without them? I know that those whom you call the children of your great Father supply your wants. But, were you not wicked as you are, you would not need them. You might live as you did before you knew them. Before those whom you call your brothers had arrived, did not your bow and arrow maintain you? You needed neither gun, powder, nor any other object. The flesh of animals was your food, their skins your raiment. But when I saw you inclined to evil, I removed the animals into the depths of the forests, that you might depend on your brothers for your necessaries for your clothing. Again become good and do my will, and I will send animals for your sustenance. I do not, however, forbid suffering among you your Father's children; I love them, they know me, they pray to me; I supply their own wants, and give them that which they bring to you. Not so with those who are come to trouble your possessions. Drive them away; wage war against them. I love them not. They know me not. They are my enemies, they are your brothers' enemies. Send them back to the lands I have made for them. Let them remain there.

Here is a written prayer which I give thee; learn it by heart, and teach it to all the Indians and children." (The Indian, observing here that he could not read, the Master of Life told him that, on his return upon earth, he should give it to the chief of his village, who would read it, and also teach it to him, as also to all the Indians). "It must be repeated," said the Master of Life, "morning and evening. Do all that I have told thee, and announce it to all the Indians as coming from the Master of Life. Let them drink but one draught, or two at most, in one day. Let them have but one wife, and discontinue running after other people's wives and daughters. Let them not fight one another. Let them not sing the medicine song, for in singing the medicine song they speak to the evil spirit. Drive from your lands," added the Master of Life, "those dogs in red clothing; they are only an injury to you. When you want anything, apply to me, as your brothers do, and I will give to both. Do not sell to your brothers that which I have placed on the earth as food. In short, become good, and you shall want nothing. When you meet one another, bow, and give one another the ..... hand of the heart. Above all, I command thee to repeat, morning and evening, the prayer which I have given thee."

202

The Indian promised to do the will of the Master of Life, and also to recommend it strongly to the Indians; adding that the Master of Life should be satisfied with them.

His conductor then came, and leading him to the foot of the mountain, told him to take his garments and return to his village; which was immediately done by the Indian.

His return much surprised the inhabitants of the village, who did not know what had become of him. They asked him whence he came; but, as he had been enjoined to speak to no one until he saw the chief of the village, he motioned to them with his hand that he came from above. Having entered the village, he went immediately to the chief's wigwam, and delivered to him the prayer and laws intrusted to his care by the Master of Life.

THE SIX HAWKS,

OR

BROKEN WING.

AN ALLEGORY OF FRATERNAL AFFECTION.

THERE were six young falcons living in a nest, all but one of whom were still unable to fly, when it so happened that both the parent birds were shot by the hunters in one day. The young brood waited with impatience for their return; but night came, and they were left without parents and without food. Meeji-geeg-wona, or the Gray Eagle, the eldest, and the only one whose feathers had become stout enough to enable him to leave the nest, assumed the duty of stilling their cries and providing them with food, in which he was very successful. But, after a short time had passed, he, by an unlucky mischance, got one of his wings broken in pouncing upon a swan. This was the more unlucky, because the season had arrived when they were soon to go off to a southern climate to pass the winter, and they were only waiting to become a little stouter and more expert for the journey. Finding that he did not return, they resolved to go in search of him, and found him sorely wounded and unable to fly.

"Brothers," he said, "an accident has befallen me, but let not this prevent your going to a warmer climate, Winter is rapidly approaching, and you cannot remain here. It is better that I alone should die than for you all to suffer miserably on my account." "No! no!" they replied, with one voice, "we will not forsake you; we will share your sufferings; we will abandon our journey, and take care of you, as you did of us, before we were able to take care of ourselves. If the climate kills you, it shall kill us. Do you think we can so soon forget your brotherly care, which has surpassed a father's and even a mother's kindness? Whether you live or die, we will live or die with you."

They sought out a hollow tree to winter in, and contrived to carry their wounded nestmate there; and, before the rigors of winter set in, they had stored up food enough to carry them through its severities. To make it last the better, two of the number went off south, leaving the other three to watch over, feed, and protect the wounded bird. Meeji-geeg-wona in due time recovered from his wound, and he repaid their kindness by giving them such advice and instruction in the art of hunting as his experience had qualified him to impart. As spring advanced, they began to venture out of their hiding-place, and were all successful in getting food to eke out their winter's stock, except the youngest, who was called Peepi-geewi-zains, or the Pigeon Hawk. Being small and foolish, flying hither and yon, he always came back without anything. At last the Gray Eagle spoke to him, and demanded the cause of his ill luck. "It is not my smallness or weakness of body," said he, "that prevents my bringing home flesh as well as my brothers. I kill ducks and other birds every time I go out; but, just as I get to the woods, a large Ko-ko-ko-ho* robs me of my prey." "Well! don't despair, brother," said Meeji-geg-wona. "I now feel my strength perfectly recovered, and I will go out with you to-morrow," for he was the most courageous and warlike of them all.

Next day they went forth in company, the elder seating himself near the lake. Peepi-geewi-zains started out, and soon pounced upon a duck.

"Well done!" thought his brother, who saw his success; but, just as he was getting to land with his prize, up came a large white owl from a tree, where he had been watching, and laid claim to it. He was about wresting it from him, when Meeji-geeg-wona came up, and, fixing his talons in both sides of the owl, flew home with him.

The little pigeon hawk followed him closely, and was rejoiced and happy to think he had brought home something at last. He then flew in the owl's face, and wanted to tear out his eyes, and vented his passion in abundance of reproachful terms. "Softly," said the Gray Eagle; "do not be in such a passion, or exhibit so revengeful a disposition; for this will be a lesson to him not to tyrannize over anyone who is weaker than himself for the future." So, after giving him good advice, and telling him what kind of herbs would cure his wounds, they let the owl go.

* Owl.

WEENG,

THE SPIRIT OF SLEEP.

SLEEP is personified by the Odjibwas under the name of Weeng.* The power of the Indian Morpheus is executed by a peculiar class of gnome-like beings, called *Weengs*. These subordinate creations, although invisible to the human eye, are each armed with a tiny war-club, or puggamaugun, with which they nimbly climb up the forehead, and knock the drowsy person on the head; on which sleepiness is immediately produced. If the first blow is insufficient, another is given, until the eyelids close, and a sound sleep is produced. It is the constant duty of these little agents to put everyone to sleep whom they encounter—men, women, and children. And they are found secreted around the bed, or on small protuberances of the bark of the Indian lodges. They hide themselves in the GUSHKEEPITAUGUN, or smoking pouch of the hunter, and when he sits down to light his pipe in the woods, are ready to fly out and exert their sleep-compelling power. If they succeed, the game is suffered to pass, and the hunter obliged to return to his lodge without a reward.

In general, however, they are represented to possess friendly dispositions, seeking constantly to restore vigor and elasticity to the exhausted body. But being without judgment, their power is sometimes exerted at the hazard of reputation, or even life. Sleep may be induced in a person carelessly floating in his canoe, above a fall; or in a war party, on the borders of an enemy's country; or in a female, without the protection of the lodge circle. Although their peculiar season of action is in the night, they are also alert during the day.

While the forms of these gnomes are believed to be those of *ininees*, little or fairy men, the figure of Weeng himself is unknown, and it is not certain that he has ever been seen. Most of what is known on this subject, is derived from Iagoo, who

* This word has the sound of *g* hard, with a peculiarity as if followed by *k*.

related, that going out one day with his dogs to hunt, he passed through a wide range of thicket, where he lost his dogs. He became much alarmed, for they were faithful animals, and he was greatly attached to them. He called out, and made every exertion to recover them in vain. At length he came to a spot where he found them asleep, having incautiously ran near the residence of Weeng. After great exertions he aroused them, but not without having felt the power of somnolency himself. As he cast his eyes up from the place where the dogs were lying, he saw the Spirit of Sleep sitting upon the branch of a tree. He was in the shape of a giant insect, or *monetos*, with many wings from his back, which made a low deep murmuring sound, like distant falling water. But Iagoo himself, being a very great liar and braggart, but little credit was given to his narration.

Weeng is not only the dispenser of sleep, but, it seems, he is also the author of dullness, which renders the word susceptible of an ironical use. If an orator fails, he is said to be struck by Weeng. If a warrior *lingers*, he has ventured too near the sleepy god. If children begin to nod or yawn, the Indian mother looks up smilingly, and says, "They have been struck by Weeng," and puts them to bed.

ADDIK KUM MAIG,*

OR

THE ORIGIN OF THE WHITE FISH.

A LONG time ago, there lived a famous hunter in a remote part of the north. He had a handsome wife and two sons, who were left in the lodge every day, while he went out in quest of the animals, upon whose flesh they subsisted. Game was very abundant in those days, and his exertions in the chase were well rewarded. The skins of animals furnished them with clothing, and their flesh with food. They lived a long distance from any other lodge, and very seldom saw anyone. The two sons were still too young to follow their father to the chase, and usually diverted themselves within a short distance of the lodge. They noticed that a young man visited the lodge during their father's absence, and these visits were frequently repeated. At length the elder of the two said to his mother:

"My mother, who is this tall young man that comes here so often during our father's absence? Does he wish to see him? Shall I tell him when he comes back this evening?" "Bad boy," said the mother, pettishly, "mind your bow and arrows, and do not be afraid to enter the forest in search of birds and squirrels, with your little brother. It is not manly to be ever about the lodge. Nor will you become a warrior if you tell all the little things you see and hear to your father. Say not a word to him on the subject." The boys obeyed, but as they grew older, and still saw the visits of this mysterious stranger, they resolved to speak again to their mother, and told her that they meant to inform their father of all they had observed, for they frequently saw this young man passing through the woods, and he did not walk in the path, nor did he carry anything to eat. If he had any message to deliver, they had observed that messages were always addressed to the men, and not to the women.

* This term appears to be a derivative from ADDIK, the reindeer, and the plural form of the generic GUMEE, water, implying deer of the water.

At this, the mother flew into a rage. "I will kill you." said she, "if you speak of it." They were again intimidated to hold their peace. But observing the continuance of an improper intercourse, kept up by stealth, as it were, they resolved at last to disclose the whole matter to their father. They did so. The result was such as might have been anticipated. The father, being satisfied of the infidelity of his wife, watched a suitable occasion, when she was separated from the children, that they might not have their feelings excited, and with a single blow of his war-club dispatched her. He then 'buried her under the ashes of his fire, took down the lodge, and removed, with his two sons, to a distant position.

But the spirit of the woman haunted the children, who were now grown up to the estate of young men. She appeared to them as they returned from hunting in the evening. They were also terrified in their dreams, which they attributed to her. She harassed their imaginations wherever they went. Life became a scene of perpetual terrors. They resolved, together with their father, to leave the country, and commenced a journey toward the south. After travelling many days along the shores of Lake Superior, they passed around a high promontory of rock where a large river issued out of the lake, and soon after came to a place called PAUWATEEG.*

They had no sooner come in sight of these falls, than they beheld the skull of the woman rolling along the beach. They were in the utmost fear, and knew not how to elude her. At this moment one of them looked out, and saw a stately crane sitting on a rock in the middle of the rapids. They called out to the bird, "See, grandfather, we are persecuted by a spirit. Come and take us across the falls, so that we may escape her."

This crane was a bird of extraordinary size and great age. When first described by the two sons, he sat in a state of stupor, in the midst of the most violent eddies. When he heard himself addressed, he stretched forth his neck with great deliberation, and lifting himself by his wings, flew across to their assistance. "Be careful," said the crane, "that you do not touch the back part of my head. It is sore, and should you press against it, I shall not be able to avoid throwing you both into the rapids." They were, however, attentive on this point, and were safely landed on the south shore of the river.

The crane then resumed his former position in the rapids.

* Sault Ste. Marie

210

But the skull now cried out. "Come, my grandfather, and carry me over, for I have lost my children, and am sorely distressed." The aged bird flew to her assistance. He carefully repeated the injunction that she must by no means touch the back part of his head, which had been hurt, and was not yet healed. She promised to obey, but soon felt a curiosity to know where the head of her carrier had been hurt, and how so aged a bird could have received so bad a wound. She thought it strange, and before they were half way over the rapids, could not resist the inclination she felt to touch the affected part. Instantly the crane threw her into the rapids. "There," said he, "you have been of no use during your life, you shall now be changed into something for the benefit of your people, and it shall be called Addik Kum Maig." As the skull floated from rock to rock, the brains were strewed in the water, in a form resembling roes, which soon assumed the shape of a new species of fish, possessing a whiteness of color, and peculiar flavor, which have caused it, ever since, to be in great repute with the Indians.

The family of this man, in gratitude for their deliverance, adopted the crane as their totem, or ancestral mark; and this continues to be the distinguishing tribal sign of the band to this day.

BOKWEWA,

OR

THE HUMPBACK MAGICIAN.

ODJIBWA.

BOKWEWA and his brother lived in a secluded part of the country. They were considered as Manitoes, who had assumed mortal shapes. Bokwewa was the most gifted in supernatural endowments, although he was deformed in person. His brother partook more of the nature of the present race of beings. They lived retired from the world, and undisturbed by its cares, and passed their time in contentment and happiness.

Bokwewa,* owing to his deformity, was very domestic in his habits, and gave his attention to household affairs. He instructed his brother in the manner of pursuing game, and made him acquainted with all the accomplishments of a sagacious and expert hunter. His brother possessed a fine form, and an active and robust constitution; and felt a disposition to show himself off among men. He was restive in his seclusion, and showed a fondness for visiting remote places.

One day he told his brother that he was going to leave him; that he wished to visit the habitations of men and procure a wife. Bokwewa objected to his going; but his brother overruled all that he said, and he finally departed on his travels. He travelled a long time. At length he fell in with the footsteps of men. They were moving by encampments, for he saw several places where they had encamped. It was in the winter. He came to a place where one of their number had died. They had placed the corpse on a scaffold. He went to it and took it down. He saw that it was the corpse of a beautiful young woman. "She shall be my wife!" he exclaimed.

He took her up, and placing her on his back, returned to his brother. "Brother," he said, "cannot you restore her to life?

---

* i. e., the sudden stopping of a voice.

212

Oh, do me that favor!" Bokwewa said he would try. He performed numerous ceremonies, and at last succeeded in restoring her to life. They lived very happily for some time. Bokwewa was extremely kind to his brother, and did everything to render his life happy. Being deformed and crippled, he always remained at home, while his brother went out to hunt. And it was by following his directions, which were those of a skillful hunter, that he always succeeded in returning with a good store of meat.

One day he had gone out as usual, and Bokwewa was sitting in his lodge, on the opposite side of his brother's wife, when a tall, fine young man entered, and immediately took the woman by the hand and drew her to the door. She resisted and called on Bokwewa, who jumped up to her assistance. But their joint resistance was unavailing; the man succeeded in carrying her away. In the scuffle, Bokwewa had his hump back much bruised on the stones near the door. He crawled into the lodge and wept very sorely, for he knew that it was a powerful Manito who had taken the woman.

When his brother returned, he related all to him exactly as it happened. He would not taste food for several days. Sometimes he would fall to weeping for a long time, and appeared almost beside himself. At last he said he would go in search of her. Bokwewa tried to dissuade him from it, but he insisted.

"Well!" said he, "since you are bent on going, listen to my advice. You will have to go south. It is a long distance to the residence of your captive wife, and there are so many charms and temptations in the way, I am afraid you will be led astray by them, and forget your errand. For the people whom you will see in that country do nothing but amuse themselves. They are very idle, gay, and effeminate, and I am fearful they will lead you astray. Your journey is beset with difficulties. I will mention one or two things, which you must be on your guard against. In the course of your journey, you will come to a large grapevine lying across your way. You must not even taste its fruit, for it is poisonous. Step over it. It is a snake. You will next come to something that looks like bear's fat, transparent and tremulous. Don't taste it, or you will be overcome by the pleasures of those people. It is frog's eggs. These are snares laid by the way for you."

He said he would follow the advice, and bid farewell to his brother. After travelling a long time, he came to the enchanted grapevine. It looked so tempting, he forgot his

213

brother's advice and tasted the fruit. He went on till he came to the frog's eggs. The substance so much resembled bear's fat that he tasted it. He still went on. At length he came to a very extensive plain. As he emerged from the forest the sun was setting, and cast its scarlet and golden shades over all the plain. The air was perfectly calm, and the whole prospect had the air of an enchanted land. The most inviting fruits and flowers spread out before the eye. At a distance he beheld a large village, filled with people without number, and as he drew near he saw women beating corn in silver mortars. When they saw him approaching, they cried out, "Bokwewa's brother has come to see us." Throngs of men and women, gayly dressed, came out to meet him. He was soon overcome by their flatteries and pleasures, and he was not long afterward seen beating corn with their women (the strongest proof of effeminacy), although his wife, for whom he had mourned so much, was in that Indian metropolis.

Meantime, Bokwewa waited patiently for the return of his brother. At length, after the lapse of several years, he sat out in search of him, and arrived in safety among the luxuriant people of the South. He met with the same allurements on the road, and the same flattering reception that his brother did. But he was above all temptations. The pleasures he saw had no other effect upon him than to make him regret the weakness of mind of those who were led away by them. He shed tears of pity to see that his brother had laid aside the arms of a hunter, and was seen beating corn with the women.

He ascertained where his brother's wife remained. After deliberating some time, he went to the river where she usually came to draw water. He there changed himself into one of those hair-snakes which are sometimes seen in running water. When she came down, he spoke to her, saying, "Take me up; I am Bokwewa." She then scooped him out and went home. In a short time the Manito who had taken her away asked her for water to drink. The lodge in which they lived was partitioned. He occupied a secret place, and was never seen by anyone but the woman. She handed him the water containing the hair-snake, which he drank, with the snake, and soon after was a dead Manito.

Bokwewa then resumed his former shape. He went to his brother, and used every means to reclaim him. But he would not listen. He was so much taken up with the pleasures and dissipations into which he had fallen, that he refused to give them up, although Bokwewa, with tears, tried to convince him of his foolishness, and to show him that those pleasures could not endure for a long time. Finding that he was past reclaiming, Bokwewa left him, and disappeared forever.

AGGODAGAUDA AND HIS DAUGHTER,

OR

THE MAN WITH HIS LEG TIED UP.

THE prairie and forest tribes were once at war, and it required the keenest eyes to keep out of the way of danger. Aggodagauda lived on the borders, in the forests, but he was in a by-place not easy to find. He was a successful hunter and fisher, although he had, by some mischance, lost the use of his legs. So he had it tied, and looped up, and got over the ground by hopping.

Use had given him great power in the sound leg, and he could hop to a distance, which was surprising. There was nobody in the country who could outgo him on a hunt. Even Paup-Puk-keewiss, in his best days, could hardly excel him. But he had a great enemy in the chief or king of the buffaloes, who frequently passed over the plains with the force of a tempest. It was a peculiarity of Aggodagauda, that he had an only child, a daughter, who was very beautiful, whom it was the aim of this enemy to carry off, and he had to exert his skill to guard her from the inroad of his great and wily opponent. To protect her the better, he had built a log house, and it was only on the roof of this that he could permit his daughter to take the open air, and disport herself. Now her hair was so long, that when she untied it, the raven locks hung down to the ground.

One fine morning, the father had prepared himself to go out a fishing, but before leaving the lodge put her on her guard against their arch enemy. "The sun shines," said he, "and the buffalo chief will be apt to move this way before the sun gets to the middle point, and you must be careful not to pass out of the house, for there is no knowing but he is always narrowly watching. If you go out, at all, let it be on the roof, and even there keep a sharp lookout, lest he sweep by and catch you with his long horns." With this advice he left his lodge. But he had scarcely got seated in his canoe, on his favorite fishing-ground, when his ear caught opprobrious strains from his enemy. He listened again, and the sound was now clearer than before—

> "Aggodagauda—one legged man,
> Man with his leg tied up;
> What is he but a rapakena,*
> Hipped, and legged?"

He immediately paddled his canoe ashore, and took his way home—hopping a hundred rods at a leap. But when he reached his house his daughter was gone. She had gone out on the top of the house, and sat combing her long and beautiful hair, on the eaves of the lodge, when the buffalo king, coming suddenly by, caught her glossy hair, and winding it about his horns, tossed her on to his shoulders, swept off in an opposite direction to his village. He was followed by his whole troop, who made the plains shake under their tread. They soon reached, and dashed across a river, and pursued their course to the chief's village, where she was received by all with great attention. His other wives did all they could to put the lodge in order, and the buffalo king himself was unremitting in his kindness and attention. He took down from the walls his pibbegwun, and began to play the softest strains, to please her ear. Ever and anon, as the chorus paused, could be heard the words—

> "Ne ne mo sha makow,
> Aghi saw ge naun.
> My sweetheart—my bosom is true,
> You only—it is you that I love."

They brought her cold water, in bark dishes from the spring. They set before her the choicest food. The king handed her nuts from the pecan-tree, then he went out hunting to get her the finest meats and water fowl. But she remained pensive, and sat fasting in her lodge day after day, and gave him no hopes of forgiveness for his treachery.

In the meantime, Aggodagauda came home, and finding his daughter had been stolen, determined to get her back. For this purpose he immediately set out. He could easily track the king, until he came to the banks of the river, and saw that he had plunged in and swam over. But there had been a frosty

---

* Grasshopper.

217

night or two since, and the water was covered with thin ice, so that he could not walk on it. He determined to encamp till it became solid, and then crossed over and pursued the trail. As he went along he saw branches broken off and strewed behind, for these had been purposely cast along by the daughter, that the way might be found. And the manner in which she had accomplished it was this. Her hair was all untied when she was caught up, and being very long, it caught on the branches as they darted along, and it was these twigs that she broke off for signs to her father. When he came to the king's lodge it was evening. Carefully approaching it, he peeped through the sides and saw his daughter sitting disconsolately. She immediately caught his eye, and knowing that it was her father come for her, she all at once appeared to relent in her heart, and asking for the dipper, said to the king, "I will go and get you a drink of water." This token of submission delighted him, and he waited with impatience for her return. At last he went out with his followers, but nothing could be seen or heard of the captive daughter. They sallied out in the plains, but had not gone far, by the light of the moon, when a party of hunters, headed by the father-in-law of Aggodagauda, set up their yells in their rear, and a shower of arrows was poured in upon them. Many of their numbers fell, but the king being stronger and swifter than the rest, fled toward the west, and never again appeared in that part of the country.

While all this was passing, Aggodagauda, who had met his daughter the moment she came out of the lodge, and being helped by his guardian spirit, took her on his shoulders and hopped off, a hundred steps in one, till he reached the stream, crossed it, and brought back his daughter in triumph to his lodge.

IOSCO;

OR

THE PRAIRIE BOYS' VISIT TO THE SUN AND MOON.

AN OTTAWA LEGEND.

ONE pleasant morning, five young men and a boy about ten years of age, called Ioscoda, went out a shooting with their bows and arrows. They left their lodges with the first appearance of daylight, and having passed through a long reach of woods, had ascended a lofty eminence before the sun arose. While standing there in a group, the sun suddenly burst forth in all its effulgence. The air was so clear, that it appeared to be at no great distance. "How very near it is," they all said. "It cannot be far," said the eldest, "and if you will accompany me, we will see if we cannot reach it." A loud assent burst from every lip. Even the boy, Ioscoda, said he would go. They told him he was too young; but he replied, "If you do not permit me to go with you, I will mention your design to each of your parents." They then said to him, "You shall also go with us, so be quiet."

They then fell upon the following arrangement. It was resolved that each one should obtain from his parents as many pairs of moccasins as he could, and also new clothing of leather. They fixed on a spot where they would conceal all their articles, until they were ready to start on their journey, and which would serve, in the meantime, as a place of rendezvous, where they might secretly meet and consult. This being arranged, they returned home.

A long time passed before they could put their plan into execution. But they kept it a profound secret, even to the boy. They frequently met at the appointed place, and discussed the subject. At length everything was in readiness, and they decided on a day to set out. That morning the boy shed tears for a pair of new leather leggings. "Don't you see," said he to his parents, "how my companions are dressed?" This appeal to their pride and envy prevailed. He obtained the leggings. Artifices were also resorted to by the others, under the plea of going out on a special hunt. They said to one another, but in a tone that they might be overheard, "We will see who will bring in the most game." They went out in different directions, but soon met at the appointed place, where they had hid the articles for their journey, with as many arrows as they had time to make. Each one took something on his back, and they began their march. They travelled day after day, through a thick forest, but the sun was always at the same distance. "We must," said they, "travel toward Waubunong,* and we shall get to the object, some time or other." No one was discouraged, although winter overtook them. They built a lodge and hunted, till they obtained as much dried meat as they could carry, and then continued on. This they did several times; season followed season. More than one winter ovetook them. Yet none of them became discouraged, or expressed dissatisfaction.

One day the travellers came to the banks of a river, whose waters ran toward Waubunong. They followed it down many

* The East—*i. e.* place of light.

220

days. As they were walking, one day, they came to rising grounds, from which they saw something white or clear through the trees. They encamped on this elevation. Next morning they came, suddenly, in view of an immense body of water. No land could be seen as far as the eye could reach. One or two of them lay down on the beach to drink. As soon as they got the water in their mouths, they spit it out, and exclaimed, with surprise, "Shewetagon awbo!" (salt water.) It was the sea. While looking on the water, the sun arose as if from the deep, and went on its steady course through the heavens, enlivening the scene with his cheering and animating beams. They stood in fixed admiration, but the object appeared to be as distant from them as ever. They thought it best to encamp, and consult whether it were advisable to go on, or return. "We see," said the leader, "that the sun is still on the opposite side of this great water, but let us not be disheartened. We can walk around the shore." To this they all assented.

Next morning they took the northerly shore, to walk around it, but had only gone a short distance when they came to a large river. They again encamped, and while sitting before the fire, the question was put, whether any one of them had ever dreamed of water, or of walking on it. After a long silence, the eldest said he had. Soon after they lay down to sleep. When they arose the following morning, the eldest addressed them: "We have done wrong in coming north. Last night my spirit appeared to me, and told me to go south, and that but a short distance beyond the spot we left yesterday, we should come to a river with high banks. That by looking off its mouth, we should see an island, which would approach to us. He directed that we should all get on it. He then told me to cast my eyes toward the water. I did so, and I saw all he had declared. He then informed me that we must return south, and wait at the river until the day after tomorrow. I believe all that was revealed to me in this dream, and that we shall do well to follow it."

The party immediately retraced their footsteps in exact obedience to these intimations. Toward the evening they came to the borders of the indicated river. It had high banks, behind which they encamped, and here they patiently awaited the fulfillment of the dream. The appointed day arrived. They said, "We will see if that which has been said will be seen." Midday is the promised time. Early in the morning two had gone to the shore to keep a look-out. They waited anxiously for the middle of the day, straining their eyes to see if they could discover anything. Suddenly they raised a shout. "Ewaddee suh neen! There it is! There it is!" On rushing to the spot they beheld something like an *island* steadily advancing toward the shore. As it approached, they could discover that something was moving on it in various directions. They said, "It is a Manito, let us be off into the woods." "No, no," cried the eldest, "let us stay and watch." It now became stationary, and lost much of its imagined height. They could only see *three* trees, as they thought, resembling trees in a pinery that had been burnt. The wind, which had been off the sea, now died away into a perfect calm. They saw something leaving the fancied island and approaching the shore, throwing and flapping its wings, like a loon when he attempts to fly in calm weather. It entered the mouth of the river. They were on the point of running away, but the eldest dissuaded them. "Let us hide in this hollow," he said, "and we will see what it can be." They did so. They soon heard the sounds of chopping, and quickly after they heard the falling of trees. Suddenly a man came up to the place of their concealment. He stood still and gazed at them. They did the same in utter amazement. After looking at them for some time, the person advanced and extended his hand toward them. The eldest took it, and they shook hands. He then spoke, but they could not understand each other. He then cried out for his comrades. They came, and examined very minutely their dresses. They again tried to converse. Finding it impossible, the strangers then motioned to the Naubequon, and to the Naubequon-ais,* wishing them to embark. They consulted with each other for a short time. The eldest then motioned that they should go on board. They embarked on board the boat; which they found to be loaded with wood. When they reached the side of the supposed island, they were surprised to see a great number of people, who all came to the side and looked at them with open mouths. One spoke out, above the others, and appeared to be the leader. He motioned them to get on board. He looked at and examined them, and took them down into the cabin, and set things before them to eat. He treated them very kindly.

* Ship and boat. These terms exhibit the simple and the diminutive forms of the name for ship or vessel. It is also the term for a woman's needlework, and seems to imply a tangled thready mass, and was perhaps transferred in allusion to a ship's ropes.

When they came on deck again, all the sails were spread, and they were fast losing sight of land. In the course of the night and the following day they were sick at the stomach, but soon recovered. When they had been out at sea ten days, they became sorrowful, as they could not converse with those who had hats on.*

The following night Ioscoda dreamed that his spirit appeared to him. He told him not to be discouraged, that he would open his ears, so as to be able to understand the people with hats. I will not permit you to understand much, said he, only sufficient to reveal your wants, and to know what is said to you. He repeated this dream to his friends, and they were satisfied and encouraged by it. When they had been out about thirty days, the master of the ship told them, and motioned them to change their dresses of leather, for such as his people wore; for if they did not, his master would be displeased. It was on this occasion that the elder first understood a few words of the language. The first phrase he comprehended was *La que notte*, and from one word to another he was soon able to speak it.

One day the men cried out, land! and soon after they heard a noise resembling thunder, in repeated peals. When they had got over their fears, they were shown the large guns which made this noise. Soon after they saw a vessel smaller than their own, sailing out of a bay, in the direction toward them. She had flags on her masts, and when she came near she fired a gun. The large vessel also hoisted her flags, and the boat came alongside. The master told the person who came in it, to tell his master or king, that he had six strangers on board, such as had never been seen before, and that they were coming to visit him. It was some time after the departure of this messenger before the vessel got up to the town. It was then dark, but they could see people, and horses, and odawbons* ashore. They were landed and placed in a covered vehicle, and driven off. When they stopped, they were taken into a large and splendid room. They were here told that the great chief wished to see them. They were shown into another large room, filled with men and women. All the room was Shoneancauda.*

---

* Wewaquonidjig, a term early and extensively applied to white men, by our Indians, and still frequently used.

* Odawbon comprehends all vehicles between a dog train and a coach, whether on wheels or runners. The term is nearest allied to vehicle.

* Massive silver.

The chief asked them their business, and the object of their journey. They told him where they were from, and where they were going, and the nature of the enterprise which they had undertaken. He tried to dissuade them from its execution, telling them of the many trials and difficulties they would have to undergo; that so many days' march from his country dwelt a bad spirit, or Manito, who foreknew and foretold the existence and arrival of all who entered into his country. It is impossible, he said, my children, for you ever to arrive at the object you are in search of.

Ioscoda replied: "Nosa,"* and they could see the chief blush in being called *father*, "we have come so far on our way, and we will continue it; we have resolved firmly that we will do so. We think our lives are of no value, for we have given them up for this object. Nosa," he repeated, "do not then prevent us from going on our journey." The chief then dismissed them with valuable presents, after having appointed the next day to speak to them again, and provided everything that they needed or wished for.

Next day they were again summoned to appear before the king. He again tried to dissuade them. He said he would send them back to their country in one of his vessels: but all he said had no effect. "Well," said he, "if you will go, I will furnish you all that is needed for your journey." He had everything provided accordingly. He told them, that three days before they reached the Bad Spirit he had warned them of, they would hear his Sheshegwun.* He cautioned them to be wise, for he felt that he should never see them all again.

They resumed their journey, and travelled sometimes through villages, but they soon left them behind and passed over a region of forests and plains, without inhabitants. They found all the productions of a new country: trees, animals, birds, were entirely different from those they were accustomed to, on the other side of the great waters. They travelled, and travelled, till they wore out all of the clothing that had been given to them, and had to take to their leather clothing again.

The three days the chief spoke of meant three years, for it was only at the end of the third year, that they came within the sight of the spirit's sheshegwun. The sound appeared to

* My father.
* A rattle.

be near, but they continued walking on, day after day, without apparently getting any nearer to it. Suddenly they came to a very extensive plain; they could see the blue ridges of distant mountains rising on the horizon beyond it; they pushed on, thinking to get over the plain before night, but they were overtaken by darkness; they were now on a stony part of the plain, covered by about a foot's depth of water; they were weary and fatigued; some of them said, let us lie down; no,no, said the others, let us push on. Soon they stood on firm ground, but it was as much as they could do to stand, for they were very weary. They, however, made an effort to encamp, lighted up a fire, and refreshed themselves by eating. They then commenced conversing about the sound of the spirit's sheshegwun, which they had heard for several days. Suddenly the instrument commenced; it sounded as if it was subterraneous, and it shook the ground: they tied up their bundles and went toward the spot. They soon came to a large building, which was illuminated. As soon as they came to the door, they were met by a rather elderly man. "How do ye do," said he, "my grandsons? Walk in, walk in; I am glad to see you: I knew when you started: I saw you encamp this evening: sit down, and tell me the news of the country you left, for I feel interested in it." They complied with his wishes, and when they had concluded, each one presented him with a piece of tobacco. He then revealed to them things that would happen in their journey, and predicted its successful accomplishment. "I do not say that all of you," said he, "will successfully go through it. You have passed over three-fourths of your way, and I will tell you how to proceed after you get to the edge of the earth. Soon after you leave this place, you will hear a deafening sound: it is the sky descending on the edge, but it keeps moving up and down; you will watch, and when it moves up, you will see a vacant space between it and the earth. You must not be afraid. A chasm of awful depth is there, which separates the unknown from this earth, and a veil of darkness conceals it. Fear not. You must leap through; and if you succeed, you will find yourselves on a beautiful plain, and in a soft and mild light emitted by the moon." They thanked him for his advice. A pause ensued.

"I have told you the way," he said; "now tell me again of the country you have left; for I committed dreadful ravages while I was there: does not the country show marks of it? and do not the inhabitants tell of me to their children? I came to this place to mourn over my bad actions, and am trying, by my present course of life, to relieve my mind of the load that is on it." They told him that their fathers spoke often of a celebrated personage called Manabozho, who performed great exploits. "I am he," said the Spirit. They gazed with astonishment and fear. "Do you see this pointed house?" said he, pointing to one that resembled a sugar-loaf; "you can now each speak your wishes, and will be answered from that house. Speak out, and ask what each wants, and it shall be granted." One of them, who was vain, asked with presumption, that he might live forever, and never be in want. He was answered, "Your wish shall be granted." The second made the same request, and received the same answer. The third asked to live longer than common people, and to be always successful in his war excursions, never losing any of his young men. He was told, "Your wishes are granted." The fourth joined in the same request, and received the same reply. The fifth made an humble request, asking to live as long as men generally do, and that he might be crowned with such success in hunting as to be able to provide for his parents and relatives. The sixth made the same request, and it was granted to both, in pleasing tones, from the pointed house.

After hearing these responses they prepared to depart. They were told by Manabozho, that they had been with him but one day, but they afterward found that they had remained there upward of a year. When they were on the point of setting out, Manabozho exclaimed, "Stop! you two, who asked me for eternal life, will receive the boon you wish immediately." He spake, and one was turned into a stone called Shin-gauba-wossin,* and the other into a cedar tree. "Now," said he to the others, "you can go." They left him in fear, saying, "We were fortunate to escape so, for the king told us he was wicked, and that we should not probably escape from him." They had not proceeded far, when they began to hear the sound of the beating sky. It appeared to be near at hand, but they had a long interval to travel before they came near, and the sound was then stunning to their senses; for when the sky came down, its pressure would force gusts of wind from the opening, so strong that it was with difficulty they could keep their feet, and the

---

* A hard primitive stone, frequently found along the borders of the lakes and watercourses, generally fretted into image shapes. Hardness and indestructibility are regarded as its characteristics by the Indians. It is often granite.

sun passed but a short distance above their heads. They however approached boldly, but had to wait some time before they could muster courage enough to leap through the dark veil that covered the passage. The sky would come down with violence, but it would rise slowly and gradually. The two who had made the humble request, stood near the edge, and with no little exertion succeeded, one after the other, in leaping through, and gaining a firm foothold. The remaining two were fearful and undecided: the others spoke to them through the darkness, saying, "Leap! leap! the sky is on its way down." These two looked up and saw it descending, but fear paralyzed their efforts; they made but a feeble attempt, so as to reach the opposite side with their hands; but the sky at the same time struck on the earth with great violence and a terrible sound, and forced them into the dreadful black chasm.

The two successful adventurers, of whom Iosco now was chief, found themselves in a beautiful country, lighted by the moon, which shed around a mild and pleasant light. They could see the moon approaching as if it were from behind a hill. They advanced, and an aged woman spoke to them; she had a white face and pleasing air, and looked rather old, though she spoke to them very kindly: they knew from her first appearance that she was the moon: she asked them several questions: she told them that she knew of their coming, and was happy to see them: she informed them that they were half way to her brother's, and that from the earth to her abode was half the distance. "I will, by and by, have leisure," said she, "and will go and conduct you to my brother, for he is now absent on his daily course: you will succeed in your object, and return in safety to your country and friends, with the good wishes, I am sure, of my brother." While the travellers were with her, they received every attention. When the proper time arrived, she said to them, "My brother is now rising from below, and we shall see his light as he comes over the distant edge: come," said she, "I will lead you up." They went forward, but in some mysterious way, they hardly knew how: they rose almost directly up, as if they had ascended steps. They then came upon an immense plain, declining in the direction of the sun's approach. When he came near, the moon spake—"I have brought you these persons, whom we knew were coming;" and with this she disappeared. The sun motioned with his hand for them to follow him. They did so, but found it rather difficult, as the way was steep: they found it particularly so from the edge of the earth till they got halfway between that point and midday: when they reached this spot, the sun stopped, and sat down to rest. "What, my children," said he, "has brought you here? I could not speak to you before: I could not stop at any place but this, for this is my first resting-place—then at the centre, which is at midday, and then halfway from that to the western edge.* "Tell me," he continued, "the object of your undertaking this journey and all the circumstances which have happened to you on the way." They complied. Iosco told him their main object was to see him. They had lost four of their friends on the way, and they wished to know whether they could return in safety to the earth, that they might inform their friends and relatives of all that had befallen them. They concluded by requesting him to grant their wishes. He replied, "Yes, you shall certainly return in safety; but your companions were vain and presumptuous in their demands. They were Gug-ge-baw-diz-ze-wug.* They aspired to what Manitoes only could enjoy. But you two, as I said, shall get back to your country, and become as happy as the hunter's life can make you. You shall never be in want of the necessaries of life, as long as you are permitted to live; and you will have the satisfaction of relating your journey to your friends, and also of telling them of me. Follow me, follow me," he said, commencing his course again. The ascent was now gradual, and they soon came to a level plain. After travelling some time he again sat down to rest, for we had arrived at Nau-we-qua.* "You see," said he, "it is level at this place, but a short distance onwards, my way descends gradually to my last resting-place, from which there is an abrupt descent." He repeated his assurance that they should be shielded from danger, if they relied firmly on his power. "Come here quickly," he said, placing something before them on which they could descend; "keep firm," said he, as they resumed the descent. They went downward as if they had been let down by ropes.

In the meantime the parents of these two young men dreamed that their sons were returning, and that they should soon see them. They placed the fullest confidence in their dreams. Early in the morning they left their lodges for a remote point

---

* This computation of time separates the day into four portions of six hours each—two of which, from 1 to 6, and from 6 to 12 A.M. compose the *morning*, and the other two, from 1 to 6, and from 6 to 12 P.M. compose the *evening*.

* This is a verbal form, plural number, of the transitive adjective—foolish.

* Midday, or middle line.

in the forest, where they expected to meet them. They were not long at the place before they saw the adventures returning, for they had descended not far from that place. The young men knew they were their fathers. They met, and were happy. They related all that had befallen them. They did not conceal anything; and they expressed their gratitude to the different Manitoes who had preserved them, by feasting and gifts, and particularly to the sun and moon, who had received them as their children.

THE ENCHANTED MOCCASINS.

ODJIBWA.

THERE once lived a little boy, all alone with his sister, in a very wild uninhabitable country. They saw nothing but beasts, and birds, the sky above them, and the earth beneath them. But there were no human beings besides themselves. The boy often retired to think, in lone places, and the opinion was formed that he had supernatural powers. It was supposed that he would perform some extraordinary exploits, and he was called Onwe Bahmondoong, or he that carries a ball on his back. As he grew up he was impatient to know whether there were other beings near them: she replied, that there was, but they lived in a remote distance. There was a large village of hunters and warriors. Being now well grown, he determined to seek his fortune, and asked her to make him several pairs of moccasins to last him on the journey. With this request she complied. Then taking his bow and arrows, and his war-club, and a little sack containing his *nawappo*, or travelling victuals, he immediately set out on his journey. He travelled on, not knowing exactly where he went. Hills, plains, trees, rocks, forests, meadows, spread before him. Sometimes he killed an animal, sometimes a bird. The deer often started in his path. He saw the fox, the bear, and the ground-hog. The eagles screamed above him. The ducks chattered in the ponds and lakes. He lay down and slept when he was tired, he rose up when he was refreshed. At last he came to a small wigwam, and, on looking into it, discovered a very old woman sitting alone by the fire. As soon as she saw the stranger, she invited him in, and thus addressed him: "My poor grandchild, I suppose you are one of those who seek for the distant village, from which no person has ever yet returned. Unless your guardian is more powerful than the guardian of your predecessors, you too will share a similar fate of theirs. Be careful to provide yourself with the Ozhebah-guhnun—the bones they use in the medicine dance*—without

* The idea attached to the use of these bones in the medicine dance is, that, by their magical influence, the actor can penetrate and go through any substance.

which you cannot succeed." After she had thus spoken, she gave him the following directions for his journey. "When you come near to the village which you seek, you will see in the centre a large lodge, in which the chief of the village, who has two daughters, resides. Before the door you will see a great tree, which is smooth and destitute of bark. On this tree, about the height of a man from the ground, a small lodge is suspended, in which these two daughters dwell. It is here so many have been destroyed. Be wise, my grandchild, and abide strictly by my directions." The old woman then gave him the Ozhebahguhnun, which would cause his success. Placing them in his bosom, he continued his journey, till at length he arrived at the sought-for village; and, as he was gazing around him, he saw both the tree and the lodge which the old woman had mentioned. Immediately he bent his steps for the tree, and approaching, he endeavored to reach the suspended lodge. But all his efforts were vain; for as often as he attempted to reach it, the tree began to tremble, and soon shot up so that the lodge could hardly be perceived. Foiled as he was in all his attempts, he thought of his guardian and changed himself into a small squirrel, that he might more easily accomplish his design. He then mounted the tree in quest of the lodge. After climbing for some time, he became fatigued, and panted for breath; but, remembering the instructions which the old woman had given him, he took from his bosom one of the bones, and thrust it into the trunk of the tree, on which he sat. In this way he quickly found relief; and, as often as he became fatigued, he repeated this; but whenever he came near the lodge and attempted to touch it, the tree would shoot up as before, and place the lodge beyond his reach. At length, the bones being exhausted, he began to despair, for the earth had long since vanished from his sight. Summoning all resolution, he determined to make another effort to reach the object of his wishes. On he went; yet, as soon as he came near the lodge and attempted to touch it, the tree again shook, but it had reached the arch of heaven, and could go no higher; so now he entered the lodge, and beheld the two sisters sitting opposite each other. He asked their names. The one on his left hand called herself Azhabee,* and the one on the right Negahnah-

231

bee.* Whenever he addressed the one on his left hand, the tree would tremble as before, and settle down to its former position. But when he addressed the one on his right hand, it would again shoot upward as before. When he thus discovered that, by addressing the one on his left hand, the tree would descend, he continued to do so until it had resumed its former position; then seizing his war-club, he thus addressed the sisters: "You, who have caused the death of so many of my brothers, I will now put an end to, and thus have revenge for the numbers you have destroyed." As he said this he raised the club and laid them dead at his feet. He then descended, and learning that these sisters had a brother living with their father, who would pursue him for the deed he had done, he set off at random, not knowing whither he went. Soon after, the father and mother of the young women visited their residence and found their remains. They immediately told their son Mudjikewis that his sisters had been slain. He replied, "The person who has done this must be the Boy that carries the Ball on his Back. I will pursue him, and have revenge for the blood of my sisters." "It is well, my son," replied the father. "The spirit of your life grant you success. I counsel you to be wary in the pursuit. It is a strong spirit who has done this injury to us, and he will try to deceive you in every way. Above all, avoid tasting food till you succeed; for if you break your fast before you see his blood, your power will be destroyed." So saying, they parted.

His son instantly set out in search of the murderer, who, finding he was closely pursued by the brother of the slain, climbed up into one of the tallest trees and shot forth his magic arrows. Finding that his pursuer was not turned back by his arrows, he renewed his flight; and when he found himself hard pressed, and his enemy close behind him, he transformed himself into the skeleton of a moose that had been killed, whose flesh had come off from his bones. He then remembered the moccasins which his sister had given him, which were enchanted. Taking a pair of them, he placed them near the skeleton. "Go," said he to them, "to the end of the earth."

The moccasins then left him and their tracks remained. Mudjikewis at length came to the skeleton of the moose, when he perceived that the track he had long been pursuing did not end there, so he continued to follow it up, till he came to the end of the earth, where he found only a pair of moccasins. Mortified that he had been outwitted by following a pair of moccasins instead of the object of his revenge, he bitterly complained, resolving not to give up the pursuit, and to be more wary and wise in scrutinizing signs. He then called to mind the skeleton he met on his way, and concluded that *it* must be the object of his search. He retraced his steps towards the skeleton, but found, to his surprise, that it had disappeared, and that the tracks of *Onwe Bahmondoong*, or he who carries the Ball, were in another direction. He now became faint with hunger, and resolved to give up the pursuit; but when he remembered the blood of his sisters, he determined again to pursue.

The other, finding he was closely pursued, now changed himself into a very old man, with two daughters, who lived in a large lodge in the centre of a beautiful garden, which was filled with everything that could delight the eye or was pleasant to the taste. He made himself appear so very old as to be unable to leave his lodge, and had his daughters to bring him food and wait on him. The garden also had the appearanc of ancient occupancy, and was highly cultivated.

His pursuer continued on till he was nearly starved and ready to sink. He exclaimed, "Oh! I will forget the blood of my sisters, for I am starving;" but again he thought of the blood of his sisters, and again he resolved to pursue, and be satisfied with nothing but the attainment of his right to revenge.

He went on till he came to the beautiful garden. He approached the lodge. As soon as the daughters of the owner perceived him, they ran and told their father that a stranger approached the lodge. Their father replied, "Invite him in, my children, invite him in." They quickly did so; and by the command of their father, they boiled some corn and prepared other savory food. Mudjikewis had no suspicion of the deception. He was faint and weary with travel, and felt that he could endure fasting no longer. Without hesitancy, he partook heartily of the meal, and in so doing was overcome. All at once he seemed to forget the blood of his sisters, and even the village of his nativity. He ate so heartily as to produce drowsiness, and soon fell into a profound sleep. Onwe Bahmondoong watched his opportunity, and, as soon as he found his slumbers sound, resumed his youthful form. He then drew the magic ball from his back, which turned out to be a heavy war-club,

LEELINAU.

A CHIPPEWA TALE.

THE Pukwudjininees, or fairies of Lake Superior, had one of their most noted places of residence at the great sand dunes of *Naigow Wudjoo*, called by the French *La Grandes Sables*. Here they were frequently seen in bright moonlight evenings, and the fishermen while sitting in their canoes on the lake often saw them playing their pranks, and skipping over the hills. There was a grove of pines in that vicinity called the manito wac, or Spirit wood, into which they might be seen to flee, on the approach of evening, and there is a romantic little lake on those elevated sand-hills, not far back from the Great Lake, on the shores of which their tracks could be plainly seen in the sand. These tracks were not bigger than little children's footprints, and the spirits were often seen in the act of vanishing behind the little pine-trees. They love to dance in the most lonesome places, and were always full of glee and merriment, for their little voices could be plainly heard. These little men, the pukwudjininees, are not deeply malicious, but rather delighted in mischief and freaks, and would sometimes steal away a fisherman's paddle, or come at night and pluck the hunter's feathers out of his cap in the lodge, or pilfer away some of his game, or fish. On one occasion they went so far as to entice away into their sacred grove, and carry off a chief's daughter—a small but beautiful girl, who had been always inclined to be pensive, and took her seat often in these lonesome haunts. From her baby name of *Neenizu*, my dear life, she was called Leelinau, but she never attained to much size, remaining very slender, but of the most pleasing and sylph-like features, with very bright black eyes, and little feet. Her mother often cautioned her of the danger of visiting these lonely fairy haunts, and predicted, playfully, that she would one day be carried off by the Pukwudjees, for they were very frolicsome, mischievous and full of tricks.

To divert her mind from these recluse moods and tastes, she

235

endeavored to bring about an alliance with a neighboring forester, who, though older than herself, had the reputation of being an excellent hunter, and active man, and he had even creditably been on the war path, though he had never brought home a scalp. To these suggestions Leelinau had turned rather a deaf ear. She had imbibed ideas of a spiritual life and existence, which she fancied could only be enjoyed in the Indian elysium, and instructed as she was by the old story-tellers, she could not do otherwise than deem the light and sprightly little men who made the fairy footprints as emissaries from the *Happy Land.* For this happy land she sighed and pined. Blood, and the taking of life, she said, the Great Spirit did not approve, and it could never be agreeable to minds of pure and spiritual moulds. And she longed to go to a region where there was no weeping, no cares, and no deaths. If her parents laughed at these notions as childish, her only resource was silence, or she merely revealed here motions in her eyes. She was capable of the deepest concealment, and locked up in her heart what she feared to utter, or uttered to deceive. This proved her ruin.

At length, after a series of conversational interviews on the subject, she announced her willingness to accede to the matrimonial proposals, and the day was fixed for this purpose. She dressed herself in the finest manner possible, putting flowers in her hair, and carrying a bunch of wild flowers, mixed with tassels of the pine-tree in her hand. One only request she made, which was to make a farewell visit to the sacred grove of the fairies, before she visited the nuptial bower. This was granted, on the evening of the proposed ceremony, while the bridegroom and his friends gathered in her father's lodge, and impatiently waited her return. But they waited in vain. Night came but Leelinau was never more seen, except by a fisherman on the lake shore, who conceived that he had seen her go off with one of the tall fairies known as the fairy of Green Pines, with green plumes nodding o'er his brows; and it is supposed that she is still roving with him over the elysian fields.

WILD NOTES OF THE PIBBIGWUN.

CONTENTS

NOTES.

THE PIBBIGWUN.*

I OPE my voice, not with the organ's tone,
　　Deep, solemn and majestic; not with sounds
Of trump or drum, that cheer armed squadrons on,
　　In coats of steel, o'er lines of bloody grounds,
Nor is my tone, the tone of rushing storms.
　　That sweep in mad career through forests tall,
Up-tearing gnarled oaks, with sounds of hellish forms,
　　That bode destruction black, and death to all.
Nor is it yet the screaming warrior, loud,
　　With hand upraised to mouth, hyena-strong,
That tells of midnight onrush, hell-endowed,
　　And bleeding scalp of aged, mild and young.
Ah no! it is a note that's only blown,
　　Where kindness fills the heart, and every thrill
Is peace and love, while music's softer tone
　　Steals on the evening air, its simple aims to fill,
Waking the female ear to carols of the Pibbigwun.

THE CHIPPEWA GIRL.

THEY tell me, the men with a white-white face
Belong to a purer, nobler race;
But why, if they do, and it may be so,
Do their tongues cry, "Yes"—and their actions, "No?"

They tell me, that white is a heavenly hue,
And it may be so, but the sky is blue;
And the first of men—as our old men say,
Had earth-brown skins, and were made of clay.

* Indian flute

238

But throughout my life, I've heard it said,
There's nothing surpasses a tint of red;
Oh, the white man's cheeks look pale and sad,
Compared to my beautiful Indian lad.

Then let them talk of their race divine,
Their glittering domes, and sparkling wine;
Give me a lodge, like my fathers had,
And my tall, straight, beautiful Indian lad.

DOUBT.

NINIMOSHA,* think'st thou of me,
When beneath the forest tree?
Do'st thou in the passing wind,
Catch the sighs I've cast behind?
Ah! I fear—I fear—I fear,
Evil bird hath filled thine ear.

Ninimosha, in the clear blue sky,
Canst thou read my constancy,
Or in whispering branches near,
Aught from thy true lover hear?
Ah! I fear—I fear—I fear,
Evil bird hath filled thine ear.

* My sweetheart

FAIRY WHISPERINGS,

Supposed to be addressed to, and responded by a young pine-tree, in a state of transformation.

SPIRIT of the dancing leaves,
Hear a throbbing heart that grieves,
Not for joys this world can give,
But the life that spirits live:
Spirit of the foaming billow,
Visit thou my nightly pillow,
Shedding o'er it silver dreams,
Of the mountain brooks and streams,
Sunny glades, and golden hours,
Such as suit thy buoyant powers:
Spirit of the starry night,
Pencil out thy fleecy light,
That my footprints still my lead
To the blush-let Miscodeed,*
Or the flower to passion true
Yielding free its carmine hue:
Spirit of the morning dawn,
Waft thy fleecy columns on,
Snowy white, or tender blue,
Such as brave men love to view.
Spirit of the greenwood plume,
Shed around thy leaf perfume,
Such as springs from buds of gold
Which thy tiny hands unfold.
Spirits, hither quick repair,
Hear a maiden's evening prayer.

* Claytonia Virginica.

240

RESPONSE.

MAIDEN, think me not a tree,
But thine own dear lover free,
Tall and youthful in my bloom
With the bright green nodding plume.
Thou art leaning on my breast,
Lean forever there, and rest!
Fly from man, that bloody race,
Pards, assassins, bold and base;
Quit their dim, and false parade
For the quiet lonely shade.
Leave the windy birchen cot
For my own light happy lot;
O'er thee I my veil will fling,
Light as beetle's silken wing;
I will breathe perfume of flowers,
O'er thy happy evening hours;
I will in my shell canoe
Waft thee o'er the waters blue;
I will deck thy mantle fold,
With the sun's last rays of gold.
Come, and on the mountain free
Rove a fairy bright with me.

SONG OF THE OPECHEE, THE ROBIN.

The Chippewas relate that the robin originated from a youth
who was subjected to too severe a task of fasting.

IN the boundless woods there are berries of red,
  And fruits of a beautiful blue,
Where, by nature's own hand, the sweet singers are fed,
  And to nature they ever are true.

We go not with arrow and bow to the field,
  Like men of the fierce ruddy race,
To take away lives which they never can give,
  And revel the lords of the chase.

241

If danger approaches, with instant alarm
   We fly to our own leafy woods,
And there, with an innocent carol and charm,
   We sing to our dear little broods.

At morning we sally in quest of the grain
   Kind nature in plenty supplies,
We skip o'er the beautiful wide-stretching plain,
   And sport in the vault of the skies.

At evening we perch in some neighboring tree
   To carol our evening adieu,
And feel, although man assert he is free,
   We only have liberty true.

We sing out our praises to God and to man,
   We live as heaven taught us to live,
And I would not change back to mortality's plan
   For all that the mortal can give.

Here ceased the sweet singer; then pluming his breast,
   He winged the blue firmament free,
Repeating, as homeward he flew to his rest,
   Tshee-ree-lee—Tshee-ree-lee—Tshee-ree-lee!

EVENING CHANT OF INDIAN CHILDREN TO THE WATASEE, THE FIRE-FLY.

FIRE-FLY, fire-fly! bright little thing,
Light me to bed, and my song I will sing.
Give me your light, as you fly o'er my head,
That I may merrily go to my bed.
Give me your light o'er the grass as you creep,
That I may joyfully go to my sleep.
Come, little fire-fly—come, little beast—
Come! and I'll make you to-morrow a feast.
Come, little candle that flies as I sing,
Bright little fairy-bug—night's little king;
Come, and I'll dance as you guide me along,
Come, and I'll pay you, my bug, with a song.

SONG OF A FAIRY CHIEF.

Addressed to the winds on transferring his sister to a position as one of the planets in the morning sky.

BLOW, winds, blow, my sister lingers
From her dwelling in the sky,
Where the moon with rosy fingers
Shall her cheeks with vermil dye.

There my earliest views directed,
Shall from her their brilliance take
And her smiles through clouds reflected,
Guide me on, by wood and lake.

While I range the highest mountains,
Sport in valleys, green and low,
Or beside our Indian fountains,
Raise my tiny hip hallo.

SONG OF A CAPTIVE CREEK GIRL,

Who was an exile in a distant northern tribe, confined on an island in Lake Superior.

To sunny vales, to balmy skies,
My thoughts, a flowery arrow, flies;
I see the wood, the bank, the glade,
Where first, a wild wood girl, I played.
I think on scenes and faces dear;
They are not here—they are not here.

In this cold sky, in this lone isle,
I meet no friends, no mother's smile.
I list the wind, I list the wave;
They seem like requiems round the grave,
And all my heart's young joys are gone;
It is alone—it is alone.

FEMALE SONG.

MY love is a hunter—he hunts the fleet deer,
With fusil or arrow, one-half of the year;
He hunts the fleet deer over mountain and lea,
But his heart is still hunting for love and for me.

My love is a warrior; when warriors go,
With fusil or arrow, to strike the bold foe,
He treads the bright war-path with step bold and free,
But still his thoughts wander to love and to me.

But hunter or warrior, where'er he may go,
To track the swift deer, or to follow the foe,
His heart's warm desire, field and forest still flee,
To go hunting his love, and make captive of me.

MALE SONG.

MY love, she gave to me a belt, a belt of texture fine,
Of snowy hue, emboss'd with blue and scarlet porcupine;
This tender braid sustain'd the blade I drew against the foe,
And ever prest upon my breast, to mark its ardent glow.
And if with art I act my part, and bravely fighting stand,
I, in the din, a trophy win, that gains Nimosha's hand.

My love, she is a handsome girl, she has a sparkling eye,
And a head of flowing raven hair, and a forehead arched and
   high;
Her teeth are white as cowry shells, brought from the distant
   sea,
And she is tall, and graceful all, and fair as fair can be.
And if with art I act my part, and bravely wooing stand,
And with address my suit I press, I gain Nimosha's hand.

Oh, I will search the silver brooks for skin of blackest dye,
And scale the highest mountain-tops, a warrior's gift to spy!
I'll place them where my love shall see, and know my present
   true;

Perhaps when she admires the gift, she'll love the giver, too.
And if with art I act my part, and bravely wooing stand,
I'll gain my love's unsullied heart, and then I'll gain her
    hand.

THE LOVE OF THE FOREST.

To rove with the wild bird, and go where we will,
Oh, this is the charm of the forest-life still!
With our houses of bark, and our food on the plain,
We are off like an eagle, and back there again.

No farms can detain us, no chattels prevent;
We live not by ploughing—we thrive not by rent;
Our herds rove the forest, our flocks swim the floods,
And we skim the broad waters, and trip through the woods.

With ships not of oak wood, nor pitchy, nor strong,
We sail along rivers, and sail with a song;
We care not for taxes—our laws are but few;
The dart is our sickle, our ship the canoe.

If enemies press us, and evil fear stray,
We seize on our war-clubs, and drive them away,
And when there is nothing to fear or withstand,
We lift the proud rattle, and dance on the land.

In feasting and dancing, our moments are gay;
We trust in the God who made heaven and day;
We read no big volumes, no science implore,
But ask of our wise men to teach us their lore.

The woods are our pastures; we eat what we find,
And rush through the lands like a rattling wind.
Heaven gave us the country; we cling to the west,
And, dying, we fly to the Lands of the Blest!

LIGHT OF CHRISTIANITY IN THE
WIGWAM.

OH why, ye subtle spirits, why
Lift I my eyes to yonder floating sky,
Where clouds paint pictures with so clear a hue?
A heaven so beautiful it must be true.

For if I but to earth withdraw my eyes,
    And fix them on the creature man
To scan his acts, the dear, fond picture dies,
    And worse he seems in thought, and air, and plan
Than the hyena, beast that only digs
For food, and not rejoices in the dart,
That stopped the warm blood current of the heart.

Had men but had just what the earth can give,
    It would be misery, and lies, and blood,
Pinching and hunger, so that he who lives
    But lives, as some poor outcast drowning in a flood.
And then—ah, tell me!—whither goes the soul?

Oh why, ye spirits blest, oh why
Is truth so darkened to the human eye?
As if a sombre cloud all heaven made black,
And the sun shone but through a chink or crack,
Within a wall, where light is but the accident of things,
And not the purport. Truth may be then as the white men
    write,
And all our tribes in a darkness set, instead of light.

NOCTURNAL GRAVE LIGHTS.

It is supposed to be four days' journey to the land of the
dead; wherefore, during four nights, the Chippewas kindle
a fire on the grave.

LIGHT up a fire upon my grave
　　　　When I am dead.
'Twill softly shed its beaming rays,
To guide the soul its darkling ways;
And ever, as the day's full light
Goes down and leaves the world in night,
These kindly gleams, with warmth possest,
Shall show my spirit where to rest
　　　　When I am dead.

Four days the funeral rite renew,
　　　　When I am dead.
While onward bent, with typic woes,
I seek the red man's last repose;
Let no rude hand the flame destroy,
Nor mar the scene with festive joy;
While night by night, a ghostly guest,
I journey to my final rest,
　　　　When I am dead.

No moral light directs my way
　　　　When I am dead.
A hunter's fate, a warrior's fame,
A shade, a phantom, or a name,
All life-long through my hands have sought,
Unblest, unlettered, and untaught:
Deny me not the boon I crave—
A symbol-light upon my grave,
　　　　When I am dead.

MANITO.

"Every exhibition of elementary power, in earth or sky, is deemed, by the Indians, as a symbolic type of a deity."—
Hist. Inds.

IN the frowning cliff, that high
Glooms above the passing eye,
Casting spectral shadows tall
Over lower rock and wall;
In its morn and sunset glow,
I behold a Manito.

247

By the lake or river lone,
In the humble fretted stone,
Water-sculptured, and, by chance,
Cast along the wave's expanse;
In its morn and sunset glow,
I behold a Manito.

In whatever's dark or new,
And my senses cannot view,
Complex work, appearance strange,
Arts' advance, or nature's change—
Fearful e'er of hurt or woe,
I behold a Manito.

In the motions of the sky,
Where the angry lightnings fly,
And the thunder, dread and dire,
Lifts his mighty voice in fire—
Awed with fear of sudden woe,
I behold a Manito.

Here my humble voice I lift,
Here I lay my sacred gift,
And, with heart of fear and awe,
Raise my loud *Wau-la-le-au.*

Spirit of the fields above,
Thee I fear, and Thee I love,
Whether joy betide or woe,
Thou, thou art my Manito.

NIAGARA, AN ALLEGORY.

AN old gray man on a mountain lived,
  He had daughters four and one,
And a tall bright lodge of the betula bark
  That glittered in the sun.

He lived on the very highest top,
  For he was a hunter free,
Where he could spy, on the clearest day,
  Gleams of the distant sea.

248

"Come out! come out!" cried the youngest one;
    "Let us off to look at the sea!"
And out they ran, in their gayest robes,
    And skipped and ran with glee.

"Come, Su;* come, Mi;† come, Hu;‡ come, Cla;"§
    Cried laughing little Er;£
"Let us go to yonder deep blue sea,
    Where the breakers foam and roar."

And on they scampered by valley and wood,
    By earth and air and sky,
Till they came to a steep where the bare rocks stood,
    In a precipice mountain high.

"Inya!"★ cried Er, "here's a dreadful leap!
    But we are gone so far,
That, if we flinch and return in fear,
    Nos** he will cry, 'Ha! ha!' "

Now, each was clad in a vesture light,
    That floated far behind,
With sandals of frozen water drops,
    And wings of painted wind.

And down they plunged with a merry skip,
    Like birds that skim the plain;
And "Hey!" they cried, "let us up and try,
    And down the steep again!"

And up and down the daughters skipped,
    Like girls on a holiday,
And laughed outright at the sport and foam
    They called Niagara.

If ye would see a sight so rare,
    Where Nature's in her glee,
Go, view the spot in the wide wild West,
    The land of the brave and free!

* Superior.   † Michigan.   ‡ Huron.
§ St. Clair.   £ Erie.
★ An exclamation of wonder and surprise.—*Odj. lan.*
** My father.—*Ib.*

But mark—their shapes are only seen
    In Fancy's deepest play;
But she plainly shows their wings and feet
    In the dancing sunny spray.

CHILEELI.

The Chippewas relate that the spirit of a young lover, who
was killed in battle, determined to return to his affianced
maid, in the shape of a bird, and console her by his songs.
He found her in a chosen retreat, where she daily resorted to
pass her pensive hours.

STAY not here—the men are base,
I have found a happier place,
Where no war, or want severe,
Haunts the mind with thoughts of fear;
Men are cruel—bloody—cold,
Seeking like lynx the rabbit's wold,
Not to guard from winds or drought,
But to suck its life's blood out
Stay not here—oh, stay not here,
'Tis a world of want and fear.

I have found those happy plains,
Where the blissful Spirit reigns,
Such, as by our wise men old,
All our fathers have foretold.
Streams of sparkling waters flow,
Pure and clear, with silver glow;
Woods and shady groves abound,
Long sweet lawns and painted ground;
Lakes, in winding shores extend,
Fruits, with flowers, inviting blend;
While, throughout the green-wood groves,
Gayest birds sing out their loves.
Stay not here, my trustful maid,
'Tis a world for robbers made.

I will lead you, soul of love,
To those flowery haunts above,
Where no tears or pain are found—
Where no war-cry shakes the ground;
Where no mother hangs her head,
Crying: "Oh, my child is dead!"
Where no human blood is spilt,
Where there is no pain, or guilt;
But the new-freed spirit roves
Round and round, in paths of loves.
Pauguk's* not admitted there,
Blue the skies, and sweet the air;
There are no diseases there;
There no famished eyeball rolls,
Sickness cannot harm the souls;
Hunger is not there a guest,
Souls are not with hunger press'd,
All are happy, all are blest.
Rife the joys our fathers sought,
Sweet to eye and ear and thought,
Stay not here, my weeping maid,
'Tis a world in glooms arrayed.

Wishes there, all wants supply,
Wants of hand, and heart, and eye;
Labor is not known—that thorn
Pricks not there, at night or morn,
As it goads frail mortals here,
With its pain, and toil, and fear;
Shadows typical and fair,
Fill the woods, the fields, the air,
Stately deer, the forests fill,
Just to have them is to will;
Birds walk kindly from the lakes,
And whoever wants them, takes;
There no drop of blood is drawn,
Darts are for an earthy lawn.
Hunters, warriors, chiefs, are there,
Plumed and radiant, bright and fair;
But they are the ghosts of men,
And ne'er mix in wars again;

* Death.

251

They no longer rove with ire,
Wood or wold, or sit by fire;
Council called—how best to tear,
From the gray-head crown its hair,
Dripping with its vital blood,
Horror—echoed in the wood.
Stay not here—where horrors dwell,
Earth is but a name for hell.

Oh, the Indian paradise is sweet,
Naught but smiles the gazers meet;
All is fair—the sage's breast,
Swells with joy to hail each guest—
Comes he, from these sounding shores,
Or the North God's icy stores,
Where the shivering children cry,
In their snow-cots and bleak sky;
Or the far receding south,
Burned with heat, and palsied drought,
All are welcome—all receive,
Gifts great Chibiabos gives.
Stay not, maiden—weep no more,
I have found the happy shore.

Come with me, and we will rove,
O'er the endless plains of love,
Full of flowers, gems, and gold,
Where there is no heart that's cold,
Where there is no tear to dry
In a single human eye.
Stay not here; cold world like this,
Death but opes the door to bliss.

ON THE STATE OF THE IROQUOIS, OR SIX NATIONS.

In 1845, the Legislature of New York directed a census of
these cantons, which evinced an advanced state of industry.

THE lordly Iroquois is tending sheep,
  Gone are the plumes that decked his brow,
For his bold raid, no more the wife shall weep—
    He holds the plough.

The bow and quiver which his fathers made;
  The gun, that filled the warrior's deadliest vow;
The mace, the spear, the axe, the ambuscade—
    Where are they now?

Mute are the hills that woke his dreadful yell—
  Scared nations listen with affright no more;
He walks a farmer over field and dell
    Once red with gore.

Frontlet and wampum, baldric, brand, and knife,
  Skill of the megalonyx, snake and fox,
All now are gone!—transformed to peaceful life—
    He drives the ox.

Algon, and Cherokee, and Illinese,
  No more beneath his stalwort blow shall writhe:
Peace spreads her reign wide o'er his inland seas—
    He swings the scythe.

Grain now, not men, employs his manly powers;
  To learn the white man's arts, and skill to rule,
For this, his sons and daughters spend their hours—
    They go to school.

Glory and fame, that erewhile fired his soul,
  And nerved for war his ever vengeful arm,
Where are your charms his bosom to control?—
    He tills a farm.

His war-scar'd visage, paints no more deform—
  His garments, made of beaver, deer, and rat,
Are now exchanged for woollen doublets warm—
    He wears a hat.

His very pipe, surcharged with sacred weed,
  Once smoked to spirits dreamy, dread and sore,
Is laid aside—to think, to plan, to read—
    He keeps a store.

This is the law of progress—kindlier arts
  Have shaped his native energies of mind,
And back he comes—from wandering, woods and darts
    Back to mankind.

His drum and rattles, both are thrown away—
His native altars stand without a blàze,—
Truth, robed in gospel light, hath found her way—
And hark! he prays!

THE LOON'S FOOT.

I THOUGHT it was the loon's foot, I saw beneath the tide,
But no—it was my lover's shining paddle I espied;
It was my lover's paddle, as my glance I upward cast,
That dipped so light and gracefully as o'er the lake I passed.
 The loon's foot—the loon's foot,
  'Tis graceful on the sea;
 But not so light and joyous as
  That paddle blade to me.

My eyes were bent upon the wave, I cast them not aside,
And thought I saw the loon's foot beneath the silver tide.
But ah! my eyes deceived me—for as my glance I cast,
It was my lover's paddle blade that dipped so light and fast.
 The loon's foot—the loon's foot,
  'Tis sweet and fair to see,
 But oh, my lover's paddle blade,
  Is sweeter far to me.

The lake's wave—the long wave—the billow big and free,
It wafts me up and down, within my yellow light canoe;
But while I see beneath heaven pictured as I speed,
It is that beauteous paddle blade, that makes it heaven in-
 deed.
 The loon's foot—the loon's foot,
  The bird upon the sea,
 Ah! it is not so beauteous
  As that paddle blade to me.

TULCO, PRINCE OF NOTTO.

Tulco, a Cherokee chief, is said to have visited, in 1838, the rotunda, or excavations, under the great mound of Grave Creek, while the Indian antiquities were collected there, and the skeleton found in the lower vault was suspended to the wall, and the exudations of animal matter depended from the roof.

'Tis not enough that hated race
Should hunt us out from grove and place,
And consecrated shores, where long
Our fathers raised the lance and song—
'Tis not enough that we must go
Where unknown streams and fountains flow,
Whose murmurs heard amid our fears,
Fall only now on foeman's ears—
'Tis not enough, that with a wand
They sweep away our pleasant land,
And bid us, as some giant foe,
Or willing or unwilling go;
But they must ope our very graves,
To tell the dead they too are slaves!
And hang their bones upon the wall,
To please their gaze and gust of thrall;
As if a dead dog from below
Were made a jesting-stock and show!

See, from above! the restless dead
Peer out, with exudation dread—
That hangs in robes of clammy white,
Like clouds upon the inky night;
Their very ghosts are in this place,
I see them pass before my face;
With frowning brows they whirl around
Within this consecrated mound!
Away—away, vile caitiff race,
And give the dead their resting-place.
They point—they cry—they bid me smite
The Wa-bish-kiz-zee* in their sight!

* White men.

Did Europe come to crush us dead,
Because on flying deer we fed,
And worshipped gods of airy forms,
Who ride in thunder-clouds, the storms?
Because we use not plough or loom,
Is ours a black and bitter doom
That has no light—no world of bliss?—
Then is our hell commenced in this.
       *   *   *   *
Nay, it is well—but tell me not
The white race now possess the spot,
That fury marks my brow, and all
I see is but my fancy's pall
That glooms my eyes—ah, white man, no!
The woe we taste is solid woe.
Comes then the thought of better things,
When we were men, and we were kings.
Men are we now, and still there rolls
A monarch's blood in all our souls!
A warrior's fire is in our hearts,
Our hands are strong in feathery darts;
And let us die as they have died
Who are the Indian's boast and pride!
Nor creep to graves, in flying west,
Unplumed, dishonored, and unblest!

ON PRESENTING A WILD ROSE

PLUCKED ON THE SOURCES OF THE MISSISSIPPI.

TAKE thou the rose, though blighted,
    Its sweetness is not gone,
And like the heart, though slighted,
    In memory it blooms on.

Thy hand its leaves may nourish,
    Thy smiles its bloom restore;
So warmed its buds may flourish,
    And bloom to life once more.

Yet if they bloom not ever,
    These thoughts may life impart
To hopes I ne'er could sever
    One moment from my heart.

Oh, then, receive my token,
    From far-off northern sky,
That speech, once kindly spoken,
    Can never—never die.

THE RED MAN.

I STOOD upon an eminence, that wide
O'erlooked a length of land, where spread
The sounding shores of Lake Superior;
And at my side there lay a vale
Replete with little glens, where oft
The Indian wigwam rose, and little fields
Of waving corn displayed their tasselled heads.
A stream ran through the vale, and on its marge
There grew wild rice, and bending alders dipped
Into the tide, and on the rising heights
The ever-verdant pine laughed in the breeze.

I turned around, to gaze upon the scenes
More perfectly, and there beheld a man
Tall and erect, with feathers on his head,
And air and step majestic; in his hands
Held he a bow and arrows, and he would have passed,
Intent on other scene, but that I spake to him:
"Pray, whither comest thou? and whither goest?"
"My coming," he replied, "is from the Master of life,
The Lord of all things, and I go at his commands."
"Then why," I further parleyed, "since thou art
So much the friend of Him, whom white men seek
By prayer and rite so fervently to obey—why, tell,
Art thou so oft in want of e'en a meal
To satisfy the cravings of a man? Why cast abroad
To live in wilds, where oft the scantiest shapes
Of foot and wing must fill thy board, while pallid hunger
    Strays

With hideous shouts, by mountain, vale, and stream?"

"The Great Spirit," he replied, "hath not alike
Made all men; or, if once alike, the force of climes,
And wants and wanderings have estranged them quite.
To me, and to my kind, forest, and lake, and wood,
The rising mountain, and the drawn-out stream
That sweeps, meandering, through wild ranges vast,
Possess a charm no marble halls can give.
We rove, as winds escaped the Master's fists—
Now, sweeping over beds of prairie flowers—
Now, dallying on the tops of leafy trees,
Or murmuring in the corn-fields, and, when tired
With roving, we lie down on beds where springs
The simple wild flower, and some shreds of bark,
Plucked from the white, white birch, defends our heads,
And hides us from the blue ethereal skies,
Where, in his sovereign majesty, this Spirit rules;
Now, casting lightning from his glowing eyes—
Now, uttering thunder with his mighty voice.

"To you, engendered in another clime
Of which our fathers knew not, he hath given
Arts, arms, and skill we know not, or if ever knew,
Have quite forgot. Your hands are thickened up
With toils of field and shop, where whirring wheels resound,
And hammers clink. The anvil and the plough
Belong to you; the very ox construes your speech,
And turns him to obey you. All this toil
We deem a slavery too heavy to be borne,
And which our tribes revolt at. Oft we stand
To view the reeking smith, who pounds his iron
With blow on blow, to fit it for the beast
That drags your ploughshares through the rooty soil.
The very streams—bright ribbons of the woods!—are yoked,
And made to turn your mills, and grind your corn;
And yet this progress stays not in its toils
To alter nature and pervert her plans.
Steam drags your vessels now, that once
Leapt in their beauty by the winds of heaven.
Some subtle principle ye find in fire,
And with a cunning art fit rattling cars
To run on strips of iron, with scream and clang

258

That seem symbolic of an angry power
Which dwells below, and is infernal called.
The war-crowned lightning skips from pole to pole
On strings of iron, to haste with quick intelligence.

"Once, nature could be hid, and fondly think
She had some jewels in the earth, but now ye dig
Into her very bowels, to recover morsels sweet
She erst with deglutition had drawn in. The rocks
Your toils dissolve, to find perchance some treasure
Lying there. Is yonder land of gold alone
Your care? Observe along these shores
The wheezing engine clank—the stamper ring.
Once, hawks and eagles here pursued their prey,
But now the white man ravens more than they.
No! give me but my water and God's meats,
And take your cares, your riches, and your thrones.
What the Great Spirit gives, I take with joy,
And scorn those gains which nothing can content.

"Drudge ye, and grind ye, white man! make your pence,
And store your purses with the shining poison.
It was not Manito who made this trash
To curse the human race, but Vatipa the black,
Who rules below—he changed the blood of innocence
And tears of pity into gold, and strewed it wide
O'er lands where still the murderer digs
And the deceptious delve, to find the cockle out
And pick it up, but laughs the while to see
What fools they are, and how himself has foiled
The Spirit of Good, that made mankind
Erst friends and brothers. Scanty is my food,
But that sweet bird, chileelee, blue of wing,
Sings songs of peace within the wild-wood dell
And round the enchanted shores of these blue seas—
Not long, perhaps, our own—which tell me of a rest
In far-off lands—the islands of the blest!"

THE SKELETON WRAPPED IN GOLD.

In digging, in 1854, a railroad in Chili, seventy feet below the surface, in a sandy plain, which had been an ancient graveyard, an Indian skeleton, wrapped in a sheet of solid gold, rolled into the excavation. Its appearance denoted an ancient Inca, of the Atacama period.

THE Indian laid in his shroud of gold,
　　Where his friends had kindly bound him;
For, in their raid so strong and bold,
　　The Spaniards had never found him.

Kind guardian spirits had watched him there,
　　From ages long—long faded,
Embalmed with gems and spices rare,
　　And in folds of sweet grass braided.

And priestly rites were duly done,
　　And hymns upraised to bless him,
And that gold mantle of the sun,
　　Put on, as a monarch to dress him.

"Sleep on," they said, in whispers low,
　　"Nor fear the white man's coming,
For we have put no *glyph* to show,
　　The spot of thy entombing.

"Inca, thy warfare here is done,
　　Each bitter scene or tender,
Go to thy sire, the shining Sun,
　　In kingly garb and splendor.

"Earth hath no honors thou hast not,
　　Brave, wise, in every station,
Or battle, temple, council, cot,
　　Beloved of all thy nation.

"Take thou this wand of magic might,
　　With signet-jewels glowing,
As heralds to the God of Light,
　　Where, father, thou art going.

"A thousand years the charm shall last,
  The charm of thy ensealment,
Till there shall come a spirit vast,
  To trouble thy concealment."

And safe he slept in Tlalcol's* train,
  With all his genii by him,
Through Atacama's pleasing reign,
  Ere Manco came a-nigh him.

That golden reign spread arts anew,
  O'er all his Andes mountains,
And temples that his sires ne'er knew,
  Arose beside their fountains.

Pizarro's bloody day flew past,
  Nor shook his place of sleeping,
Though, as with earthquakes, deep and vast,
  The land with ruins heaping.

Nor had the cherished ruler more,
  Broke the deep trance from under,
But that a stronger, sterner power,
  Arose the charm to sunder.

No gentle genii more could wield,
  The wand of his dominion;
No power of Indian guardian yield,
  Or wave her golden pinion.

It was the spirit of *progress* fell,
  And trade, and gain united,
Who swore an oath, and kept it well,
  That Tlalcol's blessing blighted.

Deep dug they down in Chili's hills,
  Deep—deeper laid their levels,
To drive those cars, whose screaming fills
  The ear, with sounds like devils.

* Tlalcol, the keeper of the dead, corresponds to the Chebiabo of the
Algonquins.

And as they dug, they sang and dug,
  As digging for a treasure,
That should, like dire Arabic drug,
  Rise, with unmeasured measure.

Old Indian arts, and Indian spells,
  And all their subtle seeming,
Passed quick away—as truth expels,
  The palsied power in dreaming.

Down rolled the cherished Indian corse,
  The sands no more could hold him,
Nor rite—nor genii—art or force,
  Nor golden shroud enfold him.

WAUB OJEEG'S DEATH WHISPERINGS.

I GO to the land where our heroes are gone, are gone,
That land where our sages are gone;
And I go with bright tone, to join hearts who are one,
That drew the bold dart at my side, at my side,
That drew the bold dart at my side.

Those lands in the bright beamy west, the west,
Those lands in the bright beamy west,
As our fathers foretold, are the plenty crowned fold,
Where the world-weary warrior may rest, may rest,
Where the war-honored hero may rest.

My life has been given to war, to war,
My strength has been offered to war,
And the foes of my land, ne'er before me could stand,
But fled as base cowards in fear, in fear,
They fled like base cowards in fear.

My warfare in life it is done, it is done,
My warfare, my friends, it is done;
I go to that Spirit, whose form in the sky,
So oft we have seen in the cloud-garnished sun,
So oft in dread lightning espy.

My friends, when my spirit is fled, is fled,
My friends, when my spirit is fled,
Ah, put me not bound, in the dark and cold ground,
Where light shall no longer be shed, be shed,
Where daylight no more shall be shed.

But lay me up scaffolded high, all high,
Chiefs, lay me up scaffolded high,
Where my tribe shall still say, as they point to my clay,
He ne'er from the foe sought to fly, to fly,
He ne'er from the foe sought to fly.

And chilren, who play on the shore, the shore,
And children who play on the shore,
As the war-dance they beat, my name shall repeat,
And the fate of their chieftain deplore, deplore,
And the fate of their chieftain deplore.

TO THE MISCODEED.*

THY petals, tipped with red, declare
The sanguinary rites of war;
But when I view thy base of white,
Thoughts of heaven's purity invite.
Symbols at once that hearts like thee
Contain *two* powers, in which we see
A passion strong to war inclined,
And a soft, pure, and tender mind.

Earliest of buds when snows decay
From these wild northern fields away,
Thou comest as a herald dear,
To tell us that the spring is near;
And shall with sweets and flowers relume
Our hearts, for all the winter's gloom.
Soon the opeecheet† comes to sing
The pleasures of an early spring;
Soon shall the swelling water's roar
Tell us that winter is no more;
The water-fowl set up their cry,

* Spring beauty, C. Virg.   † Robin.

263

Or hasten to more northern sky;
And on the sandy shore shall stray,
The plover, the *twee-tweesh-ke-way.*
Soon shall the budding trees expand,
And genial skies pervade the land;
The little garden hoes shall peck,
And female hands the moss beds deck;
The apple-tree refresh our sight,
With its fair blows of pink and white;
The cherry bloom, the strawberry run,
And joy fill all the new Seegwun.‡

THE STAR FAMILY.

WAUPEE found a deep-trod circle
    In the boundless prairie wide;
In the grassy sea of prairies,
    Without trace of path beside.

To or fro, there was no token
    Man had ever trod the plain;
And he gazed upon the wonder,
    Gazed the wonder to explain.

I will watch the place, quoth Waupee,
    And conceal myself awhile;
This strange mystery to unravel,
    This new thing to reconcile.

Tracks I know of deer and bison,
    Tracks of panther, lynx, or hind,
Beasts and birds of every nature,
    But this beaten ring is blind.

Do the spirits here assemble,
    War-dance light to trip and sing?
Gather Medas of the prairie,
    Here their magic charm to fling?

‡ Spring.

264

Waupee crept beneath the bushes,
  Near the wondrous magic ring;
Close beneath the shrubs and grasses,
  To behold so rare a thing.

Soon he heard, high in the heavens,
  Issuing from the feathery clouds—
Sounds of music, quick descending,
  As if angels came in crowds.

Louder, sweeter, was the music,
  Every moment that he stayed;
Till a basket, with twelve sisters,
  Was with all its charms displayed.

Down they came, in air suspended,
  As if by thin silver cords;
And within the circle landed,
  Gay and bright as beauteous birds.

Out they leaped with nimble gestures,
  Dancing softly round and round;
Each a ball of silver chiming,
  With the most enchanting sound.

Beauteous were they all—but one so
  More than all the other eleven,
Youngest she, he sighed to clasp her
  To his ardent, glowing breast.

Up he rose from his concealment,
  From his flower-encircled bed;
But, as quick-eyed birds, they spied him,
  Stepped into the car and fled.

Fled into the starry heavens,
  While with open ear he stood,
Drinking the receding music,
  As it left his solitude.

Now, indeed, was he a stranger,
  And a fugitive alone;
For the peace that once he cherished,
  With the heavenly car had flown.

Touched his heart was by love's fervors,
    He no longer wished to rove;
Lost the charm of war and hunting,
    Waupee was transfixed by love.

Ah! 'tis love that wins the savage
    From his wanderings, and can teach,
Where the truth could never touch him,
    Where the gospel could not reach.

Long he mourned—and lingering, waited
    Round the charmed celestial ring;
Day by day he lingered, hoping
    Once to hear those angels sing.

To deceive, the quick eyes glancing,
    An opossum's form he tries;
And crouched low, beside the circle,
    Stooped, that he might win the prize.

Soon the sounds he heard descending,
    Soon they leaped within the ring;
Joining hand in hand in dancing,
Joining hand in hand in dancing,
    Round and round—sweet revelling.

Up he rose, quick disenchanted,
    Rose and clasped his female star,
While, as lightning, quick the eleven
    Leaped, and rose within their car.

Home he took her to his wigwam,
    Sought each varied way to please;
Gave her flowers and rarest presents,
    All to yield her joy and ease.

And a beauteous son rewarded
    Love so constant, true, and mild;
Who renewed in every feature,
    Nature's lonely forest child.

But, as thoughts of youth will linger
　　Long within the heart's fond core;
So she nursed the pleasing passion,
　　Her star-home to see once more—

Made an ark of wicker branches,
　　All by secret arts and care;
Sought the circle with her earth-boy,
　　Fleeing to her Father star.

There, at length, the boy grew weary,
　　Weary e'en of heavenly spheres,
Longing for earth's cares and pleasures,
　　Hunting, feasting, joys, and tears.

"Call thy husband," quoth the star chief,
　　"Take the magic car and go;
But bring with thee some fit emblems,
　　Of the sounding chase below.

"Claw, or wing, or toe, or feathers,
　　Scalp of bird or beast to tell;
What he follows in the wood-chase,
　　Arts the hunter knows so well."

Waupee searched the deepest forests,
　　Prairies vast, or valleys low;
All to find out the rarest species,
　　That he might the star-world show.

Then he sought the ring of magic,
　　With his forest stores so rare;
And within the starry basket,
　　Rose with all his emblems fair.

Joys of greeting—joys of seeing—
　　Hand to hand, and eye to eye;
These o'ercrowned with smiles and laughing,
　　This lodge-meeting in the sky.

Then a glorious feast was ordered,
　　To receive the forest guest;
While the sweet reunion lighted,
　　Joy in every beating breast.

Broad the feasting board was covered,
  The high starry group to bind;
When the star chief rose to utter
  His congratulations kind.

"List, my guests—the Spirit wills it,
  Earth to earth, and sky to sky;
Choose ye each a claw or pinion,
  Such as ye may wish to try."

Wondrous change! by arts' transformance,
  At the typic heavenly feast;
Each who chose a wing a bird was,
  Each who chose a claw, a beast.

Off they ran on plains of silver,
  Squirrel, rabbit, elk, or deer;
White Hawk chose a wing, descending
  Down again to forests here,

Where the Waupees are still noted
  For their high essays of wing;
And their noble deeds of bravery,
  In the forest, mount, and ring.

SONG OF THE WOLF-BROTHER.

Nesia, my elder brother,
  Bones have been my forest meal,
Shared with wolves the long, long winter,
  And their nature now I feel.

Nesia, my elder brother,
  Now my fate is near its close;
Soon my state shall cease to press me,
  Soon shall cease my day of woes.

Left by friends I loved the dearest,
  All who knew and loved me most;
Woes the darkest and severest,
  Bide me on this barren coast.

Pity! ah, that manly feeling,
    Fled from hearts where once it grew,
Now in wolfish forms revealing,
    Glows more warmly than in you.

Stony hearts! that saw me languish,
    Deaf to all a father said,
Deaf to all a mother's anguish,
    All a brother's feelings fled.

Ah, ye wolves, in all your ranging,
    I have found you kind and true;
More than man—and now I'm changing,
    And will soon be one of you.

Lodge of kindred once respected,
    Now my heart abhors your plan;
Hated, shunned, disowned, neglected,
    Wolves are truer far than man.

And like them, I'll be a rover,
    With an honesty of bite
That feigns not to be a lover,
    When the heart o'erflows with spite.

Go, ye traitors, to my lodge-fire;
    Go, ye serpents, swift to flee,
War with kinds that have your natures,
    I am disenthrall'd and free.

ABBINOCHI.

A MOTHER'S CHANT TO HER SICK INFANT.

Abbinochi,* baby dear,
Leave me not—ah, leave me not;
I have nursed with love sincere,
Nursed thee in my forest cot—
Tied thee in thy cradle trim

* A child.

269

Kind adjusting every limb;
With the fairest beads and bands
Deck'd thy cradle with my hands,
And with sweetest corn panad
From my little kettle fed,
Oft with miscodeed† roots shred,
Fed thee in thy baby bed.

Abbinochi, droop not so,
Leave me not—away to go
To strange lands—they little feet
Are not grown the path to greet
Or find out, with none to show
Where the flowers of grave-land grow.
Stay, my dear one, stay till grown,
I will lead thee to that zone
Where the stars like silver shine,
And the scenes are all divine,
And the happy, happy stray,
And, like Abbinochi, play.

TO PAUGUK.

(This is the impersonation of death in Indian mythology.
He is represented with a bow and arrows.)

Pauguk! 'tis a scene of woe,
This world of troubles; let me go
Arm'd to show forth the Master's will,
Strike on thy purpose to fulfil.
I fear not death—my only fear
Is ills and woes that press me here.
Want stares me in the face, or woe,
Where'er I dwell—where'er I go;
Fishing and hunting only give
The pinching means to let me live;
And if, at night, I lay me down,
In dreams and sleep my rest to crown,
Ere day awakes its slumbering eyes,
I start to hear the foe's mad cries,
Louder and louder, as I clutch

†Claytonia Virginica.

My club, or lance, or bow and dart,
And, springing with a panther's touch,
Display the red man's bloody art.

Nay, I am sick of life and blood,
That drowns my country like a flood,
Pouring o'er hill, and vale, and lea,
Lodge, ville, and council, like a sea,
Where one must gasp and gasp for breath
To live—and stay the power of death.
Ah! life's good things are all too poor,
Its daily hardships to endure.
My fathers told me, there's a land
Where peace and joy abound in hand,
And plenty smiles, and sweetest scenes
Expand in lakes, and groves, and greens.
No pain or hunger there is known,
And pleasure reigns throughout alone—
I would go there, and taste and see
A life so beauteous, bless'd and free,
Where man has no more power to kill,
And the Great Spirit all things fills.
Blanch not, Pauguk, I have no fear,
And would not longer linger here;
But bend thy bow and aim thy dart,
Behold an honest hunter's heart:
Thereby a dart, a boon may give,
A happy life on high to live.

'Tis all the same, in countries here,
    Or where Pacific billows roar,
We roved in want, and woe and fear
    Along the Mississippi shore.
And where Missouri's waters rush,
    To tell to man that God is strong,
We shrank as from a tiger's touch,
    To hear the white man's shout or song
O not for us is peace and joy
    Arising from the race that spread,
Their purpose only's to destroy—
    Our only peace is with the dead.
Think not my heart is pale with fear,
    But strike, Pauguk—strike boldly here.

Avery Color Studios, Inc. has a full line of Great Lakes oriented books, puzzles, cookbooks, shipwreck and lighthouse maps, lighthouse posters and Fresnel lens model.

For a full color catalog call:
1-800-722-9925

Avery Color Studios, Inc. products are available at gift shops and bookstores throughout the Great Lakes region.